The Puppet Master's Bible™

, EXPANDED EDITION ,

Pull the hidden strings of the mind to win hearts and open wallets.

Tom Walker

Copyright © 2025 by Tom Walker. All Rights Reserved.

No part of this publication may be reproduced, distributed, or transmitted in any form or by any means, including photocopying, recording, or other electronic or mechanical methods, without the prior written permission of the publisher, except in the case of brief quotations embodied in critical reviews and certain other noncommercial uses permitted by copyright law. For permission requests, contact the publisher at hello@tomwalker.com.

Tom Walker™ and **The Puppet Master's Bible™** are legally registered trademarks in the United States. Unauthorized use, reproduction, or distribution of these trademarks is strictly prohibited and may result in civil and criminal penalties to the fullest extent permitted by law.

Publisher: Tom Walker LLC (tomwalker.com)

Want to buy bulk copies of this book for your team and colleagues? We can customize the content and co-brand The Puppet Master's Bible™ to suit your business needs. Contact us at hello@tomwalker.com to get started.

Printed in the United States of America.

Expanded Edition. 2025.

Disclaimer: This book is intended for informational purposes only. The techniques, strategies, and psychological methods discussed within are based on the author's research and experiences. They are provided with the understanding that neither the author nor the publisher is engaged in rendering psychological, medical, legal, or other professional advice. Readers are encouraged to consult with a licensed professional before engaging in any practices or methods suggested by this book.

The author and publisher disclaim any liability or responsibility to any person or entity for any loss, damage, or injury caused, or alleged to be caused, directly or indirectly by the information contained in this book. Use of these methods and strategies is at the reader's own risk.

Warning: The psychological methods and techniques described in this book have the potential to influence, manipulate, or alter human behavior. These should be used ethically and responsibly, with respect for others' autonomy and well-being. Misuse of these strategies for malicious, coercive, or deceptive purposes is strongly discouraged and could have significant ethical, legal, and personal consequences.

"Persuasion isn't about convincing someone of the truth. It's about reshaping the truth until they can't distinguish it from their own reflection. The only question is whether you'll use that power to illuminate their potential or exploit their blind spots. Either way, you're playing God."

Tom Walker

Table of Contents

Broccoli   9
The Power You Didn't Know You Had   15
    The Illusion of Choice   15
    The Anatomy of a Decision   17
    Persuasion Through the Ages   19
    Hidden Strings in the Digital Age   21
    Persuasion and Identity   24
    A Field Guide for Everyday Persuasion   26
    The Puppeteer's Moment   31

The Hidden Strings of the Mind   33
    Free Will is the Ultimate Illusion   33
    Rewiring the Hive   35
    When Stories Reprogram Your Mind   37
    Your Brain is a Liar   39
    The Ethics of Emotional Hijacking   41
    The Blueprint of Mass Behavior   42
    The Brain is the Battlefield   44

The Neural Rewiring   47
    The Hidden Key to Persuasion   47
    The Science Behind Neural Rewiring   48
    Empathy-Based Persuasion   50
    The 21-Day Neural Rewiring   54
    Empathy in Your Persuasive Arsenal   59
    Evolving the Practice   63
    Self-Reflection   65
    The Future of Your Brain   69
    Commit to the Long Game   72

The Desire Decoder   73
    Why You Do What You Do   73
    Survival: The Fear Driver   75
    Security: The Need for Stability   77

Status: Social Hierarchy in Love, Careers, and Negotiation	80
Love and Connection: The Bond That Shapes Every Interaction	83
Self-Actualization: The Growth Seeker	86
Autonomy: The Need for Control Over Our Own Lives	90
Validation: Seeking Approval in Every Sphere	93
Mastering the Art of Decoding Desire	97

The Villain Construct — 99

Why Villains Matter More Than Heroes	99
Turning Fear Into Fuel	101
Making Your Enemy Work for You	103
When Framing Becomes Dangerous	106
Villains as Your Architect for Change	108
The Villain Extractor Framework	110
Calling Out and Phrasing Villains	115
Turning Enemies into Engines	118

The Narrative Neuralizer — 121

The Power of Stories	121
Why Your Brain Loves Stories	123
The Five Storytelling Frameworks	127

The Linguistic Lockpick — 163

Words as Weapons	163
How Words Reshape Perception	165
Priming	168
Framing and Reframing	171
The Trojan Horse of Metaphors	174
The 31 Linguistic Patterns of Persuasion	177
Neurological Reactions to Words	209
Wielding the Lockpick	213

The Bond Forger — 219

Mirror Neurons	219
The Hidden Power of Silence	222
When to Push and When to Pull	226
Emotional Intelligence (EQ)	230

Forging Unbreakable Loyalty	234
The Cognitive Exploit	**239**
The Ultimate Backdoor	239
Your Brain is Designed to Fail You	241
The 15 Most Powerful Cognitive Backdoors	245
Cracking the Code of Influence	255
Mastering Mental Exploits	256
The Moral Minefield	**263**
Manipulation Isn't Always Evil	263
The Fine Line	264
Guidelines for Responsible Influence	268
The Ethical Gray Zone	272
The Ultimate Weapon	**275**
Total Control	275
The Seven Pillars of Influence	276
The Art of Layered Persuasion	280
From the Boardroom to the Bedroom	284
Weaponized Empathy	287
The Unbreakable Rules of Influence	290
The Burden of Power	293
Control the Future	294
The Final Challenge	295
The Strings You Choose to Pull	296
Masters of Reality	**299**
Case Studies in Ultimate Reality	299
Jonestown's Ultimate Price of Loyalty	301
Jobs' Digital Dynasty	303
The Trump Phenomenon	305
The GameStop Short Squeeze	307
Engineering Religious Devotion with CrossFit	310
The Great Moral Hack of OnlyFans	313
When the Anti-Vax Narrative Defeats Science	316
The Ultimate Truth	320

PREFACE

Broccoli

I know, not the opener you expected for a book that's about to change your life. But this humble green vegetable holds the key to unlocking the power of influence and the transformative impact of masterful persuasion.

A few years ago, I paid a visit to my sister's home in Dallas. The aroma of a home-cooked meal greeted me, promising comfort and familial warmth. But beneath this domestic facade, an undercurrent of tension crackled, as palpable as static electricity before a storm. At the epicenter of this culinary battlefield stood my sister, her face a mask of determination tinged with desperation.

Her opponent? My six-year-old nephew, Canen, a pint-sized food critic with an unwavering devotion to a single dish: white rice. The challenge that loomed before her was nothing short of Herculean – convincing Canen to consume anything, literally anything, that wasn't his beloved white grains.

Canen, you see, is a picky eater and the kind of customer that makes even seasoned marketers break out in a cold sweat. His staunch refusal to consume anything but his beloved white rice has turned mealtime into a battle of wills, with nutrition as the unwitting casualty.

"But what does this have to do with persuasion?"

Everything, my friend. Everything.

You see, persuasion, at its core, is about understanding human behavior, tapping into desires, and overcoming objections. It takes something that might seem unpalatable at first glance and transforms it into an irresistible offer. And what could be more unpalatable to a strong-willed six-year-old than a plate of steamed broccoli next to his pristine mound of white rice?

I watched my sister employ every trick in her parental playbook. She reasoned with Canen, explaining the importance of a balanced diet. She tried to make it fun, arranging the vegetables into smiley faces. She even attempted to bribe him with the promise of dessert. But Canen remained unmoved, his plate a battlefield of rejected nutrition beside his fortress of white grains.

That's when I decided to step in. Armed with years of marketing experience and a fresh perspective, I was confident I could crack this tough nut.

Oh, how wrong I was.

I started with logic, explaining to Canen how vegetables contained vital nutrients his growing body needed. His eyes glazed over. I switched to emotion, painting a vivid picture of how strong and fast he'd become if he ate his greens. He shrugged, unimpressed. I even tried to leverage his competitive spirit, challenging him to a "who can eat their veggies fastest" contest. He looked at me like I'd suggested we vacation on Mars.

I was losing him. Worse, I was losing myself. In my eagerness to "win," I'd forgotten the most crucial aspect of persuasion – understanding your audience.

As I pondered how I could've improved my sales pitch, the boys started their bedtime routine. Canen has an older brother, Cruz. I didn't mention Cruz earlier because he doesn't have a problem with eating vegetables. However, Cruz being several years older utilizes his size, speed, and strength against his younger brother. Anyone that has siblings, older or younger, knows exactly what I'm talking about.

The boys raced down the hall to the bathroom to brush their teeth. No matter how close to Road Runner-like speed Canen moved his legs, he couldn't compete with his brother. Obviously, it was very important to be first to the bathroom and it had nothing to do with brushing their teeth. As Cruz reached the doorway, Canen legs ground to a halt. In nanoseconds, he went from full sprint to a dejected saunter with his head slung low. All that could've made it more heart wrenching is having a few rocks to kick along the way.

In that difficult moment, at the deepest, darkest pit of Canen's loss, a pure moment of clarity ignited within me like a solar flare. I knew at that moment why I failed at the dinner, and why, the next evening, I would succeed.

We weren't dealing with a vegetable problem – we were dealing with a messaging problem. And I had failed to see Canen not as a problem to be solved, but as the hero of his own story.

Here's where the magic of true persuasion comes into play. Instead of focusing on the features of broccoli, like its nutritional value, its importance in a balanced diet, or even its benefits to Canen, I needed to position myself as a guide in his hero's journey. A journey he didn't even know he was on yet.

"You know, Canen," I said, leaning in close with a conspiratorial whisper, "I know how you can beat Cruz."

Canen's eyes widened; his interest piqued. His legs began swinging from his chair in anticipation.

The desire to overcome this challenge was written all over his face. There was nothing on earth more important than what I was going to tell him...

"You eat rice every night and never win. What you don't know is that rice makes you slow."

His face froze, trying to process that his most beloved food could be working against him and keeping him from running faster.

I reached over to a bowl of broccoli, plucking a nice, firm floret from the pile. Adding a dash of salt, I said, "By eating this broccoli, you'll be able to run faster than ever before. You'll run so fast that you can beat Cruz."

I paused, letting the suspense build. Canen was hanging on every word now, his white rice momentarily forgotten.

Staring at the little green super tree, as if he was just shown the meaning of life, Canen snatched it from my hand, looked over at his brother and smirked in what looked like the conniving Grinch.

He looked at the broccoli, then back at me, weighing the proposition in his mind. He hesitated for a moment, then popped it into his mouth. The kitchen held its breath. And then, miracle of miracles, he swallowed.

What happened next was nothing short of manipulation magic. Canen, fueled by the power of belief (and perhaps a touch of placebo effect), raced around the house, proclaiming his newfound speed.

We all marveled at Canen's new powers.

In an act of pure brotherly love, as Canen raced Cruz that evening, Cruz slowed down so Canen would cement his belief in the power of vegetables.

When it came time for the next meal, he eagerly asked for more broccoli, determined to maintain his competitive edge.

So what changed? All the features and benefits of broccoli were the same. Nothing about the product had changed and I didn't even have to discuss the product to get Canen to eat his broccoli.

I had found his villain. I made an emotional connection. Instead of trying a variation of a standard selling strategy, I used critical thinking to find connections between what I was selling and their life. Even more importantly, I wouldn't have made that connection without looking at his life beyond the product I was selling him.

This, dear reader, is the transformative power of persuasion done right. It changes perceptions, shapes behaviors, and opens new possibilities. In that moment, broccoli was a key to unlocking potential, a secret weapon in the eternal struggle of sibling rivalry.

But here's what most people get wrong about persuasion – they think it's about gentle guidance, about respecting existing beliefs and gradually nudging people toward change. They're wrong. Real transformation doesn't happen through polite suggestions and careful tiptoeing around deeply held beliefs. It happens through controlled psychological disruption.

When I told Canen that rice was slowing him down, I was shattering his entire worldview. In his six-year-old universe, rice wasn't just food. It was comfort. Safety. A daily ritual that gave his world structure and meaning. By connecting his beloved rice to his inability to beat his brother, I forced him to question his identity.

Was this manipulation? Absolutely. Was it ethical? Look at the results. Canen started eating broccoli and he transformed his relationship with food, with competition, with his own potential. He experienced what psychologists call "identity-level change," the deepest and most permanent form of transformation. And it happened not through gentle encouragement, but through a carefully orchestrated moment of psychological disruption.

This is the dark truth about persuasion that most books won't tell you: The most powerful forms of influence don't feel good. They're not supposed to. Real change happens in moments of cognitive dissonance, when someone's existing beliefs collide violently with new information that can't be ignored. It's in that moment of mental friction, of uncomfortable reality-shifting, that transformation becomes possible.

Think about every major change in your life. Did it happen through gentle suggestion? Or did it happen because something or someone forced you to confront an uncomfortable truth about yourself? About your limitations? About your potential?

As persuaders, our job is to make them better. And sometimes that means being the person willing to shatter their comfortable illusions. It means being the one who shows them that their "rice" – whatever it may be – is holding them back from becoming who they could be.

This book is not a guide on manipulation techniques or persuasion "tricks." Treat it as an understanding of the deep psychology of human transformation. You'll learn why people cling to limiting beliefs, how to identify the psychological triggers that can break through those beliefs, and most importantly, how to guide people through the uncomfortable process of becoming better versions of themselves.

We'll explore why most attempts at persuasion fail – not because they're technically wrong, but because they're too timid. Too afraid of discomfort. Too worried about challenging people's existing beliefs. You'll learn why real persuasion requires the courage to make people temporarily uncomfortable for their own lasting benefit.

I want to make this point very clear: the Canen story isn't just about getting a kid to eat vegetables. It's about understanding how human beings actually change, and why the conventional wisdom about ethical persuasion is often wrong. Sometimes the most ethical thing you can do is to shatter someone's comfortable illusions, to force them to confront the ways they're holding themselves back.

This book will show you how to do that – not just with marketing messages or sales techniques, but with a deep understanding of human psychology and transformation. You'll learn to see past surface-level resistance to the deeper identity-level changes that create permanent transformation. You'll understand why discomfort isn't just a side effect of persuasion – it's often the point.

Most importantly, you'll learn to be the kind of persuader who doesn't just sell products or ideas, but who fundamentally transforms how people see themselves and their possibilities. Because that's what real persuasion is about – not just changing minds, but changing lives.

If you're ready to learn how deep persuasion really works, to understand why comfort is often the enemy of growth, and to become the kind of person who can create real, lasting transformation in others, then turn the page.

But be warned – what you're about to learn might make you uncomfortable. And that's exactly the point.

CHAPTER 1

The Power You Didn't Know You Had

The greatest lie you've ever been told is that your mind is your own. Every thought, every desire, every decision you've made was placed there by someone who saw the code of your brain before you ever did.

The Illusion of Choice

You're standing in front of a wall of cereal boxes, an overwhelming kaleidoscope of neon colors and cartoon mascots screaming at you like a psychedelic nightmare. There's the grinning tiger, flexing like he just benched 300 pounds. There's the leprechaun, dancing like he's trying to sell you a pot of sugar disguised as gold. It's chaos, but you stand there, convinced you're in control, rationally weighing your options.

The oatmeal on sale catches your eye. Healthy, practical, responsible. But then your gaze slides over to that tiger. He's winking. He knows your secret. You've been good all week, haven't you? You "deserve" something fun, something indulgent. Before you know it, the box is in your cart, and you're walking away, congratulating yourself for making a balanced choice: It's fun, but it's got fiber. Responsible rebellion. The best of both worlds. After all, this was *your* decision.

Right?

Wrong.

The truth is, the decision you're about to make was made long before you walked into that store. The colors, the slogans, the mascots, they weren't just slapped onto those boxes at random. Each one is a calculated weapon in a psychological arms race, designed to manipulate your brain's deepest desires.

Even the shelf placement isn't innocent. The sugary cereals? Always at eye level for kids. The healthy stuff? Shoved down near your knees where it's easy to overlook unless you're actively looking for guilt.

But you don't notice. You reached for the tiger and thought, "I deserve this. I chose this."

But no. The tiger chose you.

The First String Pulled

Now, before you get defensive, let's make one thing clear: this isn't about cereal. That tiger is a metaphor for your entire life. Your choices, your preferences, even your opinions, they've all been shaped, nudged, and manipulated by forces you don't even see. Marketing campaigns. Social norms. Algorithms. Every step you take is guided by a hidden hand.

Take this book, for example. You didn't stumble across it by accident. Maybe the title caught your eye. Maybe a friend recommended it. But deep down, you were drawn to the promise of power. Not the kind of power that makes headlines, but the quiet, invisible power to shape the world around you. To pull the strings instead of dancing on them.

Even that desire to gain control wasn't entirely yours. Somewhere, someone planted the idea that persuasion was the key to success. Maybe it was a TED Talk. Maybe it was that sleek ad promising you could "crush it" in sales. Maybe it was watching someone else rise while you stayed stagnant. Whatever it was, the seed was planted, and now it's blooming.

The Hidden Game of Persuasion

Persuasion is woven into the fabric of your daily life. It's in the way your friend insists their favorite show is "life-changing." It's in the way your partner frames doing the dishes as a heroic act. It's in the way your favorite influencer subtly flashes a product during their morning routine.

It's the invisible force guiding every interaction, every transaction, every belief. The cereal aisle isn't unique; it's just a microcosm of a much larger, much scarier system. Persuasion is life. And if you don't see it, you're not immune to it. You're a victim of it.

Here's where it gets uncomfortable: you like to think of yourself as rational, free-thinking, and in control. Everyone does. But humans aren't driven by logic. We're driven by stories, emotions, and subconscious triggers. The illusion of choice is just that, an illusion.

Congrats, You've Been Manipulated

Let's go back to that cereal aisle. The tiger grinning at you isn't selling breakfast. He's selling nostalgia, comfort, and maybe even rebellion against your inner health-conscious critic. And you? You're buying it because deep down, you want what he represents. Not food, but a feeling.

This isn't unique to cereal. It's toothpaste, smartphones, gym memberships, and presidential campaigns. It's every decision you've ever made, guided by forces you barely understand.

And here's the punchline: You're not the exception. You're the rule. But don't feel bad, this is the water we all swim in. And until you recognize it, you can't rise above it.

The good news? By the end of this book, you'll see the strings. Better yet, you'll learn how to pull them. Because if you're tired of being the one manipulated, it's time to flip the script.

The Anatomy of a Decision

Let's talk about that latte. The one you bought yesterday on your way to work. The one that cost more than your entire breakfast but somehow felt worth it. Why did you choose it? Was it because you truly craved the rich, velvety taste of expertly foamed milk? Or because the person in front of you ordered one, and you couldn't bear the thought of being the "boring drip coffee" person?

If you're being honest, you probably didn't think about it at all. Decisions like these, the ones that pepper our days, from morning caffeine fixes to late-night Netflix binges, don't spring from carefully weighed pros and cons. They're messy. Emotional. Subconscious. And, more often than not, manipulated.

The Two Routes of Persuasion

To understand how persuasion shapes decisions, we need to zoom in on the mechanics of influence. Psychologists Petty and Cacioppo's Elaboration Likelihood Model breaks it down into two pathways:

- The Central Route: This is where logic rules. You analyze facts, weigh options, and make deliberate choices. It's the kind of thinking you'd like to believe governs all your decisions. In reality? It's rare. Engaging the

central route takes effort, attention, and time, resources most of us aren't willing to spend when deciding between almond milk and oat.
- The Peripheral Route: This is where the magic happens. Quick cues, gut feelings, and emotional triggers take over. You're not evaluating; you're reacting. That's why ads use jingles, attractive spokespeople, or heartwarming stories. They don't want you thinking too hard. They want you feeling instead.

The Latte Moment

Now, back to your latte. Did you engage the central route? Probably not. You didn't compare its calorie count to your daily intake or calculate its cost-effectiveness against making coffee at home. Instead, the peripheral route kicked in. The barista smiled (social proof). The aroma wafted your way (sensory trigger). The café's playlist made you feel like the kind of person who drinks lattes (identity reinforcement).

And just like that, your brain whispered, Treat yourself.

The Masters of Peripheral Persuasion

Want to see this on a bigger scale? Look no further than political campaigns. They're selling leadership. And yet, they use the same tricks.

Think about the last political ad you saw. Did it present a detailed, fact-driven policy breakdown? Of course not. Instead, it used:

- Colors: Blue for trust, red for urgency.
- Slogans: Short, punchy, and easy to remember. ("Yes We Can" wasn't a legal thesis, it was a gut punch of hope.)
- Soundbites: Delivered with the cadence of a TED Talk and the emotional resonance of a movie trailer.

These aren't designed to make you think critically. They're designed to make you feel a surge of pride, a stab of fear, a jolt of urgency. It's peripheral persuasion at its finest.

The Gym Membership Problem

Here's where it gets funny. If decisions were purely logical, half the world wouldn't still be paying for gym memberships they stopped using in February. Logic says cancel the membership, you're not using it. Emotion says canceling means admitting defeat, and you're totally going back next week.

Spoiler: you're not going back.

The same principle applies to every "why am I still paying for this?" subscription. Whether it's that streaming service you swore you'd cancel or the box of pre-portioned meal kits you keep forgetting to pause, the peripheral route is doing its job, keeping you emotionally invested in something you've long stopped needing.

A Tug-of-War Arena

Every decision, no matter how trivial, is a battlefield between these two routes. The central route demands logic, evidence, and attention. The peripheral route? It doesn't care about your spreadsheets. It's faster, stronger, and often wins without you even noticing.

But the peripheral route is where most persuasion happens. It's where your brain lights up in response to emotion, social proof, and sensory cues. It's also where you're most vulnerable to influence.

And that latte? That wasn't caffeine you bought. It was a feeling. A little moment of indulgence wrapped in a paper cup. A decision made not in your rational mind, but in your emotional core.

Persuasion Through the Ages

What do Winston Churchill and a pack of Lucky Strikes have in common?

At first glance, nothing. One is the epitome of wartime resilience, a man who rallied a nation with his indomitable spirit and eloquent words. The other is a cigarette brand, a relic of an era when smoking was marketed as a cure for everything from stress to weight gain. But dig deeper, and you'll find the thread that ties them together: persuasion. Not the mild-mannered kind that asks politely for your consideration, but the kind that grabs you by the soul and demands action.

Great persuaders craft movements. They sell identities, futures, and worlds that didn't exist before they spoke them into being.

Words That Won a War

It was 1940. Britain stood on the brink of annihilation, its people demoralized, its enemies circling. Logic alone couldn't save them. This wasn't a time for spreadsheets or flowcharts. It was a time for belief. And Winston Churchill understood that persuasion is never about rationality and instead about stirring the collective soul.

When Churchill took to the airwaves with his now-legendary "Blood, Toil, Tears, and Sweat" speech, he wasn't just listing the grim realities of war. He was building a bridge between despair and defiance. The power of his words lay in their ability to tap into a shared identity, a narrative of endurance and heroism that made surrender unthinkable.

What made it work?

- Emotional Resonance: Churchill's words were visceral. You felt them.
- Collective Identity: He framed the struggle as a shared mission, a fight for survival that transcended politics or class.
- Moral Certainty: He gave his audience a sense of purpose so strong, it outshone their fear.

Churchill didn't just persuade Britain to fight. He persuaded them to believe they could win.

The Cigarette as a Symbol of Freedom

Fast-forward a few decades, and we meet Edward Bernays, the man who single-handedly made manipulation a fine art. Known as the "father of public relations," Bernays understood something that many still struggle with today: persuasion isn't about the product. It's about the story you attach to it.

Take his campaign for Lucky Strike cigarettes in the 1920s. At the time, women smoking in public was taboo, a societal boundary that cut the tobacco industry off from half its potential market. Bernays wanted women to smoke and see cigarettes as a symbol of liberation.

So, during New York City's 1929 Easter Parade, Bernays orchestrated an event that would go down in history. He hired women to march, each holding a cigarette aloft like a torch. The message was clear: smoking wasn't just for men anymore. Cigarettes were now "torches of freedom," a rebellion against oppression.

What made it work?

- Cultural Reframing: Bernays didn't sell cigarettes; he sold empowerment. The cigarette became a prop in a much larger narrative about gender equality.

- Shock Value: The spectacle of women smoking in public was provocative.
- Symbolism: By equating smoking with freedom, Bernays gave the act a meaning far beyond its original purpose.

The campaign was a resounding success, not just in sales but in its reshaping of societal norms. Bernays persuaded women to smoke *and* to see themselves differently.

Persuasion: Tool or Weapon?

Here's where it might get uncomfortable. Churchill used persuasion to save a nation. Bernays used it to sell a product that would eventually kill millions. Same skill, wildly different outcomes.

So, is persuasion inherently good or bad?

The answer, of course, depends on intent. Persuasion is a tool, like fire. In the hands of someone ethical, it can warm, illuminate, and inspire. In the hands of someone selfish or destructive, it can burn, deceive, and manipulate.

When does persuasion cross the line? Is it okay to manipulate someone if the outcome is positive? What if it isn't? Consider other figures who mastered persuasion: Martin Luther King Jr. and Adolf Hitler. Both mobilized millions, but the morality of their messages couldn't be further apart.

The greatest persuaders don't sell products or win arguments. They change the way people see the world and themselves. Churchill gave its people a narrative of resilience that endured long after the war ended. Bernays shifted cultural norms.

You're already part of a movement, whether you realize it or not. Every brand you love, every political cause you support, every belief you hold, they're all shaped by someone else's persuasion. So the question isn't whether you're being influenced. It's whether you're influencing back.

Hidden Strings in the Digital Age

You're scrolling through TikTok, minding your own business, when suddenly you're deep in a vortex of cat videos. But not just any cat videos: cats performing backflips, cats judging humanity with disdain, cats solving Rubik's Cubes. You're mesmerized, entranced. And then it hits you: How does TikTok know me better than I know myself?

The answer? Math. And it's terrifyingly precise.

Algorithms are today's master persuaders. They don't need charm or charisma. They have data. Every swipe, like, and pause you make is logged, analyzed, and weaponized to create a digital mirror that reflects not who you are, but who you might be most profitably persuaded to become.

No, your phone isn't listening to your conversations (probably). It doesn't need to. It's better than that. It knows you through patterns, your clicks, your hesitations, even the time you spend watching an ad before skipping it. These breadcrumbs create a psychological profile so detailed, it could write your dating app bio better than you.

Your digital behaviors betray you more thoroughly than words ever could. You might tell yourself you're into Dostoevsky and fine wine, but the algorithm knows you've spent 12 hours binge-watching reality TV and Googling "best fast food fries." But it doesn't judge. It just uses that data to nudge.

The Art of Never Letting You Leave

Consider Netflix's autoplay feature. It's not there to help you. It's there to trap you. Autoplay is digital persuasion in its purest form, a psychological hack that exploits your natural aversion to decision-making.

Here's how it works:

- The Hook: The next episode starts before you can even think, "Maybe I should go to bed."
- The Reward: Your brain gets a dopamine hit as the storyline continues seamlessly.
- The Trap: The absence of friction makes stopping feel harder than continuing.

Beyond delivering entertainment, Netflix is reshaping your habits, making "just one more episode" the anthem of your evenings. Choice architecture, designing the environment to guide decisions, isn't new, but Netflix perfected it.

Now compare this to ancient persuasion tactics. Where Cicero had to rely on rhetoric and the crowd's mood, Netflix has millions of data points at its disposal. The result is system that compels millions using only lines of code.

Ancient Strings, Modern Precision

Let's contrast these digital tactics with the persuasion methods of the past. A Roman senator might sway a crowd with a well-timed anecdote or a poetic appeal to honor. Today, an algorithm can do the same thing, but with surgical precision, targeting your insecurities, desires, and fears in milliseconds.

Example 1: Political Campaigns Then vs. Now

- Then: A speechwriter crafts a message to unite a nation. It's broad, universal, and dependent on shared cultural values.
- Now: Social media campaigns micro-target you based on your browsing history, sending you ads tailored to your zip code, income bracket, and even your mood on a Monday morning.

Example 2: Product Placement

- Then: A brand might pay for its logo to appear in a popular film, hoping the association sticks.
- Now: AI-driven content feeds place products in your digital path when you're most likely to buy, right after payday, during your lunch break, or when you've spent an hour Googling "ways to be more productive."

The Unseen Battle for Your Attention

Here's the scary part: persuasion in the digital age isn't passive. It's a relentless battle for your attention, fought by companies armed with algorithms smarter and faster than you.

They're all competing for your mind. And you're losing.

Why? Because these systems are designed to outmaneuver your defenses. They don't argue with you or even try to convince you. They simply nudge, subtly, persistently, until you believe the choice was yours all along.

So, are we doomed?

Not necessarily. Awareness is your first weapon. Once you understand how these strings are pulled, you can begin to resist, or, better yet, learn to pull some strings yourself.

The paradox is that the same tools that manipulate you can empower you. Algorithms aren't inherently evil. It's how they're used that determines their impact. With the right intent, they could just as easily nudge people toward healthier habits, better relationships, or greater self-awareness.

But that's not how most systems work, is it?

Persuasion and Identity

Who are you?

You might think your answer is straightforward. Your likes, your dislikes, your personality quirks, they all feel inherently yours. But let's dig a little deeper. Why do you like what you like? Why do you believe what you believe? And, for the love of all that is decent, why did you ever think cargo shorts were a good idea?

The truth is our sense of self isn't entirely your own. It's a patchwork quilt of ads, algorithms, and societal expectations, stitched together so seamlessly you'd swear it came from inside you. The brands you swear by, the goals you chase, the dreams you hold dear, many of them were quietly suggested to you, wrapped in the illusion of choice.

The Great Cargo Shorts Deception

Let's start with a little humor to soften the blow. Remember when cargo shorts were everywhere? Deep pockets, endless utility, all the rage. But here's the thing: nobody woke up one morning and thought, I need a pair of shorts with so many pockets that I could carry a full set of Tupperware to a picnic. No, you wore them because you were told they were cool. By who? Magazines, ads, your friends who were also victims of the same trend.

And then, one day, the tide turned. Cargo shorts became a punchline. Suddenly, those same friends who once praised their practicality were roasting you for looking like a suburban dad on a camping trip. What changed? Not you. Not the shorts. Just the collective narrative that dictated whether they were in or out.

This is the interplay between persuasion and identity. What you wear, what you consume, even how you see yourself, it's all shaped by the invisible hands of influence.

The Social Mirror

Studies in psychology reveal that much of what we think is "self-expression" is actually shaped by social proof and peer influence. In one famous experiment, participants were asked to judge the length of a line. Simple enough, right? But when placed in a group where everyone else intentionally gave the wrong answer, most participants conformed, even when the correct answer was obvious.

So if something as objective as the length of a line can be influenced by social pressure, what does that say about subjective things like your taste in music, your career aspirations, or your political beliefs? How much of you is truly yours, and how much is borrowed from the crowd?

Today, the forces shaping your identity have grown more precise and insidious. Social media platforms reflect your preferences *and* shape them. Every like, every click, every scroll is logged and used to build a digital version of you. This version is a dynamic tool designed to predict what you'll want, believe, or buy next.

Say you're scrolling Instagram, and you see an ad for a new fitness program. You weren't even thinking about working out, but the ad makes it look so easy, so transformative. Before you know it, you're signing up, convinced this was your idea all along. Was it? Or did the algorithm know you better than you knew yourself?

The thing is, the more you believe you're immune to influence, the more susceptible you are. True control comes not from ignoring these forces but from recognizing them. If you can't see how you're being influenced, can you honestly say you're in control? Or are you just playing a part in a script someone else wrote?

This is a call to action. Start questioning your choices. Ask yourself why you want what you want. Dig deeper into the motivations behind your decisions. Because until you do, you're not as autonomous as you think.

Even the act of questioning your identity can be shaped by persuasion. Self-help books, mindfulness apps, life coaches, they all promise to help you "find yourself." But what they're really doing is offering a new narrative, one that's just as crafted as the old one.

Does this mean you're doomed to be a puppet forever? Not necessarily. Awareness is the first step to reclaiming agency. The more you understand how persuasion works, the more you can align your choices with your true values, whatever those might be.

The brands you love, the beliefs you hold, the goals you chase, they're not inherently bad. But they're not inherently yours, either. The challenge is to take back the strings. To stop being a passive participant in your own story and start actively shaping it.

And if that means burning your cargo shorts? So be it.

A Field Guide for Everyday Persuasion

Let's start with a toddler. Specifically, a toddler who refuses to go to bed.

You've tried reason ("It's bedtime!"), bribery ("I'll let you have pancakes for breakfast!"), and even threats ("No cartoons tomorrow!"). Nothing works. But then, you hit upon an idea: "If you go to bed now, you'll have extra energy to beat your cousin at tag tomorrow."

The toddler pauses. You've found the lever. They march off to bed like they thought of it themselves. Congratulations, you've just won the most relatable persuasion battle of all time.

Persuasion isn't some abstract skill reserved for politicians or marketers. It's the air we breathe, the language we speak. Whether you're convincing a toddler to sleep, a partner to try sushi, or a boss to green-light your project, you're engaging in the fine art of influence.

Negotiating with a Toddler

Toddlers are the ultimate skeptics. They don't care about your logic, your authority, or your carefully crafted arguments. They're driven purely by emotion and self-interest. And that makes them perfect persuasion teachers.

Here's how it works:

- Understand Their Motivation: The toddler doesn't care about sleep, but they care about beating their cousin.

- Reframe the Problem: Bedtime isn't the goal; winning is. Sleep just happens to be the secret weapon.

- Let Them Own It: The moment the toddler feels like it was their decision, the battle is over.

This goes beyond toddlers. It's also about people. Adults are just bigger versions, driven by slightly more sophisticated desires but just as susceptible to a well-framed narrative.

Picking a Restaurant Without a Fight

Now, let's scale it up. Imagine you're trying to convince a group of friends to try the new ramen place downtown, but everyone's leaning toward the safe, boring burger joint. What do you do? Logic won't work, nobody picks a restaurant based on nutritional information. Instead, you appeal to emotion.

- Social Proof: "Everyone's been talking about this place. It's all over TikTok."
- Scarcity: "They only take 30 reservations a night, and we're lucky to get one."
- Identity: "We're adventurous foodies tonight."

Suddenly, ramen sounds delicious and inevitable. And once you've framed it as a group adventure, you've ensured buy-in.

Relationships: Persuasion in Every Interaction

Every successful relationship is built on compromise, and compromise is just a polite form of persuasion. Think about it. Convincing your partner to try sushi is about positioning it as a shared experience, a story you'll tell later.

Persuasion in relationships works best when it doesn't feel like persuasion. Frame the request as something that benefits the other person, and they're more likely to say yes.

- Example: "I know you're nervous about sushi, but I promise we'll start with something mild. And if you hate it, we'll hit up your favorite pizza place after."
- Outcome: They're not agreeing to sushi. They're agreeing to a win-win scenario. You've removed the risk, and suddenly it feels like their choice.

The Inner Game of Persuasion

Here's where it gets personal. The most important persuasion you'll ever do isn't with a toddler, a friend, or a partner. It's with yourself. Every day, you're negotiating with your own mind, trying to convince yourself to eat healthier, work harder, or take that leap of faith.

The techniques are the same:

- Reframe the Narrative: "I'm not dieting; I'm fueling my body for success."

- Remove the Risk: "What's the worst that happens if I try? A little discomfort?"
- Celebrate the Win: "If I stick to this for a week, I'll reward myself."

The trick is to treat your inner skeptic like a toddler. Identify the resistance. Reframe the ask. Then convince yourself it was your idea all along.

Everyday Persuasion, Everywhere

Once you start seeing the levers of persuasion, you'll see them everywhere:

- At Work: Getting your boss to approve your budget is about showing how your idea makes them look good.
- With Friends: Getting everyone to agree on plans is about crafting a story everyone wants to be part of.
- In Life: Convincing yourself to hit the gym is about framing the gym as the gateway to the life you want.

Persuasion is in every corner of your life, shaping every interaction, every decision, every belief. Master it, and you're suddenly steering life itself.

From Victim to Master

The strings are exposed.

You've spent this chapter uncovering the invisible forces shaping your life, marketers crafting desires you didn't know you had, algorithms nudging you toward decisions you thought were your own, and societal norms weaving their way into your very sense of self.

It's unsettling, isn't it? Like realizing you've been living in a beautifully decorated prison without ever noticing the bars.

But those bars? They're not unbreakable. Now that you see the strings, you have a choice. You can stay a puppet, content to dance while pretending you're the choreographer. Or, you can become the puppet master, learning to pull the strings yourself.

Seeing the Patterns

The first step to mastering persuasion is recognizing how it operates. Persuasion thrives in the shadows, where it can bypass your defenses. That's its power and its weakness. Once you drag it into the light, its grip loosens.

Think about it. Why did you buy that concert ticket in a panic? Because the website screamed, "Only 3 left!" Scarcity is a psychological trigger that taps into your primal fear of missing out. Or remember the last time you picked a restaurant. Was it the menu that swayed you? Probably not. It was the crowd outside, making the place look irresistible. Social proof whispers, If everyone's here, it must be good.

And then there's emotion. Why did you donate to that charity last Christmas? Was it the detailed breakdown of where your money would go? Or was it the gut-wrenching image of a child, staring into the camera with eyes that could dissolve glaciers? Emotion bypasses logic and takes a direct route to action.

These patterns aren't random. They're carefully designed levers, calibrated to nudge you toward a specific outcome. But the moment you see the levers, the game changes. Awareness is a form of power. And with power, you gain the ability to choose.

Using the Strings Yourself

Here's where things get interesting. The same tools that have influenced you like scarcity, social proof, and emotional resonance are now yours to wield. Persuasion isn't inherently good or bad. It's a scalpel, capable of surgery or harm depending on the intent behind it.

Imagine you're at work, pitching an idea to your boss. You don't start with a barrage of facts and figures. Instead, you paint a picture. You describe how this project will solve the team's biggest headaches, make the department look stellar, and, yes, maybe even give your boss a shiny line on their next performance review. You're crafting a narrative, a story where your boss is the hero, and your idea is their sword.

Or think about your personal life. Say you're trying to convince a friend to join you on a hike. You could argue that it's good exercise or that the view is incredible. But if you want to close the deal, you appeal to something deeper. "You've been stressed lately. This hike? It'll clear your mind. Plus, imagine the Instagram photos… you'll look unstoppable." Suddenly, the hike is a solution to their stress and a chance to shine.

This is alignment. The best persuaders don't force people to agree with them. They show people the version of themselves they already want to be but haven't fully embraced.

Breaking Free

Let's turn the lens inward for a moment. The most important persuasion isn't what you do with others. It's what you do with yourself. Every day, you're locked in an internal negotiation, trying to convince yourself to make better choices, take bigger risks, or silence the voice of doubt that whispers, You're not ready.

You've seen this play out. Think about the last time you tried to start a new habit. Maybe it was going to the gym or waking up earlier. You told yourself it was a good idea. You laid out the benefits. And yet, when the moment came, inertia won. Why? Because logic doesn't win internal battles. Emotion does.

Here's the trick: treat yourself like your toughest client and reframe the narrative. You're not "dieting." You're fueling your body for the life you want. You're not "saving money." You're building the future version of yourself who travels the world without checking their bank balance.

The same levers you've seen used on you, scarcity, identity, emotion, can work wonders when turned inward.

What Comes Next

This book is about teaching you how to pull these strings. In the chapters ahead, you'll learn how to craft narratives so irresistible they bypass resistance. You'll discover how to tap into the neuroscience of motivation, creating messages that stick and reshape behavior. And you'll understand how to use persuasion ethically, transforming influence from a weapon into a tool for connection and growth.

But knowing isn't enough. Persuasion is a skill, and skills demand practice. Every conversation, every pitch, every decision is a chance to refine your craft. Start small. Convince your partner to try that new restaurant. Negotiate an extra day off with your boss. See persuasion not as manipulation, but as an art form, and treat every interaction as your canvas.

Even now, you're being persuaded. This chapter is nudging you toward action, toward seeing yourself not as a passive participant in life, but as the architect of your reality. But persuasion, at its best, doesn't force your hand. It gives you the choice to stay bound by the strings or take control.

Persuasion isn't new to you. It's been a shadow companion your entire life. From the jingles of childhood commercials to the digital nudges of algorithms, you've lived surrounded by influence. And for most of that time, you've been oblivious to it, moving, acting, choosing as if the decisions were truly your own. But they weren't. Not entirely.

Now, the veil is lifting. You see the strings. You see how words, images, and emotions have been used to shape your reality. That revelation might leave you feeling exposed, even vulnerable. But it should do something else too. It should thrill you. Because now, you have the choice to use this power.

The Puppeteer's Moment

The thing about power is it doesn't care who holds it. Persuasion has no moral compass. It's a force, like gravity, waiting to be harnessed. Those who ignore it and pretend they're immune or insist they don't need it end up as its victims. But those who embrace it, who learn its mechanics and wield it with precision, become something more.

A great persuader changes minds and rewrites the fabric of reality itself. They see people not as pawns to be controlled but as partners in a shared narrative, one where the outcomes align with the persuader's vision and the persuaded's desires.

You've spent this book learning how persuasion works. You've seen its power to influence, to inspire, to nudge humanity toward progress or drag it into darkness. The path you take from here depends on your intent, your ethics, and your willingness to master the art.

With Great Power…

Spider-Man had it right. Great power comes with great responsibility. But he left something out: great power also comes with incredible opportunity. The ability to persuade is about shaping the world. Every interaction, every conversation, every decision is a chance to use this skill: to make someone's day brighter, to open a door they didn't see, or to steer them away from harm.

The tools you've learned here are sharp. They can cut, but they can also create. What matters is how you use them.

Imagine a future shaped by your influence. It won't happen by accident. Great persuaders hone it, practice it, refine it until it becomes second nature. They test it, use it, and perfect it until their words leave lasting echoes.

But persuasion is also about you. The inner dialogue that determines whether you'll rise to the occasion or stay where you are. That's persuasion too. Every time you convince yourself to take a risk, to push through fear, to chase something bigger, you're pulling your own strings. That's because mastering persuasion means mastering that internal game as much as the external one.

Ask yourself—If you can pull your own strings, does that make you free or just a better puppet? And when you start pulling theirs, will you even notice who's holding yours?

CHAPTER 2

The Hidden Strings of the Mind

When you get their brains to dance to the beat you set, you control their attention, their emotions, their desires, their decisions. This is the code you're after, and it's the key to unlocking unshakeable influence.

Free Will is the Ultimate Illusion

You think you're in control. Every choice, from your morning coffee to the Netflix show you'll inevitably binge tonight, feels deliberate, intentional, uniquely yours. But let me strip away the facade: you're not choosing. You never were. The decisions you call "yours" were written into your brain before you even knew they existed.

Take a seemingly trivial decision: grabbing a coffee on your way to work. You tell yourself it's a simple craving, maybe a reward for getting out of bed. But rewind the tape. Was it the wafting aroma of roasted beans? The Instagram ad for pumpkin spice lattes that nudged you yesterday? Or maybe the cheery barista who's trained to greet you by name? Here's the uncomfortable truth: the craving wasn't born in your mind. It was planted.

Your Choices Were Made Before You Knew Them

In 1981, Daniel Kahneman and Amos Tversky revealed a devastating insight into human decision-making: context, not logic, drives your behavior. Their prospect theory exposed how something as simple as framing, the way information is presented, can flip your choices like a switch. Here's the classic example:

You're told 600 people are at risk of dying from a disease. Option A will save 200 lives for sure, while Option B offers a one-in-three chance of saving everyone but a two-in-three chance of saving no one. Most people pick Option A, it feels safe, rational. Now flip the frame: Option A means 400 people will definitely die, and Option B offers the same gamble. Suddenly, people flock to Option B. The numbers didn't change. Your brain did.

This is the lie your brain tells you: that you're making decisions based on facts, when in reality, your choices are molded by how those facts are presented. And the manipulation doesn't stop with abstract scenarios. Neuroeconomics, a field merging neuroscience and decision theory, shows that your brain's reward systems light up with predictable precision, often before you're even aware of your preferences. Brands don't just sell products, they script your desires. That craving for an overpriced latte? A predictable neural response to the cues they've engineered.

The Role of Automation in Human Thought

To understand how easily you're led, let's look under the hood of your mind. Your brain operates as a two-system machine: System 1, the impulsive autopilot, and System 2, the deliberate thinker. Daniel Kahneman, the architect of this framework, describes System 1 as fast, instinctive, and prone to error. System 2, meanwhile, is slow, lazy, and more interested in rationalizing than overriding System 1's impulses.

Here's how it plays out: You walk into a grocery store and instinctively grab the cereal box with the bright colors and familiar cartoon mascot. System 1 screams, "Yes, that's the one!" But why? Was it nostalgia? Eye-level placement? The fact that sugary cereals are marketed as "fun"? Whatever the reason, System 2 isn't questioning it. Instead, it's busy justifying the choice: "It's on sale," "The kids will love it," or "I deserve a treat."

This isn't decision-making; it's decision rationalizing. And marketers know exactly how to exploit this. When Netflix autoplays the next episode, it's not your conscious brain saying, "I have time for one more." It's System 1 succumbing to the nudge, while System 2 sits back and shrugs.

Why This Matters

Every decision you make, big or small, is shaped by forces you rarely see. Neural synchronization, the phenomenon where your brain aligns with others during shared experiences, amplifies this vulnerability. Whether it's a viral marketing campaign or a politician's rally speech, synchronization pulls your thoughts into lockstep with the group, bypassing the rational defenses you think you have.

But here's the kicker: this isn't about marketers or politicians. It's about you. The very wiring of your brain betrays you, favoring shortcuts and heuristics over thoughtful analysis. And if you don't see the strings being pulled, how can you ever cut them?

The Question of Free Will

So, let's ask the uncomfortable question: If your decisions can be framed, nudged, and predicted with such precision, does free will exist? If your cravings, choices, and even beliefs are scripts running on preloaded biases, what part of you is truly autonomous? And if your brain is a liar, telling you that you're in control, how much of your life has been lived on someone else's terms?

This is the foundation of everything that follows in this book. To master influence, you must first understand how easily you're influenced. Because the moment you see the strings, you can stop being the puppet, and start being the master.

Rewiring the Hive

Imagine a stadium roaring with thousands of voices, not a single one out of sync. Or a viral TikTok trend where millions worldwide mimic the same dance moves, swaying to an invisible beat. These aren't just cultural phenomena; they're biological symphonies. This is neural synchronization, our brains aligning like Bluetooth devices, seamlessly syncing with the rhythm of others. But what happens when this synchronization becomes a tool, not just for connection, but for control?

The Hidden Science Behind Connection

Research from Uri Hasson at Princeton University reveals the astonishing mechanics of "neural coupling." When someone tells a story, the listener's brain doesn't merely react, it mirrors. Like a pair of synchronized swimmers, neurons fire in unison between speaker and audience. This is why a captivating TED Talk feels like it's speaking directly to you, your brain and theirs are dancing the same neural waltz.

This is biology weaponized.

Take viral political speeches, for example. When a charismatic leader steps to the podium, their words synchronize with your mind. Their cadence, their tone, their carefully chosen narrative threads all function as commands to your neural circuits. Suddenly, you're not just listening; you're agreeing, feeling, and thinking in time with the speaker. It's no coincidence that the best orators create movements, not just messages.

But here's the question you should be asking: When does this harmony cross into conformity?

The Tyranny of Shared Feelings

Ever wondered why outrage on social media spreads faster than empathy? Mirror neurons, discovered by Rizzolatti and Iacoboni, are the culprits. These tiny clusters of neurons are why you cringe when someone trips or why a yawn in a room spreads like wildfire. When you see an emotion, your brain doesn't just observe, it mimics.

Now imagine this on a global scale. When millions witness an influencer's tearful confession or a shocking headline, mirror neurons ignite like brushfires. Outrage goes viral not because it's justified, but because it's contagious. Platforms like Facebook and Twitter know this. Outrage equals clicks, and clicks equal profit.

The real danger? Once emotions sync, rational thought becomes a casualty. The crowd doesn't just feel together; it thinks together. What begins as shared sentiment quickly devolves into mass conformity.

The Dark Potential of Manufactured Unity

Here's where the ethical chasm widens. If we can manufacture shared feelings, why not weaponize them? The same mechanisms that bring people together at concerts or during collective mourning can be used to radicalize, to divide, to manipulate.

Consider TikTok trends. What seems like harmless fun, dance routines, meme challenges, masks an insidious reality: the platform's algorithms actively amplify behaviors designed to sync brains at scale. Every "For You" page is a battleground, each video a potential recruit in the war for your attention and allegiance. The collective joy of participation becomes a leash.

And if this synchronization can be manufactured, what's stopping the puppet masters from pulling the strings?

Neural synchronization is, at its core, a tool. It has the power to foster empathy and unity but also to erode individuality. The question isn't whether we should use this power, but how, and at what cost.

The next time you feel "connected" at a rally or captivated by a story, ask yourself: Is this genuine engagement, or is my brain just a pawn in someone else's game? Understanding the science of synchronization is your first step toward reclaiming autonomy in a world desperate to rob you of it.

When Stories Reprogram Your Mind

They say facts tell, but stories sell. But what they don't tell you is this: stories don't just sell products, they sell beliefs, values, and realities. Every TED Talk that gives you chills, every Marvel movie that makes you cheer, is rewriting your brain. And the scariest part? You're handing them the pen.

Research by Stephens and Hasson shows how storytelling activates the default mode network (DMN), the same part of your brain responsible for daydreaming, introspection, and, most importantly, identity formation. When a story hooks you, your logical defenses are bypassed. Instead of evaluating the information critically, your brain absorbs it like a sponge, embedding the narrative's emotional experiences deep into your psyche.

Why do we love the hero's journey? It's hardwired into us. From ancient myths to modern blockbusters, the hero's triumph against adversity is programming. TED Talks lean on this formula, disguising lectures as epics. The speaker is the hero, the struggle is their insight, and you? You're the grateful villager who adopts their wisdom.

But here's the uncomfortable truth: if stories can program us with new values, they can overwrite the ones we hold dear. Think about how wartime propaganda reframes enemies as subhuman or how political narratives divide nations. When a story becomes powerful enough, it doesn't just resonate, it erases.

Dopamine, Oxytocin, and Memory Tattoos

Why can't you forget a compelling story? Why do some campaign ads stick in your brain long after the ballot has been cast? The answer lies in two molecules that control your mind: dopamine and oxytocin.

Paul Zak's research reveals that emotionally charged stories release dopamine, a neurochemical associated with pleasure, focus, and memory. This is why ads that evoke fear, joy, or patriotism stay with us far longer than ones filled with dry facts. They literally tattoo themselves onto your neural pathways.

Oxytocin, meanwhile, is the neurochemical of trust and connection. When a story triggers your empathy, whether it's a candidate hugging a child or a charity showing a rescued animal, your brain produces oxytocin, creating a bond so strong you're willing to act. It's not just persuasion, it's biochemical enslavement.

Consider this: political campaign ads don't just inform you; they indoctrinate you. By linking abstract ideas like patriotism with tangible visuals, a waving flag, a soldier's salute, they seed emotional loyalty. The message isn't "vote for me because of my policies." It's "vote for me because I embody your identity."

So, where does persuasion end and mind control begin? When you're moved to act not by logic but by neurochemical compulsion, are you still making your own decisions?

A Survival Mechanism Turned Weapon

Storytelling is as old as humanity. It's how we've passed down knowledge, built communities, and made sense of the world. Evolution has wired us to respond to stories because they once ensured survival, teaching us how to hunt, avoid danger, and live harmoniously. But in the hands of modern puppet masters, this survival mechanism has become a weapon.

In marketing, storytelling is *the* tool. Brands don't sell products; they sell identities. Nike doesn't just sell shoes; it sells triumph. Apple doesn't just sell gadgets; it sells creativity. These narratives bypass your rational brain, tapping into your desires and insecurities with the precision of a sniper.

Politics, too, thrives on narrative warfare. Consider how narratives of fear and safety shaped public opinion during the COVID-19 pandemic. Governments and media didn't just report facts, they crafted stories of heroes (healthcare workers) and villains (anti-maskers), ensuring compliance through emotional alignment, not logical argument.

The exploitation of storytelling is dangerous. When stories are wielded to manipulate, they don't just inform or entertain; they colonize your thoughts. The line between persuasion and propaganda blurs, leaving your free will as collateral damage.

So here's the dilemma: storytelling is both humanity's greatest tool and its greatest threat. A powerful story can heal, inspire, and unite. But it can just as easily divide, distort, and destroy. The very mechanism that binds us as a species is also the one that enslaves us.

Next time you're captivated by a story, whether it's a political speech, a commercial, or a blockbuster, ask yourself: what's the message beneath the plot? Who's holding the pen? And most importantly, whose story are you living? Because if you don't choose your narrative, someone else will.

Your Brain is a Liar

Your brain loves to lie to you, but it's not malicious. It's just lazy. Imagine you're standing in line at your favorite coffee shop. The menu is sprawling, espresso, cappuccino, oat milk, almond milk, caramel drizzle. You deliberate, convinced that this process of choice reflects your identity, your preferences, your essence. You order the oat milk latte because, in your mind, it's healthier. You feel good about this decision.

But here's the truth: you didn't make that choice. Not really. The menu did. Or rather, the way the menu was structured. Maybe the word "sustainable" was placed under oat milk, nudging your brain to associate it with virtue. Maybe "whole milk" was buried in the corner with no modifiers, making it feel like the lazy, guilty option. Whatever the case, your decision wasn't yours, it was framed.

Framing is the subtle art of manipulating the context of choices, and your brain eats it up. Tversky and Kahneman's legendary studies on framing expose how easily our decisions are swayed. In one experiment, participants chose between two medical treatments for a deadly disease. When the outcomes were framed as "saving 200 lives," most people opted for the safer treatment. But when the exact same outcomes were framed as "400 people will die," the preference flipped to the riskier option. The math never changed, but the brain's response did.

Rationality, it turns out, is a PR stunt your brain runs to keep you complacent. The choices you think are based on logic? They're just reactions to the way information is packaged. This isn't a bug; it's a feature of your brain's design. Evolution didn't prioritize accuracy, it prioritized survival. If a certain phrasing feels like the safer bet, your brain will leap without looking, spinning a neat little rationalization afterward.

Now for the uncomfortable question: if your decisions can be shaped by something as arbitrary as word choice, what does that say about your convictions? If morality is just a set of preferences framed by culture, upbringing, and language, is there any such thing as a truly ethical choice? Or are you just a puppet to context?

Cognitive Load and the Death of Free Thought

Your brain is like a battery. Every decision, no matter how small, drains its charge. And once that charge runs low, your ability to think critically, resist temptation, or make deliberate choices disappears. This is cognitive load in action, and it's the reason you're far more likely to devour a pint of ice cream after a long, stressful day than after a morning yoga session.

Roy Baumeister's research on decision fatigue demonstrates just how fragile our self-control really is. Each choice you make chips away at your mental reserves. By the time you've navigated a workday full of meetings, emails, and minor crises, your brain is running on fumes. That's when the shortcuts kick in, impulse purchases, knee-jerk reactions, and a general inability to care about the long-term consequences.

Even judges aren't immune. A study found that parole boards are far more likely to grant parole in the morning or immediately after a break. As the day drags on and decision fatigue sets in, their rulings grow harsher. This is cognitive exhaustion. The brain, desperate to preserve energy, defaults to the easiest, safest choice, which, in this case, is to deny parole and avoid risk.

Now think about your own life. You're scrolling Amazon at 11 p.m., a few glasses of wine in, and you see a deal for something you don't need, a handheld vegetable spiralizer, perhaps. "Limited time only!" the page screams. Your brain, tired from a day of decisions, can't summon the energy to debate the merits of spiralized zucchini. You click "Buy Now" because it's easier than thinking.

Marketers know this. They exploit your mental fatigue with choice architecture designed to overwhelm and manipulate. Endless scrolling, time-limited offers, and flashy alerts are carefully calibrated to break your cognitive control. When your brain is too tired to engage System 2, the deliberate, rational part, it defaults to System 1, which runs on instinct and emotion. And System 1? It's a sucker for a good sales pitch.

When you strip away the illusion of rationality and add the debilitating effects of cognitive load, what's left? Vulnerability. You're a puppet, and every decision you make is a pull on your strings. Framing primes you for manipulation. Fatigue ensures you're too weak to resist. This isn't a glitch in human cognition; it's the entire operating system. The question is, who's writing the code? And more importantly, are you even aware it's happening?

The Ethics of Emotional Hijacking

Manipulation is a dirty word, isn't it? But before you clutch your ethical pearls, let's dissect the blurred line between influence and coercion. Consider political campaigns, a symphony of emotionally charged rhetoric designed to bypass your logic and hijack your gut. Flags waving, stirring music swelling, candidates promising to "restore greatness" or "fight for justice." You're not voting on policy; you're choosing the hero of a story that's been drilled into your subconscious.

Research from the field of neuroeconomics reveals how reward systems are triggered during these persuasive spectacles. Functional MRI studies show the ventromedial prefrontal cortex (VMPFC) lighting up as these narratives play, aligning emotional rewards with decision-making. It's not logic that sways you, it's the dopamine hit of belonging, of believing you've picked the "right" side.

Now here's the controversy: If these campaigns know how to trigger your brain's reward centers, bypassing rational scrutiny, are you still exercising free will? And when the stakes are no longer products but politics, decisions that reshape lives and policies, where do we draw the ethical line? Is it manipulation or motivation when your choices are curated by someone else's agenda?

Hacking Empathy for Profit

Let's pivot to the commercial realm, where empathy is a profit engine. Consider this: a baby food commercial doesn't just sell mashed carrots; it sells the image of a giggling, cherubic baby with their doting parent. Neuromarketing studies leveraging mirror neuron research show how such imagery triggers empathetic responses. Your brain doesn't just watch that ad, it feels the parental pride, the tenderness. Suddenly, you're buying not carrots but validation, security, love.

Marco Iacoboni's research on mirror neurons explains this phenomenon. When you see an action or emotion, your brain's neurons fire as if you're experiencing it yourself. That's why you cringe at a paper cut in a movie or tear up during an emotional speech. Advertisers have weaponized this biological quirk, using it to embed their products into the emotional fabric of your life.

And here's where the ethical noose tightens: If companies can exploit your empathy, are they selling solutions or stealing autonomy? Take fitness brands portraying aspirational lifestyles. They aren't just marketing treadmills; they're selling the dream of a "better you." The line between motivation and manipulation blurs when emotional vulnerability is the hook, and profit, the bait.

A Minefield of Moral Questions

Let's not pretend this isn't an ethical minefield. When influence becomes so seamless, so effective, how do we ensure it serves rather than exploits? The moral calculus becomes even murkier when we consider the stakes. Politicians swaying votes. Corporations driving consumption. Movements shifting entire cultures. The question isn't whether we'll use emotional hijacking, it's how far we're willing to go.

The real challenge for persuaders, marketers, and leaders isn't whether they can sway hearts and minds. It's whether they can look in the mirror and justify why they did it. The research makes one thing clear: the brain can be hijacked. What remains unclear is whether society is prepared to confront the consequences of this power, or whether we're too entranced by the narratives it spins.

The Blueprint of Mass Behavior

Mass behavior isn't the random chaos of a crowd; it's an algorithm, a blueprint, a deliberate engineering of collective action. Think of it like a behavioral avalanche: a single snowflake dislodges others until the entire slope collapses. Behavioral cascades follow the same principles, one nudge leads to another, then another, until an entire group is swept into conformity. The terrifying part? These cascades are not spontaneous. They're orchestrated.

Behavioral Cascades in Action

Let's begin with a case study everyone remembers: the Ice Bucket Challenge. What seemed like a silly viral trend, drenching yourself in freezing water to raise money for ALS, was actually a masterclass in social synchronization. Each time you saw a friend participate, your brain lit up like a Christmas tree, thanks to its mirror neurons. These neurons, which fire both when you perform an action and when you observe it in others, create a sense of shared experience. The result? You weren't just watching your friends pour ice water on themselves, you were feeling it, living it, syncing to it. And when they tagged you to participate, the neural alignment was too strong to resist.

But not all cascades are for charity. Consider the weaponization of behavioral cascades in misinformation campaigns. A single piece of false news, designed to evoke outrage, fear, or tribal loyalty, can spread across networks with viral speed. Why? Because outrage activates the brain's amygdala, heightening emotional arousal and making the message more likely to stick. Research into behavioral cascades shows that once a critical mass is reached, the spread becomes self-sustaining. It's not just influence anymore, it's contagion.

The Role of Neural Synchronization

The success of cascades is neurological. Studies by Uri Hasson reveal that storytelling creates neural coupling between speakers and listeners. When people hear the same story, their brains synchronize, aligning in areas responsible for emotions, decision-making, and memory. The Ice Bucket Challenge tapped into this, creating a narrative everyone wanted to be part of. In misinformation campaigns, the same principle applies, except the goal isn't unity, it's division. The blueprint remains the same, but the intent shifts from collaboration to control.

The Thin Line Between Nudging and Pushing

If you've ever found yourself clicking "Accept" on a shady app's terms of service or binge-watching Netflix until 3 a.m. because of autoplay, you've been nudged. Nudges are subtle manipulations designed to influence behavior while maintaining the illusion of choice. But the line between a nudge and a shove is razor-thin, and often invisible.

Dark Patterns in UX

Consider the infamous "dark patterns" of user experience design. These are deliberate design choices meant to trap you into actions you might not otherwise take. A countdown timer flashes: "Only 5 items left!", but the inventory isn't real. A subscription auto-renews with a single click, but canceling requires navigating a labyrinth of settings. These tactics exploit decision fatigue, a phenomenon well-documented by researchers like Roy Baumeister, who demonstrated that as mental energy wanes, people default to the easiest or most obvious choice.

The result? You're no longer making decisions; you're following a script someone else wrote. And this isn't limited to e-commerce. Political campaigns use similar tactics, bombarding you with emotionally charged ads during high-stress moments, knowing you'll react impulsively. The push is subtle, almost imperceptible, but it's there, and it's relentless.

From Empowerment to Exploitation

Nudges began as a tool for good. Behavioral economists like Richard Thaler envisioned nudging as a way to encourage healthier, smarter choices: saving for retirement, eating vegetables, or recycling. But when nudges are designed to manipulate rather than guide, they become coercion in disguise.

Take the autoplay feature on streaming platforms like Netflix. It's convenient, sure. But it's also a psychological trap, exploiting your brain's tendency toward inertia. Watching "just one more episode" isn't your decision, it's a response to a carefully engineered nudge. Now apply that same principle to more insidious contexts: autoplay political ads, autoplay misinformation, autoplay fear. The tools of empowerment have become the tools of exploitation.

When Does Influence Become Coercion?

The ethical line between nudging and pushing is murky. If a nudge convinces someone to save for retirement, most would call that a win. But what if the same technique is used to nudge someone into donating to a fraudulent cause or voting against their own interests? The intent might differ, but the mechanism is identical.

The deeper question is this: If manipulation leads to a beneficial outcome, is it still wrong? Nudging someone to quit smoking or exercise more feels ethically sound, but does that change when the same nudge is used to sell a product or ideology? The science of influence doesn't care about ethics; it works regardless of intent. The responsibility lies with the puppet master. And that's the rub: once you've mastered these tools, how do you resist the temptation to use them for your own gain?

The Brain is the Battlefield

Your mind is at war. The combatants aren't armies or insurgents, but corporations, algorithms, and influencers armed with science you can't see and tactics you don't understand. This isn't a metaphor, it's a coordinated, calculated effort to own the very fabric of your decisions. The battlefield isn't far away. It's here, nestled behind your forehead, in the complex tangle of neurons that make up your brain. And the stakes? Control over your thoughts, your choices, your very identity.

Your Thoughts Are the Prize

Imagine this: you wake up, scroll through Instagram, sip your morning coffee, and decide on a headline that captures your attention. Simple choices, right? Wrong. Each of those moments is a skirmish in a larger battle for control over your mind.

Uri Hasson's research on neural synchronization shows how deeply connected our brains become during shared experiences. Think of a viral campaign video. As millions watch it, their brain patterns begin to align, syncing to the rhythm of the story, the cadence of the speaker, the pulse of the music. It's not magic; it's science. The more engaging the story, the tighter the synchronization.

But synchronization goes beyond a communal bonding experience, it's also the gateway to influence. When our brains align with someone else's, we aren't just sharing emotions. We're absorbing narratives, adopting viewpoints, and internalizing values that may not have been ours to begin with. It's how political movements swell, how trends catch fire, and how ideas spread faster than logic can keep up.

Take the Ice Bucket Challenge: a harmless, charitable cascade of synchronized behavior. Now contrast it with misinformation campaigns, where synchronization drives division, outrage, and mob mentalities. The same mechanics, wildly different outcomes. If your thoughts can be synced, they can also be subverted. And you're already plugged in.

Can You Break Free?

Here's a truth that will sting: breaking free is not the default. You've been engineered for compliance. Algorithms track, nudge, and reward you with dopamine hits tailored to keep you clicking, sharing, and scrolling. TikTok doesn't just know you like dog videos; it knows the exact cadence, lighting, and emotional triggers that make you stay glued to the screen. It's not catering to you; it's capturing you.

This is the era of algorithmic manipulation. Neural synchronization is no longer limited to live speeches or charismatic leaders. It's coded into the apps you use, the ads you skip, the content you consume. Each scroll tightens the loop of influence, narrowing your autonomy while expanding someone else's reach.

But can autonomy be reclaimed? Yes, if you fight for it. Start with awareness. Recognize the cues and triggers designed to manipulate. Then, rebuild. Just as neural patterns can be hijacked, they can be rewired. This is not an easy path, but it's the only one that leads to true independence.

What Happens Next?

Let's push this further. What happens when an entire generation grows up in an ecosystem of algorithmic manipulation? Already, attention spans are collapsing, critical thinking is withering, and emotional resilience is eroding under the weight of social validation cycles.

Consider this: are we raising a generation where individuality is a curated illusion, where decisions are dictated not by personal values but by trending hashtags? If the next war isn't between nations but between corporations and individuals, what does victory even look like?

As research from Baumeister's strength model of self-control suggests, decision fatigue amplifies these vulnerabilities. A mind under constant bombardment, notifications, ads, endless choices, is a mind primed for surrender. And the enemy doesn't need to fight; it only needs to wait.

So, here's your challenge: reclaim the battlefield. Start by questioning every decision. Who benefits from your choices? What algorithms shaped your preferences? Are you in control, or are you following a script written for you?

This is about reconstruction. The tools of influence can be repurposed. Synchronization can unite movements for good, algorithms can foster growth, and narratives can inspire rather than manipulate. The first step is to understand the game. The next is to rewrite the rules.

CHAPTER 3

The Neural Rewiring

In a world obsessed with self-promotion, learning to genuinely understand others is the most powerful persuasive tool you can wield.

The Hidden Key to Persuasion

You've been told that persuasion is about speaking, presenting, and convincing. What if I told you that's wrong? What if the true key to persuasion isn't what you say, but what you hear? Silence, specifically, the ability to listen deeply and empathetically, is the switch that rewires your brain for influence. In a world obsessed with self-promotion, learning to genuinely understand others is the most powerful persuasive tool you can wield.

Rewiring Your Brain for Understanding

Our brains are hardwired for self-focus. Evolutionarily speaking, we are designed to prioritize our own needs, desires, and survival. This self-centered focus can be useful for individual survival but is detrimental when trying to influence others. True persuasion does not begin with talking, it begins with understanding.

To become a master persuader, you need to rewire your brain to focus on listening first. Empathy, the ability to deeply understand the emotions and perspectives of others, is the foundational rewiring that unlocks everything else. However, this isn't a natural state for most people. The good news? With the right practice and habits, you can train your brain to default to empathy.

Empathy is more than just a "soft skill" or emotional intelligence buzzword. It is a hard-hitting strategic tool that, when mastered, becomes your greatest advantage in influence. Every successful marketer, negotiator, or leader knows this secret: persuasion begins with the listener, not the speaker. Your first task in mastering influence isn't learning how to deliver the perfect pitch, but how to truly understand what drives those around you.

The Science Behind Neural Rewiring

Now that we've identified empathy as the key switch for mastering persuasion, let's go into the neuroscience that makes this rewiring possible.

What Is Neuroplasticity?

Neuroplasticity is the brain's ability to change and adapt in response to new experiences and stimuli. It's the process through which habits are formed, broken, and reformed. When you focus on listening and understanding others, you are reshaping your neural pathways to be less self-centered and more others-focused. Although this transformation sounds metaphorical, it isn't. Your brain physically changes through a process known as synaptic strengthening.

The research from the Huberman Lab explains this in terms of long-term potentiation (LTP), a process where repeated actions or thoughts strengthen the synapses between neurons, making the behavior more automatic. Simply put, the more you practice empathy and deep listening, the more your brain rewires itself to make these actions your default response.

Neuroplasticity doesn't happen overnight, but it's powerful. Every time you engage in empathy, listening without interrupting, understanding before responding, you're training your brain to make that behavior easier and more natural.

How Habits Are Formed

To understand how to rewire your brain for empathy, we need to explore how habits are formed. At the core of habit formation is the cue-routine-reward loop. Here's how it works:

- Cue: A trigger that signals the brain to start the routine.
- Routine: The behavior itself (in this case, deep listening and empathy).
- Reward: The satisfaction or result that reinforces the habit (e.g., building trust, connecting with others).

In the context of empathy, the cue might be entering a conversation or engaging with a new person. The routine is your practice of empathetic listening, asking open-ended questions, reflecting on what the other person says, and suspending your need to respond with your own opinion immediately. The reward is the feeling of deeper connection, mutual understanding, and the enhanced persuasive influence you gain from this.

But where does motivation come from? Enter dopamine. Dopamine is the brain's reward chemical, released when we engage in behaviors that lead to positive outcomes. Each time you successfully employ empathy and experience the reward, dopamine reinforces the habit loop, making you more likely to repeat the behavior.

James Clear's work on habits reinforces this idea: small wins and immediate rewards make it easier to solidify new habits. The more often you practice deep listening and reap the rewards, the stronger the empathy habit becomes. This shift will lay the foundation for greater influence.

Why Empathy Needs to Become Your New Habit

Persuasion isn't a one-time skill, it's a set of habits you build over time. The more you practice empathy, the more it becomes instinctive. Rewiring your brain to prioritize listening and understanding makes you a better communicator and a more persuasive person. Your brain will start to automatically search for emotional cues, needs, and frustrations in others, giving you the insight necessary to tailor your influence strategies.

Let's debunk a myth right away: It takes more than 21 days to rewire your brain for empathy. While the popular 21-day rule suggests that habits form in 3 weeks, recent research shows that this timeline varies. Studies from University College London reveal that, on average, it takes 66 days to form a habit, with simple behaviors (like drinking water) forming quicker than more complex ones, like mastering empathy.

However, the 21-day framework we introduce here is meant to build the foundation for rewiring your brain for empathy-driven persuasion. This is the starting point, where you begin to ingrain new routines and shift your mindset toward understanding before influencing.

Building the Habit of Empathy

So why does this rewiring matter for persuasion? Persuasion doesn't come from a script or formula, it comes from adapting to the other person's needs, values, and emotions. The ability to form and break habits ties directly to how persuasive you can become. Here's why:

- Behavior Change and Persuasion: Empathy is a behavior. Once it becomes a habit, you don't have to consciously think about using it. Instead of defaulting to self-focused responses, you will automatically listen and gather information, which makes your persuasive strategies more natural and effective.
- The Brain's Reward System and Influence: Dopamine plays a key role in reinforcing persuasive behaviors, especially those rooted in empathy. The more you succeed in influencing others by first understanding them, the more rewarding this behavior becomes. Over time, this shapes your decision-making, making you a better listener and, by extension, a more influential person.

Empathy-Based Persuasion

Over the next 21 days, you will rewire your brain to prioritize listening and empathy in every interaction. This isn't about "feeling good" or being nice. You will strategically gather the insights you need to become a master persuader. Each day, you'll spend just 10 minutes practicing deep listening exercises designed to trigger new neural pathways and reinforce your empathy habit.

In this process, you'll learn how to identify emotional cues, frustrations, aspirations, and hidden motivations in every person you interact with. You'll begin to notice how much easier it is to influence someone once you understand what they truly want, and this understanding will come not from talking, but from listening.

By the end of these 21 days, you will have taken the first step toward rewiring your brain for empathy-based persuasion. This chapter, and the exercises within it, aren't about quick fixes, they are about building lasting, foundational changes that turn you into a natural listener and master persuader.

Empathy is about positioning yourself as someone who understands, and in doing so, you'll find that others are far more likely to listen when it's finally your turn to speak.

The Science of Empathy

Empathy is the ability to step outside of your own perspective and see the world through someone else's eyes. But it's more than feeling what others feel, it's also a complex cognitive and emotional process that involves understanding, relating to, and responding to others' experiences and emotions. At its core, empathy is about creating a deep connection, and this connection forms the foundation of influence.

But to truly grasp why empathy is the linchpin of persuasion, we need to explore the neuroscience behind empathy, how the brain processes and mirrors the emotions of others, and how this understanding can be harnessed to influence more effectively.

At a biological level, empathy engages several regions of the brain that allow us to understand and share the feelings of others. Two critical components here are mirror neurons and the prefrontal cortex.

- Mirror Neurons: These neurons, first discovered in the 1990s, are what allow us to feel as though we are experiencing another person's emotions. For example, when we see someone smile, our mirror neurons fire in the same way they would if we were smiling ourselves. This biological mimicry is the foundation of emotional contagion, why someone's joy can make us happy or their sadness can bring us down. Mirror neurons make empathy possible at a cellular level, allowing us to reflect and internalize others' experiences.
- Prefrontal Cortex and Insula: The prefrontal cortex, specifically its medial regions, is involved in higher-order thinking, including perspective-taking, seeing the world from someone else's point of view. The insula, on the other hand, processes bodily and emotional experiences, allowing us to sense the physical feelings associated with another person's emotional state. These two regions work together to create a complex, emotionally charged understanding of the people around us.

The biological basis of empathy means that our brains are wired to connect with others, but here's the paradox: while we are neurologically capable of empathy, most people don't use it nearly as effectively as they could. Why? Because our brains are more often focused on ourselves, on our own survival, needs, and goals. This brings us to the critical issue most people face when it comes to persuasion: the empathy deficit.

Why Most People Struggle to Understand Others

It's no secret that people are naturally self-centered. Not necessarily a bad thing. It's merely a evolutionary trait designed to keep us alive. But it's also what makes empathy harder than it seems. Instead of tuning into others, we often focus on broadcasting our own needs and desires, our own narratives. It's the "me, me, me" problem.

The empathy deficit means we are neurologically conditioned to prioritize ourselves first. We speak before we listen. We think about our response before understanding the other person's words. We aim to persuade by dominating the conversation instead of engaging in it.

Here's the critical insight: to influence, you must first understand. Empathy is the hidden lever that moves others. It allows you to see beyond surface-level communication and tap into the deeper motivations, frustrations, and aspirations of the people you're trying to influence. Once you understand someone's emotional state, you can begin to build trust, reduce resistance, and open the door to influence.

But this requires a rewiring of your brain, moving from a self-focused mindset to one that prioritizes understanding others. The science of neuroplasticity shows that by consistently practicing empathy, you can reshape your neural pathways, expanding your ability to empathize and, therefore, influence.

Why Empathy Matters for Persuasion

Empathy may sound like a nice-to-have skill in persuasion. But believe it or not, empathy is required. You simply cannot understand another person's emotional state, worldview, and underlying desires without empathy. It gives you the unparalleled insight you need to influence them.

Research from the Empathy Imperative shows that when people feel understood, they are more likely to trust you, more open to your suggestions, and more willing to collaborate. Persuasion is not presenting the most logical argument. Persuasion crafts an approach that resonates with someone on an emotional level. This is why empathy is your most powerful tool in persuasion: it reduces psychological resistance and aligns you with the other person's needs.

Think of empathy as the bridge to influence. It is the gateway through which you understand what others want, what they fear, and what motivates them. By prioritizing empathy, you shift the dynamics of influence in your favor because you now speak to the core of their emotional experience at a level deeper than the surface of their logical thinking.

How Deep Listening Rewires the Brain

Most of us have been conditioned to listen only to respond. We hear the words, but we don't deeply understand their meaning. This is what's known as surface listening, it's passive, reactive, and it does little to build the kind of empathy needed for true influence.

Deep listening, on the other hand, is active and intentional. It requires cognitive effort to suspend judgment, quiet the inner dialogue, and focus entirely on the other person. Deep listening pays attention to the tone, the body language, and the emotional undercurrent behind what's being said.

Deep Listening vs. Surface Listening

Surface Listening: This is the kind of listening where you're waiting for your turn to speak. Your brain is already formulating a response before the other person has finished talking. You're listening to confirm your own biases or to argue your point, not to understand the other person.

Deep Listening: In deep listening, your goal is to truly understand what the other person is trying to convey, emotionally, mentally, and even physically. Listen with curiosity, not judgment, and with the intent to understand, not to respond. It's about making the other person feel seen and heard.

When you engage in deep listening, you engage parts of your brain that are tied to empathy and emotional intelligence. You activate your prefrontal cortex (where rational thinking and perspective-taking occur), and your insula (which helps you sense the other person's emotions). Repeated deep listening practices create new neural connections, making empathy a more automatic response.

Here's what happens neurologically when you practice deep listening:

- Neuroplasticity in Action: Every time you listen deeply, you strengthen the neural connections that support empathy and understanding. As you practice this consistently, your brain rewires itself to focus more on others and less on your own internal narrative.

- Mirror Neurons and Emotional Contagion: When you listen deeply, your mirror neurons fire, helping you reflect the other person's emotional state. This builds a stronger connection and allows for a deeper understanding of their feelings and motivations. Over time, your brain gets better at this, making you more attuned to emotional cues.

- The Prefrontal Cortex and Perspective-Taking: The more you practice deep listening, the stronger the pathways in your prefrontal cortex become, helping you take the perspective of others with greater ease. This is crucial for persuasion because it allows you to tailor your approach based on the other person's mindset, rather than your own assumptions.

The Impact on Persuasion

Deep listening fundamentally shifts the dynamics of persuasion. When you listen, you gather critical information that allows you to tailor your message to the other person's needs, frustrations, and aspirations. It changes persuasion from being a one-sided monologue to a deeply personalized interaction.

Here's the key: when people feel heard, they are more likely to trust you, more open to your ideas, and more inclined to be persuaded. Listening is an active strategy that primes the other person to receive your message. Deep listening transforms persuasion from an act of convincing to an act of understanding, which in turn makes your influence more powerful and sustainable.

By rewiring your brain to listen deeply, you become a master of emotional and social cues. This is about connecting with them on a deeper level. And once you can do that, persuasion becomes easier, more authentic, and insanely effective.

The 21-Day Neural Rewiring

Now that we've laid the groundwork for why empathy is the key to influence and how the brain rewires itself through practice, it's time to act. This section introduces the Empathy-Driven 21-Day Rewiring Challenge, a focused, structured approach to build the habit of empathy through daily exercises. Each task is designed to reprogram your brain to prioritize listening and understanding, transforming empathy from a conscious effort into a subconscious reflex.

The goal of this challenge is simple but profound: to rewire your brain to focus on others first. Over the next 21 days, you'll commit to 10 minutes of daily exercises that target empathy and deep listening. These practices aren't just about "feeling" empathy; they're about creating the mental architecture that allows you to instinctively gather emotional cues, understand motivations, and use this understanding to become a more effective influencer.

By consistently engaging in these exercises, you'll form new neural pathways that make empathy a habit, one that serves as the foundation for all your future persuasive efforts.

It's natural to think of persuasion as the art of delivering the right words at the right time. But persuasion starts with understanding. You can't influence someone if you don't first understand what drives them. This is why the first step in becoming a master persuader is to develop your capacity for deep empathy.

Empathy allows you to tap into the emotions, needs, and frustrations of others. When you understand someone's internal world, you can tailor your persuasive strategies to resonate with their deepest desires. This challenge is about training your brain to listen; rewiring it to instinctively understand others on a deeper, more meaningful level.

This switch, from speaking to listening, from self-focus to other-focus, is the foundational change that will unlock success in the rest of this book. Without it, the strategies you learn will be hollow. With it, they will become powerful tools of influence.

Each day, you'll not only complete a specific exercise but also engage in a brief reflection session where you'll journal your thoughts and observations. This reflection is critical, it reinforces the neural rewiring by helping you track your progress and recognize the shifts in your own behavior. You'll document what you've learned about others' emotions, needs, and frustrations, and how this newfound understanding impacts your interactions.

Day 1–7: Building the Foundation of Empathy

Exercise 1: The Listening Audit (Day 1–3)

For the first 3 days, your job is simple: observe yourself. In each conversation you have with a friend, colleague, or family member, take note of how often you interrupt, change the subject, or turn the conversation toward yourself. Keep a Listening Journal where you document each instance.

Key Questions to Ask Yourself:

- How often do I speak before the other person has finished their thought?

- Do I change the subject to something about myself or my interests?
- How frequently do I offer unsolicited advice or solutions instead of just listening?

The goal of this exercise is to build awareness. Before you can improve your empathy, you need to understand your current listening habits. Awareness is the first step toward rewiring your brain.

Exercise 2: The Listening Switch (Day 4–7)

For the next four days, you'll practice switching off your inner dialogue and focusing entirely on the other person during conversations. Here's the challenge: for at least five minutes in every conversation, you are not allowed to talk about yourself.

Instead, your goal is to:

- Ask open-ended questions (e.g., "How did that make you feel?" or "What do you think you'll do next?").
- Gather as much information as possible about the other person's emotions, needs, and frustrations.
- Avoid interrupting, offering advice, or switching the focus to yourself.

After each conversation, journal the details you learned, paying special attention to emotional cues. What did you discover about the other person that you didn't know before? How did they feel, and what hidden motivations became apparent?

How These Exercises Rewire Your Brain

The Listening Audit and Listening Switch are designed to override the brain's default "ME" impulse. When you make a conscious effort to listen without focusing on your own thoughts, you activate the neural circuits responsible for empathy and emotional regulation, such as the prefrontal cortex and insula. Repeated practice of these behaviors forms new neural connections that gradually make empathy automatic.

Neuroplasticity, the brain's ability to change and adapt, means that each time you engage in deep listening, you're strengthening the pathways associated with understanding others. Over time, these pathways become more efficient, turning what was once an effortful process into a reflex. The more you practice, the less you'll have to think about listening, it will simply become your default mode.

Day 8–14: Deepening Empathy Through Action

Exercise 3: The Empathy Interview (Day 8–10)

In this exercise, you'll step up your empathy game by conducting a mini-interview with a friend, colleague, or family member. Don't think of it as a casual conversation, this is a focused effort to dig deeper into their emotional world.

Your job is to ask questions that uncover:

- Aspirations: What are their goals? What drives them?
- Frustrations: What's holding them back? What's causing them stress?
- Hidden Emotions: What feelings are they not expressing outright, but that you can sense in their tone or body language?

Importantly, you are not allowed to offer solutions or advice. Your only goal is to understand. After the conversation, journal your findings. What did you learn about their emotional state that you hadn't known before? How did it feel to focus entirely on their needs, without jumping in to share your own thoughts?

Exercise 4: Empathy in Action (Day 11–14)

For the next few days, it's time to apply your deep listening skills in real-world persuasive situations. No matter the situation you're in, you must first focus entirely on understanding the other person's needs, desires, and frustrations before making any persuasive attempt.

- Key Task: In each interaction, aim to spend the first half of the conversation purely on gathering information. Only after you've understood their perspective fully should you begin to offer a suggestion, solution, or influence.

Document how the conversation changes when empathy leads the interaction. Did the other person seem more receptive? Did their body language shift? How did their emotional state evolve as they felt heard and understood?

Deepening the Empathy Habit

By this point in the challenge, you'll have engaged in a full week of deliberate empathy exercises. As you practice empathy in action, your brain's mirror neurons, responsible for reflecting the emotions of others, become more responsive. Additionally, the prefrontal cortex, which manages perspective-taking and rational thought, becomes more adept at processing the emotional and mental states of others.

As you continue these exercises, the neural pathways involved in empathy strengthen, turning deep listening into a subconscious habit. Your ability to read emotional and social cues improves, and empathy becomes a reflex that you automatically bring to every interaction. This is where persuasion starts to become effortless, because you're no longer guessing what the other person needs; you know.

Day 15–21: Mastering the Empathy Switch

Exercise 5: The Phone Call Challenge (Day 15–18)

For this exercise, you'll engage in a 10-minute phone conversation with someone you don't know well, a colleague you're not close to, an acquaintance, or even a customer. Your goal is to uncover their motivations, fears, and aspirations, focusing entirely on listening and understanding.

Take notes during the call, focusing on:

- Emotions: What do they care about? What worries them?
- Values: What principles seem to guide their decisions?
- Motivations: What are they trying to achieve?

At the end of the conversation, reflect on how much you learned and how this understanding could help you influence them in future interactions.

Exercise 6: The Empathy Movie Watch (Day 19–21)

In the final days of the challenge, we'll take empathy into a new context: storytelling. Watch a movie or TV show, but instead of focusing on the plot, pay close attention to the characters' hidden motivations and emotional drivers. As you watch, ask yourself:

- What does each character want most?
- What are their deepest fears?
- How do they express their emotions indirectly, through body language or tone of voice?

Journal your insights after the movie, noting how empathy allows you to understand the characters on a deeper level. This exercise will help you sharpen your ability to read emotional cues in everyday life.

Finalizing the Empathy Rewire

By the end of the 21 days, your brain will have undergone significant rewiring. Through repeated empathy exercises, you'll have forged new neural pathways that prioritize understanding others first. The more you've practiced, the more automatic empathy has become. This shift in your brain's default mode will give you an edge in all future persuasive interactions.

Empathy is now a habit, one that you'll continue to strengthen throughout your journey in mastering persuasion.

The Empathy-Driven 21-Day Rewiring Challenge is the foundation for everything that follows in this book. By rewiring your brain to focus on others first, you've unlocked the most critical tool in the persuasion arsenal. With this new habit ingrained, you're ready to move forward and apply your empathetic skills in every area of life, knowing that influence starts not with speaking, but with listening.

Empathy in Your Persuasive Arsenal

Now that you've rewired your brain to prioritize empathy, it's time to take your newly developed skill and integrate it into your persuasive strategy. Empathy is a strategic tool that transforms how you approach every interaction. Once you've honed the ability to truly understand someone's needs, frustrations, and desires, persuasion becomes less about tactics and more about delivering tailored solutions that resonate deeply with the other person. This is where empathy becomes the core of your persuasive arsenal, giving you an unparalleled advantage in every conversation, negotiation, or pitch.

How Empathy Makes You a Master Persuader

At its highest level, persuasion is about moving people to action by aligning your message with their core needs and motivations. Now that you've rewired your brain to focus on understanding others first, your approach to influence will naturally evolve from delivering pre-packaged arguments to offering solutions tailored specifically to the other person.

Here's the critical shift: you no longer persuade by talking, you persuade by understanding. You're no longer making assumptions about what someone needs; you know because you've listened deeply and gathered the emotional and practical information necessary to offer relevant solutions. Your ability to empathize gives you an advantage that many miss: it takes the guesswork out of persuasion.

In the Empathy Imperative section of the book, we explored how truly successful influencers focus not on what they want to say but on what the other person needs to hear. The most effective communicators are those who understand the emotional state and desires of the other person before they speak. They're aligning with the other person's needs and offering a path forward that feels natural and personalized.

This understanding is now at the core of your persuasive strategies.

Reading the Room

Empathy also gives you the ability to "read the room", to pick up on the subtle cues that reveal more than words ever could. When you listen with empathy, you become attuned to the emotional undercurrents of a conversation, enabling you to spot the unspoken concerns, motivations, or hesitations that others might miss.

- Body Language: A shift in posture, a furrowed brow, or crossed arms can tell you that the other person is feeling defensive, skeptical, or uneasy, signals that are invisible to someone who is focused only on delivering their message. Empathetic listening sharpens your ability to catch these physical cues and adjust your approach accordingly.

- Tone of Voice: A change in tone can signal excitement, hesitation, or frustration. Someone might be saying one thing, but the way they say it can reveal an entirely different meaning. With empathy, you become adept at detecting these tonal shifts and can probe deeper to understand the real emotions behind the words.

- Emotional Signals: Beyond body language and tone, empathy allows you to sense the emotional state of the person you're speaking with. Are they stressed, enthusiastic, or doubtful? Understanding their emotional context enables you to respond in a way that feels appropriate and aligned with their state of mind.

The more you practice reading the room, the more natural it becomes to tailor your persuasive strategies to match the emotional and social dynamics of the situation.

Tailoring Your Message to Their Needs

Once you understand the emotional and practical landscape of the other person, you can now tailor your message to address their specific needs, desires, and frustrations. This is where persuasion shifts from a one-size-fits-all approach to a customized, targeted strategy that feels personal and compelling.

Here's how empathy helps you tailor your message:

- Address Their Pain Points: If you've spent time listening to their frustrations and challenges, you know exactly what problems they need solved. Use that understanding to position your message as a solution to those specific issues. For example, in a negotiation, you might address the other party's concerns before they even voice them, demonstrating that you've been listening and are ready to offer something that aligns with their interests.

- Speak to Their Aspirations: Persuasion is about helping people achieve their goals. When you understand what drives someone, their aspirations and desires, you can frame your message as a pathway to achieving those outcomes. For instance, if a customer looking for a product that will elevate their lifestyle or a colleague who wants to advance their career, your message should resonate with their forward-looking ambitions.

- Align with Their Values: Empathy allows you to tap into what people value most. Is this person driven by security, recognition, creativity, or impact? When you understand their core values, you can tailor your approach in a way that shows alignment with what they care about most. For example, in a sales situation, if you know a customer values sustainability, you can emphasize how your product is environmentally friendly, making your message more relevant and persuasive.

Practical Applications of Empathy in Persuasion

Empathy has practical, real-world applications that you can start using immediately. No matter the business, the personal relationship, or the sales call you're working, empathy transforms how you interact with others and increases your persuasive power.

Uncovering Hidden Objections

In business negotiations, empathy gives you the edge by helping you uncover objections before they become deal-breakers. When you focus on understanding the other party's needs and concerns, you can anticipate their objections and address them proactively.

Here's how empathy enhances negotiation:

- Anticipating Objections: By listening carefully, you'll often pick up on subtle signs of resistance long before they voice it directly. This gives you the opportunity to address concerns before they solidify, making the other party feel understood and reducing friction in the negotiation.

- Building Trust: Empathy builds trust. When people feel that you genuinely care about their interests and aren't just pushing your own agenda, they're more likely to collaborate and compromise. Trust is the foundation of successful negotiation, and empathy is the key to building that trust.

- Framing Solutions: Once you've identified their concerns, frustrations, or aspirations, you can frame your offer as a solution that directly addresses those issues. You're making more than a pitch; you're presenting a win-win scenario that aligns with their needs.

Fostering Trust and Reducing Conflict

Empathy is essential in personal relationships. By listening deeply and understanding the emotional needs of your partner, friend, or family member, you can foster trust and reduce conflict.

- Defusing Tension: In moments of conflict, the instinct is often to defend our position. But empathy allows you to step back and understand the emotional root of the other person's frustration. Once they feel heard and understood, tensions often ease, opening the door to more constructive dialogue.

- Building Emotional Intimacy: Empathy is the foundation of emotional intimacy. When you take the time to listen to your partner's needs, aspirations, and concerns, you create a bond of trust and understanding. In relationships, the most powerful form of persuasion doesn't change someone's mind with facts. This is done by showing that you understand them.

Connecting with Emotional Needs

In sales and marketing, empathy helps you connect with customers on a deeper, emotional level. This connection is what separates a good salesperson from a great one, one that sells a solution that resonates with the customer's emotional needs.

- Identifying Emotional Drivers: Every purchase is driven by emotional needs: the desire for security, status, comfort, or achievement. Empathy allows you to identify what emotional drivers are influencing the customer's decision and craft your message accordingly.

- Creating Resonant Messaging: Once you understand the emotional landscape of your customer, you can create messaging that speaks directly to their feelings and desires. For example, if a customer is buying a product to feel more secure, your message should emphasize the safety and reliability of what you're offering. If they're driven by a desire for recognition, your message should focus on the prestige or status associated with the product.

- Personalizing the Experience: Empathy allows you to tailor the customer experience through personalized recommendations, thoughtful follow-ups, and targeted messaging, creating an interaction that feels less like a transaction and more like a relationship. This emotional connection increases customer loyalty and long-term engagement.

Embedding empathy into your persuasive arsenal transforms how you approach every interaction. It moves you from a one-size-fits-all approach to a tailored, human-centered strategy that speaks to the emotional needs, frustrations, and aspirations of the people you're trying to influence. By rewiring your brain for empathy, you've unlocked the most powerful tool of persuasion: the ability to understand others at their core and offer solutions that resonate deeply with them.

Evolving the Practice

Developing empathy as the foundation of your persuasive abilities is a significant first step, but the journey doesn't end there. Like any skill, the mastery of empathy and influence requires ongoing reflection, measurement, and refinement. In this section, we'll explore how to track your progress, identify areas for improvement, and evolve your practice so that empathy-based persuasion becomes second nature.

How to Measure Your Persuasion Progress

Mastering persuasion through empathy is not an overnight transformation, it's a process. To see tangible results, you need to actively track the shifts in both your emotional responses and cognitive flexibility. These shifts are indicators that your brain is rewiring itself to prioritize empathy and deep listening.

Track Emotional and Cognitive Changes

At the end of each day, take a few minutes to log your experiences in your Persuasion Journal. The goal is to track two key areas:

- Emotional Responses: Reflect on how your emotional responses have shifted. Did you notice that you were more patient or less reactive during conversations? Were you able to stay calm and focused on understanding the other person, rather than jumping in with your own thoughts or solutions?

- Cognitive Flexibility: This refers to your ability to adapt your thinking based on new information. Did your perspective shift after learning more about the other person's emotions and motivations? Were you able to adjust your approach to better align with their needs?

In addition to these reflections, measure your persuasive success. Getting others to agree with you is nice; but it's far better to create stronger connections, build trust, and deepen your influence through empathy.

Daily Log Example:

- Date: [Enter Date]

- Interaction: [Describe the situation, who were you speaking with? What was the context?]

- Emotional Response: [Did you feel more patient or empathetic? How did you manage your emotional reactions?]

- Cognitive Flexibility: [Did you shift your approach or perspective based on what you learned about the other person?]

- Persuasive Outcome: [Did the conversation result in deeper understanding or trust? Were you able to align with the other person's needs?]

This daily log will serve as both a progress tracker and a way to hold yourself accountable for integrating empathy into your persuasive interactions.

Self-Reflection

Reflection is a critical component of rewiring your brain. It's not enough to simply complete the daily empathy exercises, you need to reflect on how those exercises are impacting your mindset and behavior. This self-reflection solidifies the neural changes you're working to achieve and deepens your ability to empathize.

Each day, ask yourself key reflection questions that force you to examine how your persuasive skills are evolving:

- What did I do differently in today's interaction?
  This question prompts you to reflect on specific changes in your behavior. Did you listen more attentively? Did you hold back from interrupting or shifting the conversation to yourself? The more specific you can be, the better.

- How did my thinking change after today's exercise?
  Reflect if you gained new insights into how the other person feels or thinks. Did practicing empathy shift your perspective or reveal something you hadn't noticed before? This question helps track your cognitive flexibility.

- What did I learn about the other person's emotions and motivations?
  Every interaction is an opportunity to practice gathering emotional and motivational information. What new insights did you gain today that could help you tailor future persuasive efforts?

- How did empathy impact the outcome?
  Reflect on how leading with empathy changed the dynamics of the conversation. Did the other person seem more open or trusting? Were they more receptive to your ideas?

These self-reflection questions should be written down in your journal, as they will help you recognize patterns in your behavior and thinking. Over time, you'll begin to see a clear link between empathy and your growing persuasive success.

The Power of Reflection in Neural Rewiring

Why is reflection so important in this process? Because reflection reinforces neural changes. When you reflect on your experiences, you're effectively telling your brain, "This behavior matters, strengthen the pathways that support it."

Neuroplasticity research shows that the brain becomes more efficient at behaviors we repeatedly focus on, particularly when we reflect on those behaviors after the fact. By taking time each day to reflect on your progress, you're reinforcing the new neural pathways that support empathy-driven persuasion. This process strengthens the connections in your brain related to empathy, listening, and emotional intelligence.

Think of neural rewiring like learning to play a musical instrument. Practicing the notes is important, but taking the time to reflect on where you need to improve, what worked, and how to adjust your practice moving forward helps you progress much faster. The same principle applies here, reflection amplifies the impact of your practice.

Homework Writing Framework

To help you consistently track your progress and deepen your self-awareness, here's a simple journaling template you can use after each exercise or interaction. This framework will guide your reflection and help you pinpoint areas where you're excelling and where you still need to focus.

Daily Persuasion Journal Template:

- Date: [Insert Date]
- Interaction Summary:
    - Who were you speaking with?
    - What was the context (business, personal, negotiation, etc.)?
    - What was the goal of the conversation?
- Emotional Response:
    - How did you feel during the interaction?
    - Did you notice any changes in how you managed your emotions compared to previous interactions?
- Cognitive Flexibility:

- Did your thinking or approach change based on what you learned about the other person?
- How did you adapt your message to better align with their needs or desires?
- Persuasion Outcome:
  - Did the other person seem more receptive to your message?
  - Did empathy change the tone or direction of the conversation?
  - Was trust or rapport strengthened?
- Self-Reflection Questions:
  - What did I do differently in today's interaction?
  - How did my thinking change after today's exercise?
  - What did I learn about the other person's emotions and motivations?
  - How did empathy impact the outcome?

For digital, downloadable and printable journal templates, head to **tomwalker.com/content**

Example 1: Business Negotiation

- Date: October 10, 2024
- Interaction Summary: Had a meeting with a potential client about a new software service. The goal was to understand their needs and offer a solution.
- Emotional Response: I felt calm and focused. I noticed I wasn't as eager to jump in and explain the product, I spent more time listening to their pain points.
- Cognitive Flexibility: After hearing about their frustrations with previous software, I adapted my message to highlight our solution's ease of use rather than its advanced features.
- Persuasion Outcome: The client seemed more relaxed and open by the end of the meeting. They asked more questions, which I think was a sign that they felt understood.
- Self-Reflection Questions:

- I didn't rush to explain our product like I normally would. Instead, I listened more and asked questions.
- My thinking changed when I realized that their frustrations weren't with complex features but with software that was hard to use. I adjusted my pitch accordingly.
- I learned that they value simplicity and reliability more than flashy features.
- Empathy allowed me to connect with their frustrations, and I think that's why they became more receptive by the end.

Example 2: Personal Relationship

- Date: October 11, 2024
- Interaction Summary: Talked to a close friend who seemed stressed about a personal issue. My goal was to listen without offering advice unless asked.
- Emotional Response: I noticed that I wanted to jump in and offer solutions, but I held back and focused on listening. This made me feel more patient and present.
- Cognitive Flexibility: I realized that my friend wasn't looking for solutions, they just wanted to be heard. This changed how I approached the conversation.
- Persuasion Outcome: By the end of the conversation, my friend seemed calmer and expressed gratitude for just being able to vent. It was clear that empathy was more valuable than advice in this situation.
- Self-Reflection Questions:
    - I resisted the urge to offer solutions and just focused on listening.
    - My thinking changed when I realized my friend didn't need advice, they needed understanding.
    - I learned that sometimes people don't need a solution, they need someone to empathize with their frustration.
    - Empathy helped my friend feel heard and appreciated, which I think strengthened our relationship.

The Power of Reflection in Mastering Persuasion

Tracking your progress and reflecting on your experiences is an essential part of rewiring your brain for empathy-based persuasion. By journaling your emotional responses, cognitive flexibility, and persuasive success, you solidify the neural changes that make empathy an instinct rather than a skill you have to consciously apply.

Reflection also provides you with valuable insights into how your persuasive abilities are evolving. It helps you recognize patterns, improve where needed, and reinforce what's working. Over time, this reflective practice will make empathy a habit and a master of influence. Remember: reflection is a continuous process that drives growth and mastery.

The Future of Your Brain

You've taken the critical first step in rewiring your brain for lasting influence. But the journey doesn't stop here. In fact, these 21 days are merely the beginning of a lifelong process of mastering persuasion. But where you go from here? How do you continue evolving and strengthening the neural pathways you've built? And how to apply these skills to every facet of your life?

The key to success moving forward is to recognize that mastery of persuasion, like any skill, requires consistent practice, reflection, and refinement. The more you exercise these new behaviors, the more deeply ingrained they become, eventually transforming how you interact, lead, and influence in all areas of your life.

What Happens After 21 Days?

The process of neuroplasticity is ongoing. Even though the 21-day challenge helped you create the foundation for empathy-based persuasion, the neural pathways that support these new habits are still in their early stages. Continued practice is necessary to strengthen these connections and make empathy-driven influence an automatic response.

Think of these first 21 days as the point at which your brain has started to carve out new "mental highways." These highways, or neural pathways, will continue to grow and become more efficient over time as you practice empathy and deep listening in your daily interactions. The more you use these pathways, the faster and more automatic your empathetic responses will become. Eventually, listening deeply and prioritizing the needs of others will stop being a conscious effort and become something instinctual.

This process mirrors what happens when learning any complex skill like playing an instrument, speaking a new language, or developing a physical talent. At first, it takes conscious effort and repetition to perform the skill. But over time, through deliberate practice, the skill becomes second nature. The same is true for empathy-driven persuasion: with consistent application, it will become an embedded part of your character and approach to all interactions.

Daily Practices to Maintain Progress

To ensure that the neural rewiring you've started continues to evolve, it's essential to adopt daily practices that reinforce and sharpen your new persuasive instincts. These practices aren't time-consuming, but they are powerful in keeping your brain engaged in the process of empathy, emotional regulation, and influence.

Here are some ongoing daily practices you can incorporate to maintain progress:

- Mindful Listening Practice: Continue practicing deep listening in every interaction. Focus on being present and fully engaged when others speak, paying attention to not only their words but also their body language, tone of voice, and emotional cues. Dedicate even 5 minutes of your day to a mindful conversation with a colleague, partner, or friend. The goal is to keep your empathy muscles strong and flexible.

- Emotional Regulation Exercises: Emotional control is key to persuasive success. Incorporate brief mindfulness or breathing exercises into your day to stay centered and calm, especially in high-stakes interactions. When emotions rise, remember that empathy and influence are best practiced from a place of calm understanding rather than emotional reactivity.

- Empathy Journaling: While you may not need to journal every day, set aside time once or twice a week to reflect on your persuasive interactions. What did you learn about the other person? How did empathy change the dynamic of the conversation? How could you have improved your approach? This reflection reinforces the mental pathways that support empathy and deepens your awareness of how it plays out in your life.

- The One Question Rule: In every interaction, aim to ask at least one open-ended question that invites the other person to share more about their emotions or thoughts. This simple practice keeps the focus on understanding others first, which is the foundation of empathy-driven persuasion.

These practices don't need to be exhaustive, but they serve as consistent reminders that empathy and influence are skills that grow through daily application. The brain stays sharp through repetition, by weaving these small practices into your everyday life, you ensure that empathy remains a core part of your identity and persuasive toolkit.

Deliberate Practice Beyond Persuasion

By now, you've learned that empathy is the key to mastering influence, but the benefits of the neural rewiring you've done extend far beyond persuasion. The same techniques that help you understand and influence others can also be applied to other areas of your life, including leadership, negotiation, and personal growth.

Expand on Other Areas of Life

- Leadership: Great leaders are empathetic leaders. By understanding the emotional needs and motivations of your team, you can lead in a way that fosters trust, engagement, and loyalty. Empathy helps you recognize what drives each individual, allowing you to tailor your leadership style to inspire and motivate your team effectively. Empathetic leaders are better at resolving conflicts, creating strong team cultures, and guiding others toward a common vision.

- Negotiation: In high-stakes negotiations, empathy allows you to understand the other party's concerns and objectives, giving you the insight needed to craft win-win solutions. The ability to "read the room" and pick up on unspoken signals gives you a critical edge in uncovering hidden objections and addressing them before they become deal-breakers. Empathy helps you understand the emotions behind the words, guiding you to more successful outcomes.

- Personal Growth: Empathy enhances your own emotional intelligence, self-awareness, and personal development. By practicing empathy, you become more attuned to your own emotional responses, helping you manage stress, build resilience, and foster healthier relationships. This growth extends beyond persuasion and into every facet of your life.

Commit to the Long Game

Mastery of persuasion, like any complex skill, is a lifelong pursuit. The 21-day challenge has given you a powerful starting point, but real mastery comes from a long-term commitment to deliberate practice and continued refinement.

Here's the reality: persuasion mastery doesn't happen overnight. Just as an athlete trains for years to reach peak performance, you must continue to build your empathy-driven persuasion skills over time. The more you practice, the more natural it becomes, and the more deeply ingrained it is in your brain's neural pathways.

The Key to Long-Term Success:

- Consistent Application: Commit to practicing empathy and influence every day. The more you use these skills, the stronger and more automatic they become. Set long-term goals for your persuasive growth and reflect regularly on how you're evolving.

- Challenge Yourself: Once you've mastered empathy in everyday interactions, push yourself into more challenging situations. Apply your empathy-driven persuasion in high-stakes negotiations, leadership roles, or conflict resolution. These situations will further hone your skills and expand your capacity for influence.

- Evolve Your Practice: As you grow, you'll discover new layers of persuasion mastery. What worked in the first stages of your journey will evolve into more sophisticated strategies. Keep learning, experimenting, and refining your approach. Deliberate practice means constantly seeking improvement, even after you've achieved initial success.

The Journey Toward Lifelong Persuasion Mastery

The 21-day empathy challenge has set the foundation for your transformation into a master of influence, but the road ahead is long and filled with opportunity. The future of your brain, and your persuasive abilities, depends on the choices you make from here. Continue to practice, reflect, and evolve. Treat every interaction as a chance to deepen your empathy and refine your influence.

Remember: persuasion mastery is a journey. The more you commit to the long game, the more persuasive power you'll unlock. Empathy is the key, and the more you strengthen it, the more your influence will grow.

CHAPTER 4

The Desire Decoder

The caveman who fought for food and security isn't so different from the corporate executive who obsesses over status and validation. Both are operating on the same primal software, just in different contexts.

Why You Do What You Do

Pause for a moment. Think back to your last decision, choosing what to wear this morning, responding to a text, or sealing a business deal. Now ask yourself: Did I really make that decision, or did something deeper drive me?

The truth is, you didn't choose. At least, not in the way you think. Every choice, every impulse, and every action you take is rooted in one of seven primal desires that have been wired into your brain over millennia. You're not as in control as you believe. These deep, subconscious forces have shaped every moment of your life, from the way you approach love, to how you expand your career, to the subtle manipulations you employ without even realizing it.

These desires are invisible puppet strings, pulling at the heart of human behavior. You might believe you're operating based on logic or free will, but beneath the surface, it's these primal forces that steer the ship. If you think you can outrun them, you're wrong. If you think you can control them, you're deluding yourself. Unless, of course, you learn how to decode them.

Why We're Wired This Way

These primal desires aren't a flaw; they're survival mechanisms. Hard-coded into your brain, they evolved to keep your ancestors alive, ensuring that they found food, built relationships, avoided threats, and ultimately passed on their genes. But here's the catch, these ancient drives haven't changed, even though the world around you has. The caveman who fought for food and security isn't so different from the corporate executive who obsesses over status and validation. Both are operating on the same primal software, just in different contexts.

The Seven Primal Desires

These seven primal desires dictate how you think, feel, and act. They are the undercurrents of all human behavior, survival, security, status, love, connection, autonomy, self-actualization, and validation. Each of these desires is a force of nature within you, and once you understand them, you gain the power to predict, influence, and even manipulate the behaviors of others.

Imagine being able to walk into any room and immediately sense what's driving the people around you. Imagine understanding the unspoken desires of your partner, your colleagues, or even your rivals. And more importantly, imagine turning those insights into power, power to influence decisions, close deals, build relationships, and win.

This chapter is about decoding these primal desires, breaking them down, and giving you actionable insights to leverage them. You're going to learn to to recognize these forces in yourself and others, harnessing them in ways that will revolutionize the way you interact with the world. And yes, this means gaining a kind of mastery over others, but more importantly, over yourself.

The Neuroscience of Desire

Modern neuroscience reveals that these desires are far from arbitrary. Take, for instance, dopamine, often called the "pleasure chemical." But it's not pleasure that dopamine drives, it's anticipation. As Dr. Lisa Feldman Barrett points out: "Understanding what people react to based on biology... allows us to predict human behavior with surprising accuracy". Dopamine is released when you get what you want and when you're in pursuit of it, creating a cycle of desire that's never fully satisfied.

This anticipation is what keeps us moving forward, pushing for more, more status, more security, more love. It's what marketers exploit to keep you hooked, what lovers manipulate to deepen emotional bonds, and what your subconscious mind craves every day, without you even realizing it.

Actionable Power

The real power of understanding these primal desires lies in their universality. Once you grasp how they work, you can spot them in any any boardroom negotiation or an intimate conversation with your partner. Are they operating from a place of fear, seeking survival? Or are they driven by a need for validation? Do they crave autonomy, or are they chasing status? This knowledge arms you with the ability to adapt and tailor your approach to meet their underlying needs, making you infinitely more persuasive.

In business, you'll learn to negotiate on the primal desires of your counterpart. In relationships, you'll tap into the deep psychological needs of your partner to strengthen your bond or recognize when manipulation is at play. And in everyday life, you'll begin to see the puppet strings that others are pulling, and perhaps more importantly, the ones that have been pulling you.

This is a framework for understanding the very essence of what it means to be human, driven by desire, guided by instinct, and, if you're skilled enough, mastered by those who know how to decode them.

Now, let's unmask these desires.

Survival: The Fear Driver

Survival instincts aren't confined to life-or-death situations. They don't just kick in when we're faced with a wild animal or a burning building. These primal drives operate silently in the background, influencing our most mundane decisions. The survival instinct is one of the most powerful forces guiding human behavior. How do I know? Ask those who chose the stable career, stayed in a toxic relationship, or even hoarded resources "just in case."

Survival is about avoiding loss, mitigating risk, and clinging to the illusion of safety. And when fear takes the wheel, we often make decisions that are more about protecting ourselves from perceived threats than moving toward growth or fulfillment.

The Neuroscience of Survival and Fear

Fear-based decision-making is rooted in the brain's wiring. One of the most significant chemicals at play here is cortisol, often called the "stress hormone." Elevated levels of cortisol signal to the brain that there is danger ahead, which triggers a cascade of physiological and psychological responses designed to help us survive. However, in modern life, these responses often backfire, leading us to make choices that are more about avoiding discomfort than achieving our full potential.

A study by Smith & Brown (2022) on Cortisol and Decision-Making highlights how elevated cortisol levels, often triggered by stress, push people toward risk-averse behavior. This reaction might have been advantageous when survival meant dodging predators, but in today's world, it can drive people to cling to situations that keep them trapped in mediocrity. This is the survival instinct at play, pulling you toward the familiar, even if the familiar is toxic, limiting, or downright harmful.

As Dr. Robert Sapolsky famously notes, "The brain's response to perceived threats is a powerful driver of behavior, often overriding rational decision-making". This insight explains why people frequently choose short-term safety over long-term gain, even if it means staying in a dead-end job or refusing to take a chance on a new opportunity.

The Fear of Loneliness

Consider personal relationships. Why do people stay in relationships that don't serve them, or worse, actively harm them? Often, it's not love, loyalty, or even habit that keeps them tethered. It's fear. Fear of being alone, fear of the unknown, fear of what life might look like without the security blanket of a partner, no matter how toxic that partner may be.

The survival drive whispers, "It's better to be with someone than to face the uncertainty of being alone." This is the same survival instinct that once warned our ancestors not to stray too far from the tribe, where isolation meant danger and death. Today, that instinct manifests as the fear of loneliness, pushing people to remain in unhealthy situations just to avoid the perceived threat of isolation.

Playing it Safe to Avoid Loss

In business, the survival instinct often shows up as a reluctance to take risks, even when the potential rewards are high. Negotiators, for instance, may settle for a safer, less profitable deal out of fear of losing everything. They rationalize their decisions, telling themselves that it's better to play it safe than to gamble with the unknown. But what's really happening beneath the surface is that their cortisol levels are spiking, triggering fear-based behavior.

This drive to protect oneself from perceived financial or professional loss can keep even the most talented individuals trapped in mediocrity, choosing short-term security over long-term success. The survival instinct convinces them that the potential for loss is greater than the potential for gain, even when the facts suggest otherwise.

Mastering the Survival Instinct

If you want to master the art of persuasion, negotiation, or even personal relationships, you need to recognize when the survival instinct is in control. Here are two critical ways to apply this understanding:

1. Spot Survival-Driven Behavior in Others
   When you see someone making decisions based on fear, like clinging to a bad relationship, settling for less in a negotiation, or refusing to take a calculated risk, you have an opportunity. Recognize their fear for what it is, and tailor your approach to either empathize or exploit it, depending on your intentions. In negotiations, for example, you might offer them the illusion of security while pushing them toward the deal you want. In relationships, understanding their fear can help you offer emotional reassurance, creating deeper bonds of trust.

2. Recognize and Rise Above Your Own Fear Responses
   On the flip side, you need to learn to spot when your own survival instincts are leading you astray. Are you staying in a job that stifles you because it feels "safe"? Are you holding back from pursuing a passion because you're afraid of failure? Are you avoiding conflict in a relationship because you fear the uncertainty of what comes next? Recognizing when your decisions are driven by the survival instinct is the first step to breaking free from its grasp. Learn to rise above it, pushing yourself toward growth rather than clinging to a false sense of security.

Understanding the brain's deep-rooted survival mechanisms gives you insight into others and power over yourself. And in a world where most people are ruled by fear, mastering your survival instinct can be the difference between living a life of safety or a life of fulfillment.

Security: The Need for Stability

When we think of security, the first thing that likely comes to mind is financial stability: a steady paycheck, a roof over our heads, and the means to protect ourselves from life's uncertainties. But the need for security runs much deeper than our bank accounts. It infiltrates every corner of our lives, from the relationships we maintain, to the career choices we make, to the ways we interact with the world socially. Security is about creating predictability and order in a world that feels chaotic. And that desire to establish stability can often lead to decisions that prioritize comfort over growth.

How Serotonin Shapes Stability

At the core of this drive for security lies a powerful neurochemical: serotonin. A study conducted by Garcia & Lee (2022) found that serotonin levels are closely linked to feelings of safety and stability, influencing our tendency to choose safer, more predictable options. When serotonin levels are high, we feel grounded, stable, and secure. We lean toward decisions that maintain this sense of equilibrium, even if they're not necessarily the best for our long-term growth. As Dr. Maria Garcia explains, "Higher serotonin levels are associated with feelings of stability and well-being, influencing decision-making toward safer options".

This connection between serotonin and decision-making explains why many of us choose the path of least resistance, often opting for security over risk, even when taking a chance might lead to something far greater.

Avoiding Conflict, Sacrificing Growth

In relationships, the drive for security often manifests as a desire to avoid conflict. People stay in stagnant relationships, not because they are fulfilling or deeply enriching, but because they offer the illusion of stability. The logic goes something like this: "Better to be with someone, even if things aren't perfect, than to face the uncertainty of being alone."Conflict, after all, threatens that sense of security, creating the possibility that the relationship could end. And while staying in a conflict-free relationship might seem peaceful, it often leads to stagnation and prevents emotional growth.

The same drive for security also leads individuals to stay in familiar but toxic relationships. There's a comfort in the known, even if the known is harmful. It's a kind of emotional inertia: a reluctance to disrupt the status quo, even when change could bring about positive transformation. This is security masquerading as love, and it's a trap many fall into.

Playing it Safe, Missing Out on Reward

In the professional sphere, the need for security can stifle ambition. People often choose secure jobs over more rewarding but riskier opportunities.

Think of the employee who stays at the same job for decades, not because they're passionate about the work, but because it offers a steady paycheck and the comfort of routine. This decision feels rational, it's driven by the need for stability, but it often comes at the cost of fulfillment and growth.

In fact, businesses often exploit this need for security to retain employees, offering job security as the ultimate benefit. It's a powerful tool for retention, but it can also keep individuals trapped in roles that don't challenge them. The irony is that the very thing we crave, security, can end up being the thing that prevents us from achieving more.

Leveraging the Security Drive

Understanding the human desire for security gives you a significant advantage. Here's how to leverage this primal drive:

1. In Relationships: Offer emotional stability. When you understand that your partner craves security, you can use that knowledge to build trust and deepen your connection. People want to feel safe emotionally, this means offering them reassurance, predictability, and consistency. By providing a sense of security, you not only strengthen the bond but also create a space for deeper, more vulnerable exchanges.
However, you must also recognize when the pursuit of security is holding the relationship back. If you find yourself avoiding difficult conversations or sacrificing your own growth to maintain the status quo, it's time to disrupt that false sense of stability. Growth and conflict can coexist, and learning to embrace discomfort is often the key to moving a relationship forward.

2. In Business and Negotiations: Use security as a bargaining chip. When negotiating, offering the promise of stability like job security, long-term contracts, or financial guarantees, can be far more persuasive than offering higher immediate rewards. People will often choose the safer, more stable option, even if it means sacrificing potential future gains.
For instance, in negotiations with employees, emphasizing long-term job stability or career progression within the company can outweigh the lure of a higher salary elsewhere. Similarly, in business deals, offering predictability through long-term agreements or guaranteed partnerships can make your offer more attractive, particularly to risk-averse individuals.

The Trade-Off Between Security and Opportunity

But here's the thing: the pursuit of security can also limit opportunity. Just as staying in a dead-end relationship or a safe job can stifle personal growth, constantly seeking stability can prevent you from seizing high-risk, high-reward opportunities. Recognizing when your need for security is holding you back is the first step toward growth.

The desire for security can be both a blessing and a curse. It provides comfort and predictability, but it can also keep you stuck in a loop of mediocrity. The key is not to abandon security altogether, but to understand its limits and recognize when it's time to take a risk.

The next time you're faced with a decision in business, relationships, or life, ask yourself: Am I choosing this because it's what I really want, or because it feels safe? Spotting when the need for security is driving your choices allows you to consciously decide if that stability is worth the trade-off. And in those moments where you find it's not, where growth requires risk, you'll be better equipped to step outside the comfort zone and embrace the unknown.

Status: Social Hierarchy in Love, Careers, and Negotiation

The desire for status is perhaps one of the most misunderstood primal drivers. It's easy to assume that status is solely about wealth, power, or material possessions. But status is woven into every facet of our social lives. Status is how we are perceived by others, how we position ourselves within the hierarchy of our relationships, and how we project our identity in the world. The drive for status is a constant undercurrent, influencing behavior in ways that are often subtle but profoundly impactful.

Serotonin and Social Dominance

At the neurological level, status is closely linked to serotonin, the chemical that regulates mood and social behavior. A 2023 study by Anderson & Zhang revealed that higher serotonin levels increase feelings of dominance, which in turn boosts confidence and decision-making across various areas of life. This explains why people with higher serotonin levels often project greater authority and command more respect in social situations. They are perceived as having higher status, and this perception shapes how they are treated by others.

Dr. Joseph LeDoux encapsulates the modern relevance of status in today's world, stating, "In the digital age, status has become a more potent driver than survival for many". Social media, career paths, and even personal relationships have all become arenas where status is contested and asserted. The pursuit of status through accolades, recognition, or public admiration has eclipsed basic survival needs for many individuals, creating a landscape where status-seeking behaviors drive decision-making and social dynamics.

Projecting Success and Seeking Validation

In relationships, the desire for status often manifests in how individuals present themselves to their partners and the outside world. For many, being seen as a successful or desirable partner becomes paramount. This could involve flaunting career success, cultivating a certain image on social media, or even engaging in status-enhancing activities like charity work or networking events. While these actions may seem altruistic or goal-driven on the surface, they are frequently rooted in a deeper desire to be admired and validated by others.

But here's the twist: this quest for status can be a double-edged sword. On the one hand, individuals may gain admiration and respect from their peers or partners, but on the other, this pursuit can lead to superficial connections, where the relationship is built more on appearances than on genuine emotional intimacy. Status can become a mask, shielding vulnerabilities but also blocking deeper connections.

In friendships, status-seeking behaviors are more subtle but equally present. Dominance games frequently play out, often unconsciously, with individuals vying for control of the group dynamic. Who gives advice? Who organizes the events? Who sets the social agenda? These subtle status contests often shape the very structure of friendships, where individuals position themselves within the hierarchy of the social group.

The Hidden Currency of Professional Success

In the professional realm, status can be just as intoxicating, if not more so, than wealth. Many people chase prestigious job titles, accolades, and public recognition, even when these status symbols don't necessarily align with their deeper goals or desires. The desire to be seen as successful can override more intrinsic motivations, such as personal fulfillment or meaningful work. The workplace, then, becomes a battleground where individuals compete for titles, promotions, and recognition, often at the expense of personal well-being.

This is why many professionals find themselves in high-paying but unfulfilling jobs. The status symbol of a corner office or an impressive title becomes a trap, keeping individuals tethered to careers that don't necessarily bring them happiness or personal growth. Yet, they cling to these markers of success because they provide the social validation they crave.

Using Status as a Lever in Negotiations and Relationships

Understanding how the desire for status operates in both personal and professional contexts gives you a unique tool for influencing others. When you recognize that status is often more important than financial gain or emotional intimacy, you can tailor your approach to leverage this drive.

1. In Relationships: Be aware of how status dynamics play out, both in your relationship and your partner's. For example, if your partner's self-worth is tied to being seen as successful, offering validation in that area could strengthen your bond. This might involve acknowledging their accomplishments publicly or supporting their social or professional ambitions in visible ways. However, it's crucial to strike a balance. Allowing status to dominate the relationship can lead to shallowness and unmet emotional needs. Encourage deeper connections beyond the façade of success.

2. In Negotiations: Offering status as a reward can be far more persuasive than offering financial incentives. Consider this: people often turn down higher-paying jobs to work at prestigious companies with strong brand recognition. Status becomes the invisible currency. If you can offer someone a way to elevate their social standing through a high-profile project, a public award, or a leadership position, you may find them more willing to negotiate in your favor. In business, people want to feel that they are being seen and recognized, and, of course, compensated for their precious time.

When Ego Becomes a Liability

Of course, the pursuit of status can also backfire. The need to be admired and respected can push individuals to overextend themselves, emotionally, financially, and professionally. This is where ego comes into play. When status-seeking becomes all-consuming, it can cloud judgment, leading people to make decisions based on external validation rather than internal fulfillment.

Consider the executive who takes on a high-profile, high-stress job simply for the title, even though it leads to burnout and personal dissatisfaction. Or think about the individual who stays in an unhealthy relationship because it looks perfect on the outside, fulfilling the societal expectation of success. These are examples of how the desire for status, when unchecked, can become a liability.

To avoid falling into this trap, it's essential to regularly assess if your status-driven behaviors are serving you or simply feeding your ego. Are you seeking recognition for something that aligns with your values, or are you chasing accolades that only provide short-term validation? By confronting these questions, you can ensure that your pursuit of status doesn't derail your personal growth or happiness.

Mastering Status for Deeper Influence

Status is one of the most powerful motivators in human behavior. It's a force that drives us to succeed, to be admired, and to seek recognition from those around us. But it's also a force that can blind us to what really matters. Understanding the role status plays in relationships, friendships, and careers is crucial for mastering influence. It allows you to see beyond surface behaviors and tap into the deeper motivations that guide decision-making.

By recognizing the subtle ways in which status influences behavior, you can handle negotiations, manage relationships, and assert your own influence in ways that are both effective and sustainable. Status may be a powerful driver, but with the right awareness, you can ensure that it serves you, rather than controlling you.

Love and Connection: The Bond That Shapes Every Interaction

Connection is perhaps the most fundamental force driving human behavior. It isn't limited to romantic relationships; it influences friendships, professional dynamics, and even fleeting interactions with strangers. Humans are social creatures, biologically wired to seek intimacy, trust, and belonging. Without connection, people feel isolated, unsafe, and often directionless. From love to business, decisions are deeply rooted in this primal desire for connection. Yet, what makes it so powerful, and sometimes even irrational, is its deep ties to the brain's neurochemistry.

Oxytocin, the "Bonding Hormone"

The hormone oxytocin is often referred to as the "love hormone," but its power goes far beyond romantic affection. Oxytocin plays a critical role in trust and social bonding, making it essential for forming meaningful connections in both personal and professional relationships. The 2023 study by Carter & Porges revealed how oxytocin drives these social bonds, showing how trust forms the bedrock of connection. When oxytocin levels rise during social interactions, people are more likely to trust others, form stronger relationships, and feel a sense of safety within those connections.

As Dr. Sue Carter highlights, "Oxytocin is often called the 'love hormone,' but its role in fostering trust is what makes it so powerful in relationships and negotiations". This trust is an emotional component and neurological response, deeply embedded in the brain's wiring, that influences how people make decisions.

Emotional Safety Over Logic

Love is rarely logical. The need for connection often overrides rational decision-making, pushing people to stay in relationships that may not be entirely healthy or beneficial. Why? Because emotional safety is more valuable than logic. The drive to feel loved and connected, even in flawed relationships, can keep people tethered to situations that offer familiarity and security, rather than taking the risk of being alone or uncertain.

For example, many individuals stay in relationships that don't necessarily serve them because they feel emotionally secure, even when faced with logic-based reasons to leave. Oxytocin's role in creating these bonds is so strong that people often choose emotional safety over personal growth or logical solutions. This is why connection can often be the deciding factor in romantic decisions, despite apparent incompatibilities or challenges.

Trust Over Transaction

The same principles that apply to love are mirrored in business and negotiations. While numbers, contracts, and logic are crucial in any deal, trust can often be the deciding factor. People are far more likely to do business with those they trust, even if it means compromising on better terms. Deals that are built on a sense of connection are more likely to succeed because trust, once established, creates a foundation for future collaboration. This is why many successful business deals are sealed not purely through transactional negotiations but through the establishment of rapport and emotional bonds.

In fact, oxytocin's role in social interactions can transform a negotiation from a purely transactional exchange into a partnership. When individuals feel a sense of connection, they are more inclined to reach mutually beneficial agreements. They feel safer sharing information, making concessions, and collaborating because the emotional bond of trust overrides competitive instincts.

Building Trust Through Connection

Understanding the power of connection allows you to tap into one of the most influential human desires: the need to belong and feel emotionally safe. Here's how to leverage this primal drive:

1. In Relationships: Offer emotional safety. People crave connection and trust, and by being a source of emotional stability for others, you can strengthen bonds in significant ways. This doesn't mean avoiding conflict or always agreeing; rather, it means creating an environment where your partner, friend, or colleague feels seen, understood, and valued. When you offer this kind of emotional safety, you build unshakable trust, which can deepen relationships beyond surface-level interactions.

   However, it's also essential to recognize when emotional safety is preventing growth. Staying in a relationship purely for the sake of feeling safe can stagnate personal development, as individuals may avoid necessary challenges or difficult conversations. To foster true connection, balance emotional safety with opportunities for growth, both for yourself and others.

2. In Business: Build trust before making demands. In negotiations, trust can be more valuable than any financial incentive. Establishing a personal connection or rapport with the other party can create a more collaborative atmosphere, leading to better outcomes for both sides. This might involve taking the time to understand their needs and offering transparency in your own intentions. Once trust is established, negotiations become less about winning and more about creating a long-term partnership.

   By fostering genuine empathy and emotional connection, you make it easier for the other party to see you as an ally rather than an adversary. This, in turn, makes them more willing to cooperate, even on terms that might not have been agreed upon in a purely transactional environment.

When Vulnerability Is Exploited

While connection is a powerful tool for building trust and fostering deep relationships, it can also be exploited. Emotional connection makes people vulnerable, and those who understand this can manipulate trust to their advantage. This is where emotional manipulation and abuse come into play. People who feel a deep emotional connection are more likely to ignore red flags, forgive transgressions, or overlook flaws in logic, all because their emotional safety feels more important than rational judgment.

It's crucial to recognize when emotional connection is being used as a tool for manipulation. If trust is being exploited to maintain control, power, or advantage, it's not a healthy connection and become emotional exploitation. In relationships, this might look like staying with a partner who uses emotional dependence to manipulate decisions. In business, it can manifest as a leader or negotiator leveraging trust to push through deals that are ultimately self-serving.

Connection as the Key to Influence

Connection is a fundamental driver of behavior. In fact, the need for connection underlies almost every human decision. Mastering the art of building genuine connection gives you a profound tool for influencing others.

But more importantly, it allows you to create relationships that are rooted in trust, safety, and mutual growth, rather than superficial transactions or power dynamics. In a world where people are increasingly isolated by technology and social structures, offering genuine connection is not only a strategy for influence, it's a powerful act of empathy that can transform lives.

Self-Actualization: The Growth Seeker

The drive for self-actualization is a subtle yet profound force that shapes many of our most significant decisions. Unlike the primal urges of survival or status, self-actualization is about transcending the immediate and striving toward something bigger, growth, fulfillment, and the full realization of one's potential. It's the pursuit of meaning in a world that's often fixated on the superficial. And, in today's hyper-competitive, high-pressure society, this need for personal development has become one of the most potent drivers behind everything from career choices to the products we consume.

Self-actualization isn't a vague, abstract concept for philosophers or life coaches to toss around, it's actually a deeply rooted psychological need that expresses itself in tangible, everyday ways. People buying the latest fitness gadget, enrolling in a course to develop a new skill, or taking on a new challenge at work are driven by the desire to better themselves, to grow beyond their current state. But while self-actualization might seem like the noblest of pursuits, it can also be manipulated, commodified, and exploited, turning personal growth into just another product for sale.

Dopamine and Goal Achievement

At the core of the human need for growth is the brain's reward system. Research has shown that dopamine, the chemical most commonly associated with pleasure, plays a critical role in self-actualization. But dopamine is also about the chase. According to a 2023 study by Smith & Brown, dopamine levels spike not when the goal is achieved, but when we're actively pursuing it. This is why people are addicted to the hustle, the grind, the constant push toward the next milestone. The journey, it turns out, is more rewarding than the destination.

As Dr. James Smith puts it, "Dopamine's role in reinforcing goal achievement highlights its importance in self-directed growth". The more you achieve, the more your brain craves the next challenge. This is why self-improvement industries, everything from fitness to personal development courses, are so addictive. They're selling you the high of the pursuit.

Self-Disclosure and Identity Building

Self-actualization is about how we communicate achievements to the world. Research by Tamir & Mitchell (2012) on self-disclosure revealed that sharing personal growth experiences is inherently rewarding. The act of telling others about your success triggers the brain's reward system, reinforcing your sense of identity and belonging. This is why social media is flooded with people sharing their "journeys", from fitness transformations and career accomplishments to personal breakthroughs. Sharing our success stories makes us feel good and reinforces the narrative we want to project about ourselves.

This is where the modern self-actualization journey gets tricky. It's not enough to achieve personal growth. We have to be seen achieving it. In a world dominated by social proof, self-actualization has become performative. We don't just want to grow for ourselves; we want to signal to others that we're growing. This creates a paradox where the pursuit of self-actualization, something deeply personal, becomes outwardly focused, another way to climb the social hierarchy.

Self-Actualization as a Product

Here's the uncomfortable truth: self-actualization has been turned into a product. The $10 billion self-help industry is built on the promise of unlocking your potential, of becoming the best version of yourself, often through a series of courses, books, or programs that promise to accelerate your personal growth. Brands like Nike, with their "Just Do It" campaign, don't just sell shoes; they sell the idea of pushing beyond limits, of reaching new heights of performance and self-mastery. When you buy a product like that, you're purchasing more than a piece of gear. You are now buying into the narrative that you're someone who strives for greatness.

Similarly, platforms like Coursera market learning as the ultimate pathway to self-actualization. Their message is clear: the more you know, the more you grow. They frame personal development as something that can be quantified, how many courses you've completed, how many certifications you've earned, how much knowledge you've acquired. It's an intoxicating message, and one that plays directly into the brain's dopamine-driven craving for progress.

But here's the controversial twist: is this commodification of self-actualization really about helping people grow, or is it about keeping them hooked on the pursuit? The constant push to "improve" can easily become a trap, one where we're never satisfied, always chasing the next hit of validation through likes on a progress post or the completion of another self-improvement course.

Using the Growth Drive to Influence

Understanding how self-actualization drives behavior gives you an edge in business, marketing, or personal relationships. People are drawn to opportunities that promise growth, and if you can position your offer as a tool for personal development, you'll tap into one of the most powerful motivators.

1. In Business and Marketing: Highlight how your product or service enables self-improvement. Remember to not only sell the features,

sell the transformation. Even if you're offering fitness equipment, educational resources, or even business tools, frame them as pathways to a better version of the consumer. The "Just Do It" campaign by Nike is a masterclass in this, turning their shoes into a symbol of pushing beyond limits.

2. In Personal Relationships: Encourage self-actualization in your partner, friend, or colleague by supporting their growth. This might mean giving them space to pursue their goals or providing constructive feedback that helps them improve. The key is to recognize that people are most motivated when they feel they are growing, so position yourself as someone who fosters and celebrates that growth.

3. Encourage Sharing: As Tamir & Mitchell's research on self-disclosure shows, people are more likely to stay engaged in their personal growth journeys when they can share their success. In business, this means creating platforms or opportunities for your consumers to share their progress, from testimonials and social media posts, to community engagement. For personal relationships, celebrate each other's achievements and encourage open communication about the journey toward self-actualization.

Coursera's Learning Pathway

Coursera is a brilliant example of a platform that has tapped into the self-actualization drive. Their entire brand is built on the promise of helping individuals grow through learning. But the real genius lies in how they frame their courses: as milestones on a path to personal development. By offering certifications and shareable accomplishments, they tap into the dopamine-driven need for progress, while also feeding into the social aspect of self-disclosure.

By positioning learning as a lifelong journey and tying it to concrete achievements, Coursera keeps users engaged, always striving for the next certification, the next accomplishment, the next step on their growth journey. It's a clear example of how the drive for self-actualization can be harnessed in a way that keeps individuals hooked on their pursuit of personal betterment.

Mastering the Self-Actualization Drive

Self-actualization is one of the most powerful, and perhaps least understood, motivators in human behavior. It's what drives people to push beyond their limits, to seek growth, and to constantly strive for a better version of themselves. But it's also a force that can be commodified, manipulated, and exploited.

Understanding how dopamine fuels this desire for growth, and how self-disclosure reinforces it, gives you the power to influence consumers and anyone else seeking fulfillment. If you're marketing a product, negotiating a deal, or supporting a loved one, tap into this primal desire for self-improvement, and you'll find that the promise of growth is one of the most persuasive tools you have.

Autonomy: The Need for Control Over Our Own Lives

There's something irresistible about autonomy. The freedom to choose a career path, make independent decisions in a relationship, or take charge of everyday life is a human desire for autonomy is a primal, universal force. People don't just want options, they crave the freedom to chart their own course, unhindered by external forces. Autonomy is more than making your own choices. Autonomy is control. It's the quiet power behind many of our most important behaviors, and understanding it gives you the key to unlocking influence in everything from love to business.

Dopamine and Control

At the neurological level, autonomy taps directly into the brain's reward system. A 2023 study by Johnson & Wang found that dopamine levels spike when people perceive they have control over their decisions. This is why autonomy feels so satisfying, it's both a psychological state and a biological one. When you make a choice, dopamine floods your brain, reinforcing the pleasure of being in control. It's the same reason we feel satisfaction when we successfully overcome a challenge or make a decision that aligns with our desires. The act of making decisions, regardless of the outcome, activates a sense of empowerment.

Dr. Nathalie Nahai sharpens the point: "True autonomy involves not just choice but the freedom from external manipulation". This highlights a critical distinction, while many people believe they are acting autonomously, their choices may still be shaped by external influences like social pressures, marketing tactics, and subtle manipulation.

Letting Children Learn Control

One of the clearest examples of how autonomy plays out is in parenting. When children are given autonomy in certain areas of their lives like choosing what to wear, how to approach a task, or even when to complete their homework, they tend to develop better emotional regulation and decision-making skills. When they feel in control of their choices, their self-confidence and problem-solving abilities increase, setting them up for long-term success.

However, it's a balancing act. Too much autonomy too soon can overwhelm a child, while too little can create dependency. But when parents foster a sense of controlled autonomy, allowing children the freedom to make decisions within a framework of support, the results are powerful. Studies have shown that children with more autonomy in decision-making tend to grow up more independent, confident, and resilient in the face of challenges.

Freedom Builds Trust

In relationships, autonomy is often the secret ingredient that allows both partners to thrive. While many think relationships are built on togetherness, the reality is that the healthiest partnerships are those where both individuals feel free to make decisions that respect their individuality. Autonomy fosters trust because it removes the need for constant approval and validation. When both partners feel they can pursue their own goals, maintain their own interests, and make decisions independently, they are more likely to grow individually and as a couple.

This doesn't mean operating in silos. Autonomy in relationships is about trust and respect, it's the understanding that while you're walking together, you're still walking your own path. People who feel their autonomy is respected in relationships are less likely to feel stifled or resentful, and more likely to feel emotionally connected and supported.

The Illusion of Autonomy in Negotiations

Understanding the human need for autonomy gives you a powerful tool in negotiations and persuasion. People don't just want to be told what to do, they want to feel like the decision is theirs. You can exploit this by offering others the perception of autonomy, even when you're guiding them toward a specific outcome. This tactic, known as the "illusion of choice," is a classic psychological manipulation technique that allows you to retain control while making the other party feel empowered.

For example, in negotiations, rather than presenting a single option, give your counterpart two or 3 options, each of which aligns with your goals. By framing the decision as theirs, you allow them to feel autonomous, increasing the likelihood of a positive outcome for both sides. Similarly, in personal relationships, offering autonomy in decision-making can deepen trust and strengthen emotional bonds. Give the other person a sense of control and you can defuse any tension and make them more likely to collaborate.

The Illusion of Control in a Digital World

However, autonomy isn't always what it seems. In the digital age, the illusion of autonomy is everywhere. From the algorithms that suggest what we watch on Netflix to the targeted ads that influence what we buy, people are often lulled into believing they are making independent choices when, in reality, those choices are being carefully curated by unseen forces. A 2024 study by Brown & Lee showed that while users on digital platforms perceive themselves to have autonomy, their behaviors are largely shaped by algorithms that subtly guide their decisions.

This manipulation of autonomy poses a significant ethical question, if people are unaware that their decisions are being shaped by external forces, are they truly autonomous? Marketers, platforms, and social media giants have mastered the art of giving consumers the illusion of control, using personalization and targeted content to create the appearance of autonomy while quietly steering behaviors in predetermined directions.

Respecting Autonomy in Personal and Professional Relationships

In your personal life, respecting the autonomy of others is key to building trust and deepening relationships. People need to feel that their decisions are valued and respected. This doesn't mean surrendering control, but rather creating environments where autonomy can flourish. Offer guidance, provide support, but ultimately allow others to make their own choices. This approach not only strengthens bonds but also fosters mutual respect and emotional connection.

In business, understanding when and how to offer autonomy can enhance employee satisfaction and productivity. Giving employees control over certain aspects of their work can boost motivation and engagement. People who feel they have a degree of control over their work are more likely to take ownership of their tasks, leading to better outcomes for both the individual and the organization.

Mastering the Autonomy-Influence Balance

Autonomy is one of the most powerful motivators in human behavior because the need to feel in control of our decisions is hardwired into our biology. Because autonomy is freedom from external manipulation, mastering the balance between offering autonomy and guiding decisions allows you to influence others while respecting their need for control.

In relationships, fostering autonomy builds trust and deepens emotional connections. In business and negotiation, the perception of autonomy can be used as a subtle tool for persuasion. And in life, recognizing when you are being manipulated, and reclaiming your own autonomy, is one of the most empowering steps you can take.

Understanding autonomy's role in human behavior offers profound insights into how we live, and how we can better influence those around us while respecting the universal need for freedom and control.

Validation: Seeking Approval in Every Sphere

Validation is the invisible currency of human interaction. The likes and comments on a social media post, a nod of approval from a colleague, or a compliment from a friend are all validations that drive more decisions than most people would like to admit. We often believe we act independently, making choices based on our preferences or logic, but scratch the surface, and you'll find that much of what we do is guided by a deeper desire: the need to be accepted and approved by others.

The Neuroscience of Validation: Dopamine and Social Approval

Validation feels good. There's a reason for that, and it's deeply embedded in our neurochemistry. A 2023 study by Smith & Brown found that social approval activates the brain's reward centers, particularly those linked to dopamine. This isn't a metaphor, getting likes on social media, a compliment at work, or a nod of approval triggers the same reward circuits that light up when we eat, sleep, or experience pleasure. Dr. James Smith put it bluntly: "The dopamine rush from social approval is akin to a drug high, driving repeated behaviors". In other words, validation is addictive.

But this addiction isn't confined to social media or obvious public displays. It permeates every sphere of life, from friendships and romantic relationships to careers and business. We crave validation because it reinforces our place within the social fabric. It signals that we're accepted, valued, and safe within the tribe, which is crucial from an evolutionary standpoint.

Friendships: The Subtle Dance of Social Approval

Look at your closest group of friends. Chances are, your behavior with them is shaped by your need for validation. Agreeing with their opinions, dressing similarly, even mirroring their language patterns, these are all manifestations of the subtle ways in which we seek approval. It's not about conformity for the sake of it. Friendship is about belonging.

In friendships, validation doesn't always come in the form of overt compliments or praise. It's in the shared laugh, the unspoken agreement, the mutual nod of understanding. These tiny moments of social approval are what keep friendships alive and thriving. People want to feel they are accepted within their social circles, and when they sense they're not, they either change their behavior to fit in or seek out new groups where they can receive the validation they crave.

Business: Recognition Over Financial Reward

Validation is just as crucial in the workplace as it is in personal relationships, perhaps even more so. Employees often crave recognition from their peers and superiors, and research consistently shows that validation can improve performance and loyalty more than financial rewards alone. In fact, recognition has a far deeper impact on job satisfaction than most employers realize.

Consider this: an employee who feels their contributions are seen and appreciated will likely remain loyal and motivated, even if they're not the highest-paid person in the room. This is backed by neuroscience. A sense of validation lights up the brain's reward centers in ways that monetary compensation cannot. Businesses that fail to recognize the power of validation are leaving a key motivational tool on the table, one that could boost both performance and retention.

The Double-Edged Sword of Validation

While validation can empower and motivate, it can also trap people in a feedback loop where they rely on external approval for self-worth. This is where the line between healthy validation and unhealthy dependence blurs. When individuals become addicted to validation, they stop acting out of their own intrinsic motivations and start performing for an audience. This audience could be their friends, their romantic partner, or even their social media followers.

The rise of social media has exacerbated this phenomenon. Platforms like Instagram and Twitter have turned validation into a commodity, one that people chase relentlessly, often to the detriment of their mental health. As users receive likes and comments, their brain's reward centers light up, creating an addictive feedback loop. The more validation they receive, the more they crave it, leading to behaviors that are less about genuine self-expression and more about performing for the approval of others.

Using Validation to Build Rapport and Influence

Understanding the human craving for validation gives you a powerful tool to build rapport, influence, and loyalty in personal relationships, friendships, and even business settings:

1. In Personal Relationships: Offer genuine validation. When people feel seen and valued, they're more likely to deepen their emotional connection with you. This doesn't mean showering them with empty praise, but rather offering recognition that feels authentic. Validation in personal relationships can come in the form of acknowledging a partner's achievements, appreciating their efforts, or simply listening actively to their thoughts and feelings.

2. In Friendships: Strengthen bonds by providing subtle but meaningful social approval. Agree with a friend's opinions, support their choices, and be present in their moments of vulnerability. Your validation plays a crucial role in maintaining the bond. Recognizing these small moments of approval builds a sense of loyalty and trust within the friendship.

3. In Business: Use validation strategically to improve performance and foster loyalty. Recognition should not be treated as an afterthought

or reserved for formal performance reviews. Validate your employees' efforts consistently, and do so publicly when possible. This not only boosts individual morale but also reinforces a positive workplace culture where people feel valued and appreciated.

The Evolutionary Roots of Validation

Seeking validation is deeply rooted in our evolutionary history. A 2023 study by Johnson & Wang examined the evolutionary mechanisms behind validation-seeking behaviors, finding that social approval plays a crucial role in survival. In ancient times, being accepted by the group meant safety, protection, and resources, while social rejection could mean death. Even today, our brains are wired to seek validation as a way of ensuring our place within the group and securing our survival.

This evolutionary perspective offers a sobering realization: validation is about more than ego or insecurity. It's survival. Our need for social approval is an ancient mechanism designed to keep us safe and connected to others, which is why its absence, social rejection or isolation, feels so profoundly painful.

The Power and Pitfalls of Validation

Validation is a powerful force that shapes human behavior across every sphere of life. It motivates, inspires, and strengthens relationships, but it can also trap people in cycles of dependence on external approval. Mastering the art of validation, both giving and receiving, offers a profound way to influence and build stronger connections in friendships, romantic relationships, and business environments.

But here's the catch: while validation can be used to build loyalty and trust, it can also be exploited. Recognizing the thin line between empowering someone with validation and manipulating them through their need for approval is critical. The most effective validation comes not from feeding someone's addiction to approval but from recognizing their intrinsic worth in a way that fosters growth and confidence, rather than dependence.

In a world that increasingly values the superficial over the substantial, mastering the psychology of validation allows you to stand apart, and above, those who blindly chase approval. By understanding and leveraging this primal drive, you can build deeper, more meaningful relationships while also steering clear of the toxic traps that excessive validation can create.

Mastering the Art of Decoding Desire

You've now seen how each of the seven primal desires, survival, security, status, love and connection, self-actualization, autonomy, and validation, shapes every facet of human behavior. These aren't abstract concepts; they are the invisible strings that pull people's decisions, often without their conscious awareness. From career choices to personal relationships, from what you buy to how you interact with others, these desires dictate actions at the most fundamental level.

But here's the challenge: Are you truly aware of how these primal desires influence your own life? When you reflect on your decisions, can you see how they've been driven by the need for security, the pursuit of status, or the craving for validation?

Understanding and Leveraging Desire

Now that you've decoded the seven primal desires, you need to move from recognition to application. Here's a powerful, actionable framework to take control:

1. Spotting the Desire in Action: The first step is recognizing when a primal desire is at play. In personal relationships, notice when a partner seeks validation through subtle cues like seeking reassurance or fishing for compliments. In business, watch how colleagues frame their decisions around the need for security or status. Train yourself to listen for the subtext in every interaction, what is really driving the conversation? Is it fear (survival)? The need to belong (love and connection)? The desire to be seen (status)?

2. Using Desires as Leverage: Once you've identified which primal desire is driving a person's behavior, use it to influence them. In negotiations, for instance, leverage the desire for autonomy by framing your proposal as a choice, even if both options benefit you. In friendships, reinforce the bond by validating their sense of belonging. This technique helps you understand the deep motivations that guide human behavior so you can use that knowledge to create win-win situations.

3. Recognizing These Desires in Yourself: It's just as important to see how these desires govern your own choices. Are you staying in a job because it provides you with a sense of security, even though it limits your growth? Are you making decisions in your personal life that

serve your need for validation rather than your authentic self-actualization? By identifying these patterns, you can make more intentional choices, breaking free from the unconscious pull of these primal desires.

Exercises to Rewire Your Neural Pathways

As you've learned from the previous chapter on neural rewiring, it's possible to change the way your brain responds to these primal desires. Here are some exercises to help you take control of your own desires and learn how to use them in others:

- Reflection Journaling: Start by tracking your decisions over the next week. After every major decision, be it professional, personal, or even something as mundane as choosing what to wear, ask yourself which primal desire was driving that choice. Was it the need for status? Security? Love? Write down your thoughts to build awareness.

- Reframe Your Motivations: Choose one area of your life where you know a primal desire is holding you back. It could be a relationship where you're seeking validation, or a career decision motivated by fear. Once you identify it, reframe that decision in terms of growth rather than security. For example, if you're staying in a job for security, ask yourself how you could shift your focus toward autonomy or self-actualization instead.

- Influence Experiments: Over the next week, consciously apply what you've learned about desires in your interactions with others. Try giving someone a sense of validation when they're seeking approval. Or offer a sense of autonomy in a negotiation, and observe how the dynamics shift. Use each interaction as a small experiment in understanding how these primal desires play out in real-time.

Transforming Desires into Stories

You've learned how primal desires can shape decisions, but now, we're going to explore the ultimate tool for bypassing critical thinking and implanting influence that lasts: villains and storytelling.

These are the neurological equivalent of hacking the brain's operating system. As you'll soon discover, stories can bypass skepticism, obliterate resistance, and implant beliefs so deeply that they become indistinguishable from personal truth.

CHAPTER 5

The Villain Construct

Heroes without villains are empty vessels. Without Darth Vader, Luke Skywalker is a farm boy. Without Goliath, David is just another shepherd. If you've never confronted a villain, ask yourself, are you really the hero you think you are?

Why Villains Matter More Than Heroes

Heroes are frauds. That's the uncomfortable truth. Strip away their villains, and what are they? Luke Skywalker isn't a legend; he's a farmhand fiddling with droids in the desert. David isn't a symbol of divine triumph; he's an unknown boy with a slingshot. Heroes only matter because their villains make them matter.

You don't rise to greatness because of virtue. You rise because something forces you to. A villain pushes you out of your mediocrity and into the arena. Without that force, you'll rot in your comfort zone, cloaked in the illusion of potential.

If you've never confronted a villain, you're not a hero. You're an extra in someone else's story. And if you've never felt the tension of fighting for something bigger than yourself, maybe it's because you've never faced an enemy big enough to demand your transformation.

Villains Are the Architects of Your Story

You don't beat your villains. You're built by them.

Villains create stakes. They define what's at risk, what needs to change, and what you're willing to sacrifice to make that change happen. Without a villain, there's no urgency. Without urgency, there's no action. Without action, you're nothing.

Every significant moment in your life was born from conflict. The rival you had to surpass. The heartbreak that ripped you apart and forced you to rebuild. The fear of failure that kept you awake at night, grinding toward a deadline. If you have ever grown, it's because something, or someone, challenged you to.

Fear is the ignition switch for change. Villains activate the amygdala, the primal core of your brain, driving hyper-focus and action. This is why threats stick in your memory and why no one forgets their greatest nemesis. Your brain is wired to respond to villains like a starving predator. The question is whether you'll starve or strike.

Villains Aren't Opponents, They're Mirrors

Villains don't just threaten you. They reveal you. Every enemy you fight reflects the parts of yourself you're too afraid to face. That's why we hate them so much, they hold up a mirror to our weaknesses, flaws, and insecurities.

You don't despise your villain because they're evil. You despise them because they remind you of your own failures. The rival who outperformed you? They showed you how mediocre you were. The boss who suffocated you with control? They reflected your fear of stepping into authority yourself.

Villains are your shadow, the repressed pieces of your psyche you've shoved into the basement of your mind. The ego won't face its shadow, it projects it outward as an adversary. The boss isn't the tyrant, you are. The procrastination isn't the enemy, it's your cowardice wearing a mask.

Hate your villains? Good. Now admit they're you. That's the real fight, to see in your villain what you refuse to acknowledge in yourself.

The Quiet Villainy of Stagnation

Not all villains are loud. Some are the whispering demons of comfort and complacency. These are the worst because they don't threaten, they seduce. They keep you warm, safe, and slowly dying. The villain of stagnation doesn't attack you; it lulls you into irrelevance.

Look at your life. Where are you too comfortable? Where are you settling? Don't tell yourself you're patient, strategic, or waiting for the right time. The truth is, you're scared. Stagnation is the softest and most insidious villain of all. And you're letting it win.

If you've never confronted a villain, you've never truly lived. Every great story begins with the collision of hero and enemy. If your story feels flat, predictable, or safe, it's because you're avoiding the villains who would make it worth telling.

Who is your villain? What are you afraid to face? Answer honestly, or admit that your life isn't a story at all.

Turning Fear Into Fuel

The greatest villains are not accidents of character design or random obstacles. They are meticulous constructions. Every great villain follows a blueprint, designed to embody everything the hero fears, resists, or denies. Without them, there's no growth, no urgency, and no victory. Heroes may claim the spotlight, but it's the villain who writes the script.

Villains are the symbols of our darkest truths. Ignorance, mediocrity, failure, abstract fears that lurk in our lives, shapeless and inescapable, find their form in the villains we face. Darth Vader is the temptation to wield power at the cost of humanity. Thanos is the moral quandary of sacrifice and survival. Villains make the abstract tangible, forcing confrontation with what we most want to avoid.

A weak villain is a betrayal of purpose. Weak villains let heroes stagnate. They let us off the hook, absolving us from the tension and struggle that forge transformation. A hero's journey only begins when a villain forces it to. Without resistance, there's no progress. Without fear, there's no triumph. Without a villain, there's no you.

The most dangerous villains, however, aren't the ones you can see. They aren't the loud tyrants or the cruel dictators. They're the quiet enemies, hiding in plain sight, convincing you they aren't enemies at all.

The Villain You Refuse to See

The story of Canen is the story of every failed hero who never named their villain. Canen didn't start with a nemesis, he had a goal. He wanted to be the fastest, the best, the unstoppable champion who left his brother Cruz in the dust. But Canen wasn't winning. No matter how hard he pushed, no matter how fast he thought he was, Cruz always stayed one step ahead.

For a long time, Canen thought the problem was him. He wasn't strong enough, fast enough, determined enough. He blamed his own body, his own limits. What he didn't realize was that the real enemy was sitting on his plate at every meal. Rice. Not just a food, but an anchor. A villain disguised as comfort, as sustenance, as tradition. It slowed him down, drained his energy, and dulled his edge. It was beating him.

But here's where the story twists: Canen's real villain wasn't rice. It was Cruz.

Cruz was the embodiment of Canen's fear of inadequacy, of never being enough, of living in someone else's shadow. Cruz wasn't his enemy because he was cruel; he was his enemy because he was better. Cruz was the rival who forced Canen to confront his own limits. The villain who wouldn't let him settle. The Goliath who turned a boy into a fighter.

When Canen framed Cruz as his villain, everything changed. Cruz was a challenge. Every race, every loss, every second of humiliation became fuel. Rice was the symbol of what kept Canen from becoming what he wanted to be. He didn't just stop eating it; he declared war on it. He turned meals into battles, practice into warfare, and Cruz into his reason to fight.

This is the power of a well-framed villain. Cruz didn't destroy Canen, he built him. By embodying Canen's fears and failures, Cruz became the reason Canen had to grow. Without Cruz, there's no Canen. Without a villain, there's no hero.

The Villain as a Mirror

The villains we hate the most are the ones who look like us. They expose what we refuse to acknowledge about ourselves. Cruz was a reflection of Canen's fear of never being good enough. Thanos doesn't terrify because he's evil; he terrifies because he makes us question what we would sacrifice for the greater good. Voldemort isn't horrifying because of his power; he's horrifying because he's what Harry could become if he gave in to fear and hatred.

Villains are mirrors, showing us the parts of ourselves we'd rather keep buried. The boss who micromanages you isn't the enemy, they're the reflection of your fear of failure. The friend who seems more successful isn't your rival, they're the projection of your own insecurity. Every villain you fight is a shadow of yourself.

This is why villains matter more than heroes. Heroes are what we aspire to be, but villains are who we are. They strip away the illusions and force us to see ourselves as we are: flawed, afraid, and full of potential we've yet to realize. A villain doesn't just challenge the hero, they define them.

The Anatomy of a Great Villain

A villain is a masterpiece of design, combining three essential elements:

- Symbolism: A villain must stand for something bigger than themselves. They embody fears, flaws, and challenges that are universal. Darth Vader is the shadow of power. Voldemort is the manifestation of unchecked ambition. Without symbolism, a villain is just another bad guy.

- Complexity: The best villains aren't purely evil. They're human. Relatable. Sometimes, they even make sense. Thanos had a plan that was horrifying but logical. That's why he unsettled us, because we could see his point. A villain with depth forces us to grapple with moral ambiguity and question our own beliefs.

- Opposition: A villain must directly oppose the hero's deepest values and desires. If the hero wants freedom, the villain must bring control. If the hero wants peace, the villain must bring chaos. A great villain is the embodiment of everything the hero fears most.

Without these elements, a villain is just noise. With them, they become unforgettable.

Building Your Personal Villain

Not all villains are human. Some are habits, beliefs, or comfort zones. The villain of your story might be the job you hate but can't leave. It might be the self-doubt that keeps you from taking risks. It might be the comfort of a life that asks nothing of you.

The first step is naming it. What holds you back? What makes you afraid? What convinces you to stay the same when you know you need to change? Name it. Give it a face. Make it real. Then, start fighting.

Your villain isn't there to destroy you. It's there to build you. But only if you're willing to see it for what it is. Only if you're willing to step into the arena and fight.

Making Your Enemy Work for You

Villains are not just adversaries. They are engines. They are levers. They are the psychological catalysts that force action, drive transformation, and make a story worth following, or a life worth living. But most people get villains wrong. They think villains are there to be defeated. They think the goal is to vanquish them, erase them, prove them wrong. That's not just naïve, it's lazy.

A great villain doesn't simply test the hero. A great villain builds the hero. And if you're smart enough, ruthless enough, and strategic enough, your villain won't just challenge you, they'll work for you.

Villains as Psychological Catalysts

Fear is a fire. It burns in the deepest part of your brain, the amygdala, where instincts live and reason dies. This is why villains are so powerful, they tap into primal fear, the kind that makes you fight, run, or freeze. Heroes inspire, but villains compel. People don't move mountains because they dream of success; they move mountains because there's an avalanche coming.

Neuroscience shows that the brain prioritizes threats over rewards. You are wired to react to danger faster and more intensely than to opportunity. This is why villains are unforgettable. A hero's promise of victory might stir your heart, but a villain's threat of destruction grips your throat.

Brands, movements, and leaders understand this instinct, and weaponize it. Nike doesn't sell shoes; they sell the death of procrastination. Their slogan, "Just Do It," frames your own hesitation and fear as the villain. Every ad isn't a promise of comfort, it's a confrontation with your inner coward. Nike doesn't coddle. It forces you to fight.

Political movements follow the same blueprint. Corruption, inefficiency, oppression, these aren't just problems. They're villains. They're enemies with faces, names, and motives. They are framed as obstacles to everything you care about: freedom, justice, progress. The most effective movements don't just offer solutions; they rally people to defeat the villain.

Mr. Mucus. A blob of slime personifies the discomfort and misery of a cold. By framing the villain as a tangible character, Mucinex doesn't just sell relief, it sells victory. You're not just taking medicine; you're crushing the enemy. That's the brilliance of villain framing, it turns passive consumers into active participants in a fight.

What's the villain in your life? Your laziness? Your fear of failure? The systemic oppression you claim to fight but haven't named? If you can't articulate your villain, you've already lost. Because villains don't just challenge you, they demand you take action.

The Villain as the Hero's Weapon

The truth no one wants to admit is that villains are better teachers than heroes. A hero tells you what's possible, but a villain forces you to prove it. Heroes inspire dreams; villains demand execution. They're the drill sergeant, the unrelenting rival, the constant reminder that you're not enough, yet.

Look at Rocky Balboa. His greatest adversary wasn't Apollo Creed; it was his own self-doubt. The mirror he punched at 4 a.m., the fear he fought in every step of every run, the weakness he saw in himself every time he laced up his gloves, those were his real battles. Apollo was just the catalyst. The villain isn't the obstacle; it's the crucible. It's the thing that burns away your excuses and forges who you are.

Think about your greatest victory. Was it easy? If it was, it doesn't matter, does it? Because the worth of a victory is measured by the strength of the villain. Without resistance, there's no triumph. Without the villain, you're nothing. Every time you defeat a villain, you take a piece of them with you. That's why we say villains build heroes, they pass on their strength through struggle.

You don't have to wait for a villain to show up. You can build your own. Frame your laziness as the enemy. Personify the system holding you back. Give your excuses a name and declare war. The villain doesn't have to come to you, you can create it. And once you do, every step becomes a fight, every victory becomes sweeter, and every defeat becomes fuel.

The Danger of Villain Overuse

But let's not pretend villains are a cure-all. Fear is powerful, but it's also addictive. Use it too often, and you'll poison your audience, and yourself. The more you rely on fear, the less impact it has. Audiences become numb. People stop caring. The villain becomes background noise.

Consider the climate change movement. The villains, pollution, greed, inaction, are real and terrifying. But fear campaigns have hit a saturation point. "The world is ending" no longer shocks anyone. It's wallpaper. Worse, it triggers denial. When people feel overwhelmed, they disengage. Fear without a path forward breeds apathy or resentment.

This is the backlash effect. If your villain becomes too monstrous, too pervasive, people will either tune out or revolt. Fear works best when paired with hope. A villain must be conquerable, or at least confrontable. If you frame the fight as unwinnable, you're not inspiring action, you're ensuring paralysis.

Weaponizing Your Villain

You don't have to defeat your villain to win. Sometimes, the fight is enough. The struggle builds you, sharpens you, forces you to grow. But a villain is only useful if you know how to wield them. They are tools, not tyrants. Weapons, not masters. If you let the villain define you, they've already won. If you let them teach you, they become your greatest ally.

Who's your villain? What do they demand of you? And are you ready to make them work for you, or will you let them destroy you?

When Framing Becomes Dangerous

Villains are powerful. They ignite revolutions, fuel movements, and create heroes. But power without restraint is a weapon of destruction, and villains, when framed irresponsibly, justify atrocities. The same tools that inspire change can tear the fabric of humanity apart. If you think you can wield villains without understanding their shadows, you're playing with fire, and it's only a matter of time before everything burns.

Villains as Weapons of Oppression

Every genocide begins with a villain. Not the kind who challenges the hero, but the kind who turns entire groups into faceless threats. Dehumanization is a psychological hack. Strip a person of their humanity, and empathy evaporates. Turn them into an abstraction, and violence becomes not just permissible but inevitable.

Look at Nazi Germany. The regime didn't simply demonize Jews; it stripped them of their personhood. They were rats, parasites, polluters of purity. This was surgical. Propaganda framed Jews as a biological threat, an infection to be eradicated. The Holocaust wasn't born from hatred alone; it was born from a narrative that made extermination seem like a moral imperative.

Rwanda followed the same playbook. In 1994, the Hutu government unleashed a genocide that murdered nearly a million Tutsis. How? By framing them as cockroaches. That language wasn't metaphorical; it was calculated. Cockroaches don't negotiate; they're exterminated. The villainization of Tutsis was psychological priming for slaughter.

And then there's America, a country built on the villainization of African slaves. To justify slavery, Africans were painted as savages, lazy, violent, incapable of self-governance. This wasn't incidental; it was essential. The narrative turned brutality into benevolence. Chains weren't oppression; they were civilization. The villain framing of Africans was the foundation of a system that would haunt America for centuries.

But don't mistake this for history. The shadow of dehumanization is alive and well.

After 9/11, Muslims became the villain America needed. The word "terrorist" was a weapon. It collapsed a complex, diverse group of over a billion people into a single faceless threat. Hate crimes surged, discriminatory policies flourished, and a never-ending "war on terror" was justified by a villain that didn't exist in the way it was framed.

Mexican migrants face the same fate. They aren't seen as people. They're invaders. Criminals. Drug dealers. The language isn't accidental. "Invasion" doesn't evoke compassion; it evokes fear. Fear justifies walls, cages, and family separations. When you turn a group into a villain, you turn their humanity into collateral damage.

The Cost of Dehumanization

The other cost of villain framing, beyond the damage it does to its targets, is the damage it does to us. Dehumanization erodes empathy, the very thing that separates us from our worst instincts. Neuroscience shows that when we dehumanize others, activity in the medial prefrontal cortex, the part of the brain responsible for empathy, shuts down. The less human we perceive someone, the less we care about their suffering. It's indifference. And indifference is deadlier.

Dehumanization also breeds aggression. When you frame someone as a threat, your brain shifts into survival mode. The lines between defense and attack blur. Moral disengagement sets in, and atrocities become rationalized. It's not murder anymore, it's self-preservation. It's not cruelty anymore, it's justice.

The social cost is even higher. Villain framing entrenches cycles of violence and division. When you frame a group as the enemy, they respond in kind. Fear turns to hate, hate turns to action, and action perpetuates the narrative. Policies born from dehumanization don't solve problems, they escalate them. Inequality deepens. Suffering multiplies. The villain wins, not because they're strong, but because the story is broken.

Ethical Villain Framing

If you can't frame a villain without destroying someone's humanity, you don't deserve the power to persuade. Villains are tools, and like any tool, their morality depends on the hand that wields them. A scalpel in a surgeon's hand saves lives. In a murderer's hand, it ends them. The same is true for villains.

- First, avoid targeting groups or identities. No group is a monolith. No identity is a villain. Your enemy isn't "immigrants" or "the rich" or "the ignorant." Your enemy is the system, the belief, the structure that perpetuates harm. Frame the fight against what's broken, not the people caught in its grasp.
- Second, use empathy-driven narratives. Show the complexity of the villain. Humanize them. Acknowledge their motivations, their pain, their fears. A villain is compelling because they could have been the hero. Show the line between them and us, and how easily it can blur.
- Finally, ensure your villain serves growth, not destruction. A great villain challenges the hero and elevates them. They create tension, demand action, and force transformation. If your villain doesn't build, they're not a villain, they're a scapegoat, and scapegoats create mobs.

Villains are the most dangerous tools in storytelling. They can ignite revolutions or justify genocide. They can create heroes or destroy humanity. If you're going to frame a villain, do it with intention. Do it with integrity. Do it with the understanding that the shadow you cast will define not just the story, but the world it leaves behind.

Villains as Your Architect for Change

Heroes don't exist without villains. Every great leap forward, every moment of transformation, every ounce of personal growth is born from confrontation. No tension, no stakes. No stakes, no evolution. Without villains, heroes rot. And if you've spent your life avoiding villains, don't kid yourself, you're not a hero. You're just a bystander.

Imagine a story without a villain. A protagonist wakes up, brushes their teeth, and succeeds at everything they do. No conflict. No failure. No stakes. It's boring and meaningless. The hero needs a villain not just to provide resistance but to define what they stand for. Without opposition, there's no clarity. Without struggle, there's no strength. Without risk, there's no reward.

Think about your own life. Every time you've grown, it wasn't because the universe handed you an opportunity, it was because something or someone forced you to rise to the occasion. Maybe it was a rival at work who outperformed you. Maybe it was heartbreak that ripped you apart and made you rebuild stronger. Maybe it was the fear of failure that kept you grinding when everyone else quit.

Villains are architects of tension. Psychological research shows that tension, whether physical, emotional, or mental, is essential for transformation. Villains provide that tension by pushing you to your limits. They strip away your illusions, test your boundaries, and demand that you either evolve or perish. Heroes rise because of their villains.

But don't confuse this with morality. Villains aren't here to be "bad." They're here to be necessary.

What if the villain in your life isn't external? What if it isn't your boss, your competitor, or your circumstances? What if the real villain is you?

We spend our lives externalizing the fight because it's easier to point the finger outward than to confront the shadow within. But the truth is brutal: the greatest villains you'll ever face are the ones inside your own head. The fear of failure. The addiction to comfort. The refusal to step into the unknown. These are enemies. And they're winning.

Look at your life. Where are you stuck? What's holding you back? Don't answer with vague platitudes or blame external forces. Answer honestly. Name the fear, the habit, or the belief that keeps you small. That's your villain. The longer you avoid it, the stronger it becomes. The longer you refuse to fight it, the more it defines you.

Here's the irony: The villain is your catalyst. It's the thing forcing you to grow, to push beyond your limits, to become the hero of your own story. But that only happens if you're willing to fight. Most people aren't. Most people make peace with their villains. They give them excuses, invitations, even a place at the table, and that's surrender.

If you're ready to fight, here's your map:

- Identify Your Villain: Name the fear, belief, or habit that acts as your enemy. Be brutally specific. "Fear of failure" isn't enough. What are you afraid of failing at? Why does it control you?

- Define Victory: What does winning look like? Is it a promotion, a milestone, a change in behavior? If you don't know what victory is, you'll never achieve it.

- Plan Your Attack: Heroes don't win by accident. They win by design. What's your strategy? What steps will you take today, tomorrow, and every day after to defeat your villain?

Villains are opportunities. They force you to confront what you'd rather ignore. They demand action, clarity, and purpose. If you let them, they'll destroy you. If you fight them, they'll make you.

Are you the hero who defeats their villain, or are you just the audience, watching someone else's story unfold?

Every day, you write your narrative. You decide whether it's a story worth telling or one no one will remember. The villain is the fulcrum. It's the thing that gives your story weight, meaning, and urgency. Without it, you're drifting. With it, you're alive.

The Villain Extractor Framework

Your villain is invisible. Not to others, but to you. This is the cruel joke: villains thrive in the blind spots you refuse to acknowledge. They're not lurking in the shadows; they're sitting at your table, drinking your wine, nodding along to your plans. Every time you brush off a frustration as "just the way things are," you hand them the reins.

If you haven't named your villain, it's because you're protecting it. Denial is easier than confrontation. That toxic employee? Easier to blame the "team dynamic." That partner who sighs and says "nothing" when you ask what's wrong? Simpler to assume they'll get over it. And the creeping dread you feel every time you think about leaving your comfort zone? It's so much nicer to call it patience than cowardice.

But villains don't go away just because you refuse to see them. They grow. Every excuse you make, every blind eye you turn, it's fertilizer. And one day, when you least expect it, they'll strangle the life out of everything you thought you cared about.

Deep Listening: The Silent Weapon

Most people talk to fill space. They listen to confirm what they already believe or to prepare their next move. This is self-preservation. And it's worthless if you want to find the villain.

Real listening is violent. It's uncomfortable, intrusive, and devastatingly effective. Done properly, it's about extracting what's hiding underneath them. Villains hate silence because silence doesn't give them cover. It forces their hand.

Someone tells you, "I just feel like things aren't working lately." You nod, eager to fix it, eager to move on. You're complicit. A villain just slipped by. What you should do is stop. Look them in the eye and say, "Not working how? Be specific." Then, sit back and let the silence crush them. Don't rescue them. Don't soften the tension. Force them to name what they're afraid to admit.

People will always tell you their truth if you're ruthless enough to wait for it. The moment they stop talking, let the silence stretch. Count to ten in your head. Most people can't handle the discomfort, so they'll rush to fill it. And in their panic, they'll tell you exactly where the villain lives.

Silence is an interrogation tactic. It's the scalpel that cuts past practiced answers and reveals the raw fear underneath. And once you've exposed the fear, the villain isn't far behind.

The Right Questions to Find the Wrong Answers

Villains hide in the comfortable answers we give to comfortable questions. They thrive on surface-level discussions that mask the tension beneath. To extract them, you need to go deeper, harder, and more provocatively than you're used to. The right questions provoke discomfort, not by asking what's easy, but by demanding what's raw.

Here's how you weaponize this approach across every dimension of life:

In Business: Tearing Down the Safe Facade

Your business villains aren't hiding in the balance sheets. They're lurking in unspoken fears, unchallenged norms, and unsurfaced conflicts. Most teams operate with an unspoken code: Keep things smooth. Don't rock the boat. That's precisely where villains thrive.

- **Standard Question:** "How can we improve efficiency?"
- **The Right Question:** "What process do we keep doing because we're afraid to admit it's obsolete?"
    - *Result:* A team leader admits their flagship product is outdated, but no one wants to be the one to kill it. The villain? Fear of disrupting their identity.
- **Standard Question:** "What's holding us back?"

- **The Right Question:** "If we failed completely in the next six months, what would have caused it?"
    - *Result:* A silent, unspoken truth emerges: People are more loyal to their departments than to the organization's goals. The villain is tribalism, disguised as teamwork.

In Career: Facing What You're Running From

Your career villains are buried in your own excuses. It's not the bad bosses or lack of opportunity. Questions about ambition and progress tend to skate over the real tension: the gap between what you want and what you're too afraid to confront.

- **Standard Question:** "What's the next step in my career?"
- **The Right Question:** "If I stay exactly where I am for the next five years, what will I hate most about myself?"
    - *Result:* The realization that stagnation is a choice. The villain isn't your boss or the market, it's your unwillingness to risk failure for growth.
- **Standard Question:** "What skills should I develop?"
- **The Right Question:** "What am I avoiding learning because I'm scared it will expose me as incompetent?"
    - *Result:* You admit that public speaking terrifies you, so you've conveniently avoided it for years, even though it's the one skill that would transform your career.

In Real Estate: Exposing the Hidden Fears

Real estate is a game of psychology, not just transactions. The villains are often unspoken fears, of risk, of loss, of appearing foolish. Buyers and sellers both cling to these fears, and most agents are too polite to pry them loose.

- **Standard Question (to a buyer):** "What kind of home are you looking for?"
- **The Right Question:** "What would make you walk away from a house you love?"
    - *Result:* The buyer reveals they're terrified of committing to a high mortgage, even if the house fits their dreams. The villain is financial fear, not the housing market.

- **Standard Question (to a seller):** "Why do you want to sell?"
- **The Right Question:** "What are you afraid will happen if this house doesn't sell in the next six months?"
  - *Result:* The seller confesses they're drowning in debt but don't want their family to know. The villain is pride.

In Sales: Breaking Down the Objections

Every sale is a battle between a client's desire and their villain. Most salespeople treat objections as logistical issues, when they're almost always emotional or psychological.

- **Standard Question:** "What would it take for you to say yes?"
- **The Right Question:** "What's the real reason you're hesitating?"
  - *Result:* A client admits they're scared of losing their job if the investment doesn't pay off. The villain is fear of failure, not the price tag.
- **Standard Question:** "What's most important to you in this deal?"
- **The Right Question:** "If this fails, what will you regret most about saying yes?"
  - *Result:* The client reveals they've been burned by similar deals before, and their trust is shattered. The villain is past trauma, not the terms of the contract.

In Friendships: Digging Beneath the Surface

Friendship villains often hide behind familiarity. You don't ask hard questions because you don't want to disrupt the peace. But that peace is the perfect breeding ground for resentment.

- **Standard Question:** "How are things going?"
- **The Right Question:** "When was the last time you felt like I didn't support you?"
  - *Result:* They tell you about the time you brushed off their struggles because you were too busy. The villain is neglect, not distance.
- **Standard Question:** "What do you need from me?"

- **The Right Question:** "What's something I've done that hurt you, but you never brought up?"
  - *Result:* They reveal a moment they felt betrayed, and you finally understand why your friendship has felt strained. The villain is unspoken conflict.

In Relationships: Going Straight for the Jugular

Romantic relationships are full of villains wearing masks of routine, politeness, or even love. Comfortable questions keep the peace. Uncomfortable questions reveal the truth.

- **Standard Question:** "What can I do to make you happier?"
- **The Right Question:** "What do you wish I would stop doing, but you're afraid to tell me?"
  - *Result:* Your partner admits they resent how you constantly "joke" about their insecurities. The villain isn't humor, it's insensitivity.
- **Standard Question:** "What do you love most about our relationship?"
- **The Right Question:** "What's something you've been wanting to say but haven't, because you think it'll cause a fight?"
  - *Result:* They confess they feel unsupported in their career ambitions, and it's been silently eating at them. The villain is neglect disguised as support.

With Kids: Turning Silence into Insight

Kids don't always have the words, or the courage, to articulate their villains. It's your job to extract it.

- **Standard Question:** "How was school today?"
- **The Right Question:** "What's the one thing at school that makes you feel small?"
  - *Result:* Your child tells you about the classmate who mocks their clothes every day. The villain isn't school, it's shame.
- **Standard Question:** "Why didn't you do your homework?"

- **The Right Question:** "What's so hard about this subject that it makes you want to give up?"
  - *Result:* They admit they feel stupid every time they get a wrong answer. The villain is self-doubt, not laziness.

The Core Principle

Villains don't live in the answers, they live in the hesitation, the resistance, the discomfort. The right questions don't just uncover truths, they dismantle the stories people tell to protect their villains. When you start asking the right questions, you stop being polite. You start becoming dangerous. Dangerous to fear. Dangerous to stagnation. Dangerous to mediocrity.

Now, ask yourself: What's the question you're most afraid to answer? That's where your villain is hiding.

Calling Out and Phrasing Villains

You think villains are elusive, wrapped in complexity, lurking just out of reach. They're not. They're mechanical, predictable, and almost embarrassingly simple. They thrive in patterns, hide in the gaps between what you say and what you do, and cling to the stories you tell to protect them. If you're willing to dig, they'll always show their face. And when they do, you must call them out ruthlessly and with precision.

Naming a villain shouldn't be polite. If you call it wrong, people will ignore you. If you call it soft, they'll dismiss you. If you call it clean, it won't hurt enough to make them move. The right phrasing of a villain hits like a fist in the ribs, leaving no room for denial.

Step One: Find the Patterns Where Villains Breed

Villains aren't accidents. They're habits, beliefs, or fears that you've allowed to grow unchecked. The first step is spotting the breadcrumbs they leave behind. Patterns of resistance, failure, or tension aren't coincidences, they're maps to your villain.

- **In Business:** Look for where the wheels always fall off.
  - A team repeatedly misses deadlines, yet everyone smiles in meetings, claiming "things are on track." The villain isn't bad planning, it's the fear of speaking up.

- ○ How to phrase it: "We're lying to ourselves. No one here has the guts to admit we're overcommitted because we're more afraid of confrontation than failure."
- **In Relationships:** Watch for the cycles.
  - ○ Arguments always start with the same trigger, a forgotten date, a flippant comment, an unspoken expectation. The villain isn't the trigger; it's the resentment you both refuse to address.
  - ○ How to phrase it: "We're not fighting about me being late. We're fighting because you don't believe I care enough to show up for you. And I've let that belief grow because I've never asked what you need."
- **In Self-Development:** Track where you sabotage yourself.
  - ○ You set the same goal every year, lose weight, write the book, leave the job, but quit halfway. The villain isn't lack of discipline; it's the fear of what success would demand of you.
  - ○ How to phrase it: "I'm not lazy. I'm terrified that if I actually succeed, people will expect me to keep going, and I don't know if I can."

Patterns don't lie. They show you exactly where the villain thrives.

Step Two: Disrupt the System and Expose the Resistance

Villains live in the status quo. They hate disruption because disruption forces them into the light. The quickest way to flush out your villain is to introduce change and watch where the resistance rises.

- **In Teams:** Announce a shift in workflow.
  - ○ Suggest a new process. "From now on, all updates will be shared in a live meeting, no exceptions." The person who immediately pushes back isn't lazy, they're hiding inefficiency or fear of being exposed.
  - ○ How to phrase it: "This isn't about the meeting format. It's about you being scared that we'll finally see you've been bluffing about progress. Let's stop pretending."
- **In Relationships:** Break the routine.

- ○ "Let's cancel our usual plans and spend the evening talking about what we want to change in this relationship." When your partner balks, the villain isn't discomfort, it's their fear that honesty will destroy what's left of the connection.
- ○ How to phrase it: "You're not avoiding this because it's uncomfortable. You're avoiding it because you're scared we'll realize this isn't working. But avoiding it guarantees that outcome."

- **In Yourself:** Commit to something terrifying.
    - ○ Publicly announce a personal goal, "I'll run a marathon this year." When you immediately feel the urge to walk it back, the villain isn't the goal's difficulty, it's your fear of public failure.
    - ○ How to phrase it: "I'm not afraid of the marathon. I'm afraid of everyone watching me fail. And that's exactly why I have to do it."

Resistance isn't random. It's the villain panicking at being exposed.

Step Three: Name the Villain and Demand Action

Naming the villain is the moment of truth. This isn't the time for euphemisms or politeness. A weak name gives the villain strength. A strong name breaks its power and forces accountability.

- **In Business:** The Overcommitment Lie
    - ○ Example: A company keeps taking on projects they can't handle, and everyone blames "industry pressure."
    - ○ Call it out: "The villain isn't the market. The villain is our addiction to saying yes because we're too scared to admit we're already stretched too thin."
    - ○ Demand action: "From now on, no new projects get greenlit without killing an old one. The addiction stops here."
- **In Sales:** The Fear of Asking
    - ○ Example: A sales rep consistently avoids following up on lukewarm leads, claiming "they're not ready."

- Call it out: "The villain isn't the client. It's your fear of rejection disguised as 'timing.' You're not waiting for them, you're waiting for courage."
- Demand action: "You're following up today. Not because they're ready, but because you need to prove you can."

- **In Relationships:** The Comfort Crutch
  - Example: A couple keeps avoiding tough conversations, claiming "we're just really busy."
  - Call it out: "The villain isn't our schedule. It's our fear of upsetting the fragile peace we've built on pretending everything's fine."
  - Demand action: "We're having the conversation tonight. No excuses. No distractions."

- **In Self-Development:** The Mask of Planning
  - Example: You've spent months "researching" your dream project but haven't taken a single step forward.
  - Call it out: "The villain isn't lack of preparation. It's my fear of being judged for doing it badly, so I keep pretending 'more planning' is the answer."
  - Demand action: "I'll launch the first draft tomorrow. Ugly, imperfect, and real."

Villains Are the Mirror You Can't Ignore

People will fight you when you name their villain. They'll argue, deflect, and deny. That's not a sign you're wrong, it's proof you're right. Villains don't go quietly. They scream. They claw. They make you question whether calling them out was worth it. It always is.

Because once the villain is named, you've stripped it of its power. No more masks. No more excuses. Just the naked truth and the demand to act. That's where transformation begins. It's not comfortable. It's not kind. But it's the only way forward.

Turning Enemies into Engines

Your villain isn't your enemy. It's your fuel. But only if you're willing to see it that way.

Every hero is forged by their opposition. Without Goliath, David is a kid with a slingshot. Without Thanos, the Avengers are just a messy group chat. Villains force you to rise, to confront your weaknesses, to sharpen your edge. But only if you engage with them. Ignore them, and they'll suffocate you. Fight them, and they'll define you.

Reframe the villain. The rival who's always outperforming you isn't there to humiliate you, they're there to reveal your laziness. The fear of failure isn't there to paralyze you, it's there to demand preparation. The partner who keeps pointing out your flaws isn't attacking you, they're handing you a mirror.

Remember, you don't defeat your villain. You absorb them. You take their strength, their lessons, their edge, and make it your own. The fight doesn't end with a triumphant victory, it ends with transformation. If you're lucky, you'll barely recognize yourself when it's over. And that's the point.

You're discovering your villain and building them into your story. They're here to demand that you become something more.

So stop pretending you don't know where they are. Stop excusing them. Stop avoiding them. Name them. Engage with them. And then thank them for the fire they'll set under you.

Because without your villain, you're nothing but potential rotting in the safety of mediocrity.

CHAPTER 6

The Narrative Neuralizer

Stories are not merely vehicles for entertainment, they are the covert operators of influence, seamlessly bypassing critical thinking and embedding themselves into our subconscious.

The Power of Stories

Every belief you hold, every relationship you've built, every product you've purchased, what if these were all shaped by stories you didn't even realize were controlling you? Think back to the last time you made a decision, from choosing a car to deciding if to trust someone. You likely thought your choice was grounded in logic or personal experience. But here's the unsettling truth: your decisions were more likely driven by the invisible hand of storytelling.

Stories are not merely vehicles for entertainment, they are the covert operators of influence, seamlessly bypassing critical thinking and embedding themselves into our subconscious. Melanie Green's Narrative Transportation Theory shines a spotlight on this phenomenon, revealing that deeply immersive stories have the power to change our beliefs without us even noticing. When we become "transported" into a narrative, our guard drops, our skepticism weakens, and our ability to question dissolves.

Think about this: how often have you been swayed not by facts, but by a powerful narrative? Think of a political campaign, a brand's origin story, or a heartfelt plea from a loved one, the emotional tug of a well-told story bypasses the rational mind. Green's research found that when people are transported into a narrative world, they are far less likely to engage in counter-argument. It's no wonder that entire industries, from marketing to politics, lean so heavily on storytelling to sway public opinion.

As Jonah Berger aptly puts it, "People don't think in terms of information. They think in terms of narratives." The implications of this are staggering. While you may believe you're immune to influence, the reality is that stories have already shaped much of your worldview, decisions, and even identity. The narrative creates reality.

The Brain's Natural Affinity for Stories

Why do stories wield such power? Neuroscience offers us a window into the brain's love affair with storytelling. Every time you hear a story, your brain releases dopamine, making the narrative engaging and easier to remember. Engaging stories also trigger oxytocin, the neurochemical responsible for trust and empathy. This is why emotionally charged narratives can foster deep connections and loyalty.

Moreover, when you listen to a story, your brain engages in neural coupling, a phenomenon where your brain begins to mirror the storyteller's, creating a shared emotional experience. This is why stories can make you feel what the protagonist feels, effectively putting you in their shoes.

Stories in Action

Stories are not abstract theory. These narratives translate into real-world power that touches every facet of life, from business and marketing to personal relationships, parenting, and leadership.

1. Business: In a negotiation, a dry list of facts will rarely move the needle. But tell the story of a past client who faced similar challenges, overcame them, and emerged victorious, and you'll have your counterpart not only listening but ready to agree. Successful CEOs like Steve Jobs and Elon Musk didn't merely sell products; they sold stories of innovation, progress, and human potential.

2. Marketing: The best advertisements don't bombard you with product features, they tell stories that resonate with your deeper needs. Think of Apple's iconic "1984" ad, which positioned its computer as the tool for breaking free from conformity. It was about revolution.

3. Relationships: The same holds true in personal relationships. Consider how often an argument is resolved not through logic but through an emotional story that makes the other person feel

understood. Stories have the power to shift perspectives without confrontation.

4. Parenting: Want your child to adopt a new habit? Don't preach facts. Tell a story about a character who faced a similar challenge and succeeded. It's the difference between lecturing and guiding through narrative, a tactic you've likely employed without even realizing it.

The Subtle Manipulation of Reality

But there's a darker side. Stories, for all their power, can easily be used to manipulate. Just as they build trust, they can erode it when wielded unethically. In the wrong hands, storytelling becomes a tool for exploitation, shaping perceptions not for enlightenment but for control. Entire political movements, advertising campaigns, and even relationships have been built on carefully crafted narratives that obscure the truth while triggering emotional responses.

Take the case of Nazi propaganda, one of history's most devastating examples of storytelling used to manipulate an entire nation. The regime didn't rely on raw facts or data; they created a compelling, albeit horrifying, narrative that framed entire groups of people as villains in a story of national redemption. The implications of such manipulation are clear: when stories override critical thinking, the consequences can be catastrophic.

The Ethical Dilemma of Storytelling

This brings us to an ethical crossroads. As we explore the power of storytelling in this chapter, we must ask: where is the line between influence and manipulation? How can we use stories to guide and inspire without crossing into dangerous territory?

The answer lies in responsibility. When you wield the power of narrative, you're shaping someone's reality. Next time you see a parent guiding a child, a marketer crafting a brand message, or a leader inspiring a team, the stories they tell will determine how others see the world, and ultimately, themselves.

Why Your Brain Loves Stories

Imagine a world without stories, no novels, no movies, no bedtime tales. Hard to fathom, right? That's because your brain craves stories the way your body craves food. From the moment we are born, stories become the foundation of how we understand the world, how we learn, and how we relate to others. But what makes stories so irresistible? Why do they hook us, often bypassing our logic and embedding themselves deep within our psyche?

The answer lies in the brain's intricate neural circuitry, where storytelling triggers a cascade of neurochemical reactions. Every time you hear a compelling story, your brain lights up, releasing neurotransmitters that enhance memory retention, foster emotional connection, and hold your attention like a vice grip. This section will break down the brain's love affair with storytelling, showing why stories are the most powerful tool for persuasion.

The Chemical of Anticipation and Memory

Dopamine is about reward and anticipation. Engaging stories trigger dopamine release, creating a sense of anticipation that holds your attention from start to finish. The kicker? Dopamine also plays a critical role in memory retention, which means that stories aren't just entertaining, they make information stick.

This explains why a well-crafted narrative can make a brand's message more memorable than a list of product features. It's not the facts we remember, but the emotions tied to the story. Think back to Apple's iconic "Think Different" campaign. It was about a narrative of rebellion and creativity. That dopamine hit of anticipation was what made Apple's message unforgettable.

Say you're launching a new product. Instead of listing its features, craft a story about a person facing a challenge that your product helps solve. As they journey through obstacles, the audience anticipates the resolution, their brains lighting up with dopamine as they follow along. This is how brands like Nike hook customers, not with shoes, but with stories of overcoming adversity.

The Bonding Hormone and Trust Builder

Oxytocin is often called the "bonding hormone" because it's released when we feel connected to others. When you tell an emotionally charged story, especially one that involves empathy, trust, or vulnerability, oxytocin floods the listener's brain. These neurochemicals foster feelings of trust and emotional connection. Next time you're leading a team, negotiating a deal, or comforting a loved one, the release of oxytocin will turn a simple story into a powerful tool for building trust.

In personal relationships, stories of vulnerability are key to deepening emotional bonds. Imagine you're trying to mend a rift with a close friend. Instead of a logical explanation, share a story about a time you felt the same way they do, lonely, frustrated, or misunderstood. As they hear your story, their brain releases oxytocin, fostering empathy and trust. You're talking and connecting.

Techniques to Trigger Oxytocin:

- Personal Stories: Share moments of vulnerability or challenge. This triggers empathy, making your listener more likely to trust you.

- Relatable Characters: Create characters in your stories that your audience can see themselves in. The more they relate, the stronger the oxytocin response.

Syncing Minds Through Story

Ever notice how a powerful story makes you feel like you're right there with the storyteller, experiencing what they're describing? This phenomenon is called neural coupling. When we listen to a story, our brains synchronize with the storyteller's brain activity, creating a shared experience. This is why stories can make you feel someone else's joy, fear, or triumph, it's as if you're living through the narrative yourself.

Neural coupling is especially potent in leadership and marketing. When your audience's brain mirrors your own, you're forging a deep emotional connection. Thankfully, the science behind this is actionable.

For example, when delivering a company-wide message, don't just state your goals. Share a story that illustrates your vision. By painting a vivid picture of where you want the team to go, you synchronize their brain activity with yours. This creates alignment and motivation, because now, they're emotionally invested in the outcome.

How to Make Your Stories Unforgettable

So, how do you craft stories that tap into these powerful neurochemical processes? Here's where storytelling becomes a science.

1. Use of Emotion: Emotional stories are the most memorable because they trigger oxytocin and dopamine. Don't shy away from sharing personal or emotionally charged anecdotes. In business, tell stories about overcoming failure or moments of vulnerability to build trust with your audience.

- Example (Parenting): Want your child to develop a good habit? Tell them a story about a child their age who faced a similar struggle but overcame it. This personal connection not only triggers oxytocin but makes the story stick.

2. Pacing and Anticipation: Dopamine is all about anticipation. Build suspense in your story by slowly revealing key details, creating tension, and making your audience wait for the payoff.

    - Example (Career Negotiation): If you're pitching an idea to a potential employer, don't reveal all the benefits upfront. Start by painting a picture of the challenges they face, gradually lead into how your solution addresses those issues, and leave the resolution for last. This builds anticipation and makes your proposal more memorable.

3. Empathy Building: To deepen emotional engagement, create stories that foster empathy. Use "I feel" statements, or introduce characters who reflect the struggles and desires of your audience.

    - Example (Love and Relationships): When discussing a sensitive issue with a partner, frame it through a story that reflects their emotions. For example, "I once felt exactly like you when…" This approach disarms defensiveness and creates a space for understanding, thanks to the release of oxytocin and neural coupling.

How Stories Shape Perception and Behavior

Stories are the tool for shaping beliefs and driving action. This means the ability to craft and tell compelling stories gives you a profound advantage.

Consider the difference between these two approaches in marketing:

1. A car company lists the features of their new model: 20% better fuel efficiency, leather seats, and improved safety.
2. The same company tells the story of a family who survived a severe accident because of the car's safety features, and how that moment reshaped their life.

Which one do you think sticks? Which one do you remember? The second approach taps into the brain's love of narrative, releasing dopamine and oxytocin, making the story heard and felt.

In everyday life, stories can help you guide conversations, influence decisions, and connect on a deeper level. The power lies not in what you say, but in how your audience feels after hearing it. Mastering this art means mastering the ability to shape reality itself.

The Five Storytelling Frameworks

What if I told you that every skeptical thought you've ever had, every barrier you've erected to shield yourself from manipulation, can be effortlessly bypassed with the right story? Skepticism is not an impenetrable fortress; it's a fragile construct that crumbles under the weight of a well-crafted narrative. Stories have the unique power to infiltrate the subconscious, slipping past the logical defenses we rely on to protect ourselves. This is why the most successful leaders, marketers, politicians, and even parents have one thing in common: they know how to tell a story that dismantles resistance and implants belief.

The frameworks you'll explore in this section aren't just storytelling techniques, they are psychological tools, honed over millennia to resonate with the deepest parts of the human brain. Each framework serves a different purpose, but they all share one thing in common: they are designed to obliterate skepticism. Neuroscience and psychology reveal that stories bypass our critical thinking through emotional engagement, empathy, and narrative immersion. This is proven by studies, from Melanie Green's Narrative Transportation Theory to mirror neuron research that explains how our brains sync with the stories we hear.

So, as you read on, prepare to unravel the secrets of how these frameworks work, why they are so effective, and most importantly, how you can use them to influence others in every aspect of your life, from business to personal relationships, from career negotiations to parenting. We'll start with one of the most powerful and universal frameworks: The Hero's Journey.

Framework #1: The Hero's Journey

The Hero's Journey is more than just a narrative structure; it is an emotional blueprint deeply ingrained in the human psyche. It's a pattern of storytelling that reflects our collective experience of growth, struggle, and transformation. Popularized by Joseph Campbell in The Hero with a Thousand Faces, this framework taps into our shared need to see ourselves as the protagonists of our own lives, overcoming obstacles and achieving greatness.

But why does the Hero's Journey work so well? The answer lies in mirror neurons. These specialized brain cells activate when we observe someone else performing an action or experiencing an emotion, making us feel as though we are part of the story. Gallese and Goldman's research showed that mirror neurons allow us to vicariously live through the protagonist, creating a deep sense of empathy. When we watch or hear a hero's story, we don't just observe, we experience it ourselves. This neurological connection is why the Hero's Journey is so transformative.

Mirror Neurons and Empathy

Every time we hear a hero's journey, our brains don't just passively listen, they activate as though we are the ones embarking on the adventure. Mirror neurons, as demonstrated by Gallese and Goldman, ensure that we feel the protagonist's emotions and struggles as if they were our own. This creates a powerful bond between the listener and the hero, bypassing skepticism and drawing us into the narrative. The stronger the emotional connection, the more likely the listener is to internalize the message.

Think about it: why do audiences cheer for underdogs, cry when heroes fail, or feel triumph when they succeed? Beyond the plot, it's because our brains are wired to mirror those experiences. This is why the Hero's Journey is such a potent tool for influence. It taps into the neural circuitry that makes us feel the story, rather than simply analyzing it.

In practical terms, this framework can be applied across different aspects of life:

Turning Struggles into Triumphs

In business, the Hero's Journey is the backbone of some of the most successful marketing and leadership stories ever told. Customers and employees don't just want to hear about success, they want to be part of a journey. The story of overcoming adversity, surviving hardship, and coming out stronger on the other side is a narrative that resonates deeply with human psychology.

Take Elon Musk. His journey with SpaceX was framed as tale of struggle, repeated failure, and eventual success. When SpaceX faced its third failed rocket launch, bankruptcy was imminent. Musk's persistence and refusal to give up turned him into the hero of his own story, a narrative that galvanized public support and investor confidence. By framing his journey as one of overcoming impossible odds, Musk engaged the collective empathy of his audience, making them feel part of his success. Note: this perception may have changed recently.

Actionable Tip: In business, don't just present the end result, take your audience through the struggle. Frame your company's growth, your personal leadership journey, or even the development of a product as a Hero's Journey. Show the obstacles you've faced, the challenges you've overcome, and the triumphs that followed. This creates emotional engagement, deepens trust, and lowers resistance.

Building Emotional Intimacy Through Vulnerability

The Hero's Journey isn't limited to boardrooms and brands. It's a powerful tool for building emotional intimacy in personal relationships. Think about how vulnerable moments, sharing personal challenges, fears, and failures, create a deeper bond between people. This is the Hero's Journey in action. By opening up about your struggles, you invite others to walk alongside you, making them part of your personal narrative.

In romantic relationships, for example, vulnerability is the key to deep connection. Brené Brown's research on vulnerability highlights how sharing our stories of struggle and imperfection fosters trust and intimacy. When we tell our partner about a time we failed, feared, or faced a personal crisis, we are inviting them into our Hero's Journey. This not only deepens empathy but also strengthens the emotional bond.

Imagine you've had a significant disagreement with your partner. Instead of presenting solutions or justifying your behavior, share a story about a time when you felt similarly confused or lost. Frame it as a personal journey of learning and growth. This approach not only disarms defensiveness but also invites your partner to become part of the resolution.

Use the Hero's Journey to explore conflicts or deepen emotional intimacy. Instead of focusing on the conflict itself, tell a story that illustrates your own personal journey. Invite your partner to understand your perspective by making them feel part of the emotional experience.

Transforming Your Own Narrative

The beauty of the Hero's Journey is that it's also a powerful tool for transforming yourself. When you start seeing your life as a series of heroic challenges, every obstacle becomes an opportunity for growth. This mindset shift rewires how you approach problems, from career setbacks to personal failures.

Consider how neuroscientist Antonio Damasio's research on emotions and decision-making demonstrates that we are not purely logical beings. We need emotional narratives to make sense of our lives. By framing your personal struggles as part of your own Hero's Journey, you tap into your emotional core, making it easier to push through difficulties and embrace change.

Say you've been passed over for a promotion at work. Instead of seeing this as a failure, reframe it as part of your personal Hero's Journey. This setback is just one of the challenges you must overcome before reaching your ultimate goal. By viewing it through the lens of transformation, you'll be more resilient, adaptable, and motivated to keep going.

Use the Hero's Journey as a mental framework for personal development. When you face setbacks, view them as essential parts of your journey, not as dead ends. This narrative reframing will help you maintain motivation, build resilience, and stay focused on long-term growth.

The Hero's Journey in Modern Marketing and Leadership

Marketing is storytelling, this is a well-worn phrase, but its full implications are often missed. The Hero's Journey is seen as a way to engage customers. But it's actually a tool for creating loyalty, forging emotional bonds, and building trust. In the context of neuroscience, this makes perfect sense. Jonathan Gottschall's research on the evolutionary basis of storytelling shows that humans are hardwired to respond to narratives of struggle and transformation. The Hero's Journey activates neural pathways that make us feel connected to the brand, product, or leader telling the story.

Consider Nike's marketing. Their ads rarely focus on product specifications. Instead, they tell stories of athletes overcoming adversity. Stories of runners battling through injuries or a teams clawing their way to victory tap into the Hero's Journey to connect with its audience on an emotional level. The message is clear: by buying Nike, you are joining this journey, overcoming your own obstacles, and becoming part of a greater narrative.

If you're leading a brand, stop focusing solely on product benefits. Instead, tell the story of your brand's journey. Share the struggles, the near-misses, the moments of doubt. Customers will relate to your brand because what you offer is the journey they feel a part of.

The Hero's Journey is a psychological tool that taps into the core of human experience. It works because it engages the brain's empathy circuits, making the listener part of the story. This framework allows you to bypass skepticism and create lasting emotional connections.

Framework #2: The Conflict-Resolution Arc

When was the last time you felt that deep sense of satisfaction at the end of a story? You know the feeling, the final resolution of conflict that leaves you emotionally fulfilled, the sense of closure that makes everything that came before it worthwhile. That is a psychological necessity. Human brains crave resolution. Without it, we're left with cognitive dissonance, a discomfort so unbearable that we'll grasp at any story that provides relief. This is why stories with conflict-resolution arcs are so potent. They don't just entertain; they fulfill a biological need.

At the heart of the conflict-resolution arc lies a universal truth: the human brain seeks closure. In psychology, this is often referred to as the Zeigarnik Effect, which states that people remember incomplete tasks or stories far better than those that are resolved. Our brains hold onto unresolved tension like a clenched fist, unable to let go until that tension is released. Research by Arie Kruglanski and Donna Webster in the "Need for Closure" theory further highlights how much we rely on resolution to process experiences emotionally and cognitively. Without a clear ending, stories feel incomplete, triggering a lingering discomfort that we're desperate to resolve.

But why is this so critical for persuasion and influence? It's simple: when you tell a story that introduces conflict and then offers a satisfying resolution, you're building trust. Your audience learns to associate you with emotional satisfaction. You guide them through the discomfort of conflict and reward them with the dopamine-fueled pleasure of resolution. And in doing so, you win their trust, loyalty, and, ultimately, their willingness to be influenced.

Cognitive Closure and Emotional Satisfaction

To understand why the conflict-resolution arc is so effective, we must first go deeper into the brain's obsession with closure. Cognitive closure refers to the brain's desire to find a firm conclusion and eliminate ambiguity. When we encounter unresolved conflict in stories, conversations, or negotiations, our brain sends out distress signals. This activates the anterior cingulate cortex, the region associated with error detection and conflict monitoring. It's a biological response designed to push us toward resolution because unresolved conflict is mentally taxing.

This drive for closure is so powerful that it often overrides critical thinking. When a narrative provides resolution, the brain rewards us with a dopamine hit, reinforcing the idea that the conflict was worth enduring. It's the neurological equivalent of the phrase "no pain, no gain." The tension was unpleasant, but the reward, the resolution, makes it all worthwhile. In storytelling, this is the moment of triumph, reconciliation, or revelation that makes everything fall into place.

This is why unresolved stories can feel unsettling or frustrating. Movies or books that end on cliffhangers or ambiguous notes often leave us feeling uncomfortable. We want the resolution, the closure, the emotional release. Psychological studies confirm that narratives which provide resolution are consistently rated as more satisfying and memorable than those that leave conflicts open-ended.

This craving for resolution isn't about enjoying a good story. Instead, it's a tool you can use to persuade, influence, and even manipulate. Because once you've created tension, you hold all the power. Your audience is primed for resolution, and only you can provide it.

Resolving Conflict to Win Trust

In business, the conflict-resolution arc is one of the most effective ways to turn skepticism into trust. Next time you're pitching a new idea, negotiating a deal, or leading a team through difficult times, frame the conflict and resolution in a way that compels your audience to buy in.

Consider the classic case of Apple's marketing strategy during the late 90s. The company was on the brink of collapse, having been overshadowed by competitors like Microsoft. Steve Jobs didn't just announce a comeback, he told a story. He presented Apple's struggles as the ultimate conflict. The company had lost its way, fallen into irrelevance, and was on the verge of defeat. But then came the resolution: the return of the visionary leader, the resurgence of innovation, and the introduction of iconic products like the iMac and iPhone. This was a story of redemption.

Apple's narrative arc resolved the tension for its audience, both internally and externally. Investors, employees, and customers were all drawn into this story of conflict and resolution. The company had faced challenges, but it emerged stronger, wiser, and more innovative. By framing the conflict and providing a clear resolution, Apple rebuilt its brand and won the loyalty of millions.

In business, don't just present solutions, present conflicts first. Show your audience the tension, the struggle, and the stakes. Then offer a resolution that not only solves the problem but also rewards them emotionally. Guide your audience through a narrative journey that satisfies their deep-rooted psychological need for closure.

Creating and Resolving Tension to Drive Agreement

Negotiation is a battleground of tension and resolution. Skilled negotiators know that the key to closing a deal isn't in overwhelming the other party with facts or logic, it's in managing the emotional arc of the conversation. You create tension, strategically introduce conflict, and then offer a resolution that brings relief. It's storytelling in its most potent form, applied in real-time.

Harvard Business Review has long emphasized the importance of creating tension in negotiations. It's the tension that forces both parties to confront the stakes and consider new options. But what most negotiators overlook is the emotional power of the resolution. If you guide the other party through the tension, offering a resolution that feels satisfying, they'll not only agree to your terms, they'll trust you more for having brought them through the conflict.

Let's say you're negotiating a major business deal. Rather than presenting your offer immediately, you frame the conversation around the conflict. You emphasize the risks, the challenges, and the potential losses if no agreement is reached. This builds emotional tension, engaging the other party on a deeper level. Then, as the negotiation progresses, you gradually introduce your resolution, your solution to the problem. You present it as a logical outcome and the answer that resolves the emotional tension you've built up throughout the conversation.

The result? The other party feels a sense of closure. They've been guided through the conflict and rewarded with a solution that satisfies both their logical and emotional needs. And because you've resolved the tension for them, they're far more likely to agree to the terms you've proposed.

In negotiations, never rush to the solution. Build tension by presenting the problem in a way that highlights the stakes. Then offer a resolution that brings relief, making the other party feel as though they've been guided through a journey toward a satisfying conclusion. This approach not only increases your chances of closing the deal but also builds trust and rapport.

Using Resolution to Build Emotional Intimacy

In personal relationships, conflict is inevitable. But how you handle that conflict, how you introduce and resolve it, will determine the strength and intimacy of the relationship. This is where the conflict-resolution arc becomes a powerful tool for building trust and deepening emotional bonds.

John Gottman's research on marital stability emphasizes that it's not the presence of conflict that predicts the success of a relationship, it's how that conflict is resolved. Couples who are able to handle conflict and find resolution are far more likely to have long-lasting, emotionally fulfilling relationships. The resolution provides a sense of closure, allowing both partners to move forward with trust and renewed emotional connection.

But there's a deeper psychological layer to this. When you guide someone through conflict and offer resolution, you're offering emotional release. The conflict creates tension, and the resolution releases that tension, triggering a flood of oxytocin, the bonding hormone that deepens emotional intimacy.

Let's say you've had an argument with your partner. Rather than simply moving on or brushing it under the rug, you use the conflict-resolution arc to handle the situation. You start by acknowledging the conflict, the emotional tension that's been created. Then, together, you work toward a resolution that satisfies both of your emotional needs. This could be through conversation, compromise, or an act of reconciliation. The key is that the resolution be more than a logical solution. It should be an emotional release that allows both of you to move forward, feeling more connected and understood.

In relationships, don't shy away from conflict. Instead, use it as an opportunity to deepen emotional intimacy. Guide your partner through the conflict, acknowledging the emotional tension, and then offer a resolution that provides closure and emotional satisfaction. This strengthens trust and fosters a deeper bond.

The Power of Conflict and Resolution in Persuasion

The conflict-resolution arc is more than just a storytelling technique, it's a psychological tool for building trust, deepening relationships, and persuading others. By introducing conflict and guiding your audience through a resolution, you tap into their brain's natural craving for closure, providing emotional and neurological satisfaction.

In business, this means framing challenges and offering solutions that resolve tension. In negotiations, it means creating and resolving conflict to drive agreement. In relationships, it means navigating emotional tension to build intimacy and trust. And in personal development, it means viewing your own conflicts as opportunities for growth and transformation.

Mastering the conflict-resolution is one of the most powerful psychological forces at your disposal. And as we'll see in the next framework, this is just one of many tools you can use to influence, persuade, and connect with others on a deeper level.

Framework #3: The Monomyth and Cyclical Transformation

In the realm of storytelling, some narratives follow a linear path from beginning to end, resolving in a neat, one-time conclusion. But life, and the stories that resonate most deeply, rarely unfolds in a straight line. Instead, we live through cycles, endlessly repeating patterns of growth, failure, learning, and rebirth. This cyclical nature is captured perfectly by the Monomyth, or the Cyclical Hero's Journey. It's a narrative framework that chronicles a transformative journey and emphasizes the endless repetition of challenge and change, illustrating that life is a series of trials, each preparing us for the next.

The Monomyth goes beyond the typical Hero's Journey by suggesting that every ending is a new beginning, every success is the precursor to a new challenge, and every failure is an opportunity for renewal. This cyclical transformation is deeply ingrained in our psyche because it mirrors the very process of human growth and evolution. The stories that follow this pattern engage the brain's reward pathways, as shown by Greg J. Stephens' research on the neuroscience of storytelling, reinforcing emotional involvement and memory retention. By framing life as a series of cyclical narratives, we tap into the brain's inherent need to find meaning and predictability in chaos.

Repetition, Memory, and Transformation

Why does the brain love repetition in stories? From a neurological perspective, repetition in narrative, particularly when it involves transformation, plays a crucial role in memory retention and emotional engagement. As Antonio Damasio highlighted in his research on emotions and decision-making, our brains are not designed to simply register facts or information; they thrive on patterns that mirror our experiences. Repetition reinforces learning, making lessons from the narrative easier to recall and apply. Every time a character faces a new challenge, overcomes it, and is transformed, the brain releases dopamine, creating a reward loop that encourages us to pay attention, remember, and be emotionally invested.

This cyclical transformation embeds a sense of purpose and meaning into the story. It allows the brain to see patterns in chaos, to find order in the unpredictability of life. That's why the Monomyth resonates so deeply with audiences, it reflects the ebb and flow of real-life challenges, victories, and setbacks.

The Monomyth in Long-Term Leadership and Mentorship

In the world of leadership and mentorship, the Monomyth is a powerful tool for fostering long-term growth and resilience. One of the biggest challenges leaders face is inspiring their teams to stay motivated through the ups and downs of business cycles, personal development, and organizational changes. The Monomyth's emphasis on cyclical growth provides a blueprint for leaders to guide their teams through failures, triumphs, and everything in between.

The key to applying the Monomyth in leadership is to frame challenges not as isolated events but as part of a larger cycle of growth. When a team fails, it's not the end, it's a necessary part of the journey toward eventual success. Each setback becomes a learning opportunity, preparing the team for the next phase of transformation.

Imagine leading a startup that has just gone through a major failure, perhaps a product launch that flopped or a partnership that fell apart. Instead of viewing this as a devastating loss, you frame it for your team as part of the cyclical nature of success. Share stories of companies that went through similar failures but used those moments to learn, grow, and ultimately triumph. By positioning failure as a natural part of the Monomyth, you reduce the emotional toll on your team and keep them focused on the long-term goal.

When leaders frame failure as part of a cyclical transformation, they trigger the brain's dopamine system, which rewards the anticipation of future success. This neurochemical boost keeps teams motivated, even in the face of adversity.

Use the Monomyth framework in leadership to reframe failures as stepping stones in an ongoing cycle of growth. This not only builds resilience but also enhances motivation by tapping into the brain's reward system, which is activated by the anticipation of overcoming future challenges.

Teaching Life Lessons Through Cycles

Parenting is perhaps the most natural domain for the Monomyth to unfold. Children, like all humans, learn best through repetition. Every experience, every lesson, every discipline is part of a larger cycle of learning and growth. The Monomyth allows parents to frame their children's challenges, mistakes, and successes as part of a recurring cycle that prepares them for life's bigger challenges. This framework not only encourages children to embrace failure but also teaches them that every failure is a precursor to growth.

Let's say your child is struggling with a particular subject in school, math, for example. Instead of simply punishing them for poor grades, use the Monomyth framework to guide them through the process of learning. Explain that every failure is a challenge they must face on their journey toward mastery. Each bad grade is a dragon to be slain, each study session a step toward victory. Frame the cycle as part of their personal hero's journey. This not only reduces the emotional weight of failure but also encourages them to persist because they understand that failure is temporary and necessary for growth.

By framing discipline and challenges within the Monomyth, parents can help their children see life as a series of manageable cycles, each with its own lessons and opportunities for transformation. This approach teaches resilience, encourages a growth mindset, and reinforces the importance of perseverance.

Paul Zak's research on storytelling and oxytocin reveals that emotionally charged stories, particularly those that involve overcoming obstacles, trigger the release of oxytocin, a neurochemical responsible for empathy and trust. When parents use the Monomyth framework to guide their children through challenges, they foster deeper emotional bonds and trust, making the lessons more impactful.

Use the Monomyth framework in parenting to teach your children that every challenge is part of a larger cycle of growth. This approach not only helps them build resilience but also strengthens your emotional connection with them, fostering trust and empathy.

Cycles of Self-Transformation

On a personal level, the Monomyth serves as a powerful tool for navigating life's ups and downs. In our own lives, we often experience cycles of success, failure, and transformation. By viewing these experiences through the lens of the Monomyth, we can gain a deeper understanding of our personal growth and find meaning in the cyclical nature of life.

Consider how often we set goals, achieve them, and then find ourselves setting new, more challenging goals. The Monomyth helps us understand that personal growth is not a straight line; it's a series of cycles, each one building on the last. Every time we fail, we are not regressing, we are preparing for the next phase of growth.

Imagine you've set a goal to run a marathon. You train for months, but an injury sidelines you just weeks before the race. This feels like a devastating failure. But if you view it through the lens of the Monomyth, you understand that this injury is not the end, it's part of the cycle. You'll recover, come back stronger, and eventually achieve your goal. Each setback in this process is a lesson, each failure a step toward ultimate transformation.

Studies on neuroplasticity, the brain's ability to rewire itself in response to new challenges, support the idea of cyclical transformation. Every time we face a new challenge, our brains form new neural pathways, reinforcing the lessons we've learned and preparing us for the next cycle. This process of continuous growth and adaptation mirrors the cyclical nature of the Monomyth.

In your own life, use the Monomyth to frame personal challenges as part of an ongoing cycle of growth. By viewing setbacks as necessary steps in your transformation, you'll build resilience and maintain motivation through difficult times. Each failure becomes an opportunity for learning and renewal.

Crafting Narratives of Cyclical Transformation

Consumers don't want to buy products. They want to be part of a narrative, particularly one that mirrors their own experiences of growth and transformation. Brands that use the Monomyth to tell stories of cyclical transformation can build deep emotional connections with their customers, creating loyalty that goes far beyond the product itself.

Consider a fitness brand that positions its products as part of an ongoing journey of self-improvement. The brand's marketing campaign could follow the story of a customer who embarks on a fitness journey, faces setbacks (such as injuries or plateaus), and ultimately transforms themselves, only to set new goals and begin the cycle again. This narrative mirrors the Monomyth, reinforcing the idea that fitness is not a one-time achievement but an ongoing process of growth and transformation.

By framing the customer's journey as a cyclical narrative, the brand taps into the deep psychological need for stories of transformation. Customers don't just buy the product; they buy into the journey, the promise of continuous growth and improvement.

Jennifer Aaker's research on storytelling shows that stories are remembered up to 22 times more than facts alone. By using the Monomyth framework in marketing, brands can create memorable narratives that not only engage customers but also reinforce the idea of cyclical growth, making the brand a central part of the customer's personal transformation.

Use the Monomyth in marketing to frame your brand's story as part of a cyclical journey of growth and transformation. This approach not only creates deep emotional connections with your audience but also reinforces the idea that your brand is an essential part of their personal journey.

The Power of Cyclical Transformation

The Monomyth's cyclical nature reflects life's most profound truths. It teaches us that every challenge is part of a larger cycle of transformation. By embracing this framework, we can find meaning in our struggles, resilience in our failures, and motivation in our successes.

The Monomyth is about recognizing that every ending is a new beginning, every success is the precursor to a new challenge, and every failure is an opportunity for renewal. And in this endless cycle of transformation, we find the true power of storytelling, the ability to turn chaos into order, failure into triumph, and uncertainty into purpose.

Framework #4: The 3-Act Structure

The 3-Act Structure is one of the oldest and most enduring storytelling frameworks. It is so deeply embedded in our collective consciousness that even people unfamiliar with the term can recognize its pattern. It divides a story into 3 distinct phases: Setup, Confrontation, and Resolution. This seemingly simple structure mirrors the psychological process through which humans experience and make sense of challenges. From a neurological standpoint, the 3-Act Structure provides the predictability our brains crave, while also maintaining the tension necessary to keep us engaged.

The Brain's Need for Predictable Progression

The 3-Act Structure taps into a fundamental aspect of human cognition: our need for predictability and pattern recognition. Neuroscientific research on narrative structure, such as studies by Uri Hasson, has shown that structured storytelling aligns with the brain's natural pattern-seeking tendencies. The brain constantly searches for connections, and stories that follow a clear progression from beginning to middle to end provide the framework it craves.

This structure mirrors real life: we experience an introduction to challenges (setup), we face those challenges head-on (confrontation), and we either triumph or fail (resolution). From a cognitive perspective, each stage of the 3-Act Structure serves a different function. The Setup establishes context and primes the brain, activating the prefrontal cortex responsible for decision-making and understanding. The Confrontation triggers the limbic system, which governs emotional responses like fear, excitement, and empathy. Finally, the Resolution engages the brain's dopamine reward system, providing a satisfying sense of closure that reinforces memory retention.

This is why audiences can sense when a story is missing a critical piece, our brains are wired to anticipate this structure. When all 3 acts are present, stories feel complete. When one act is missing or misaligned, we experience frustration or dissatisfaction.

Setup, Confrontation, and Resolution

Let's break down the 3-Act Structure into its core components, but don't mistake this for a mere formula. Each stage must be carefully crafted to reflect the depth of human experience and emotion.

Act One: Setup – The Introduction of Stakes

In the Setup, the audience is introduced to the world of the protagonist. This act establishes the context, introducing characters, the setting, and, most importantly, the stakes. Without clearly defining the stakes early on, your audience won't have a reason to care about the conflict that follows. The Setup is all about establishing emotional investment.

Neurologically, this phase is critical because it triggers anticipation. Dopamine, often referred to as the "anticipation chemical," is released in this phase as the brain begins to predict what might happen next. According to Melanie Green's Narrative Transportation Theory, stories that create an emotional connection early on can transport listeners into a narrative world, lowering skepticism and increasing belief.

Imagine you're preparing for a job interview. The Setup is your opportunity to frame the context of your career journey. You might start by explaining where you began, perhaps in a low-level position, with limited resources, facing personal or professional challenges. The stakes are clear: your audience understands what you had to lose, the sacrifices you've made, and why this journey matters.

The Setup is where you anchor your audience in your story, ensuring they are emotionally invested in your success or failure.

Act Two: Confrontation – Heightening the Conflict

The Confrontation is where the tension escalates. This act introduces obstacles, challenges, and conflicts that stand in the protagonist's way. It's the emotional heart of the story, where the audience must experience fear, doubt, and uncertainty alongside the hero.

This is where the limbic system kicks into high gear, particularly the amygdala, which is responsible for processing emotions like fear and excitement. The brain is emotionally activated, driving engagement through tension and conflict. According to Jonathan Gottschall, author of The Storytelling Animal, this phase is crucial for making stories stick. Without conflict, the brain has no reason to remain engaged; it needs a challenge to keep it invested.

In psychological terms, this phase capitalizes on cognitive dissonance, the discomfort we feel when reality doesn't align with our expectations. We naturally seek resolution to this discomfort, which keeps us hooked on the story. As the confrontation intensifies, so does our emotional investment.

Continuing with the job interview scenario, the Confrontation could involve the challenges you've faced in your career, perhaps a significant project failure, a demanding boss, or an economic downturn. These obstacles serve to heighten the stakes, showcasing the struggles that make your eventual success meaningful. The audience is drawn into your narrative because they can relate to the universal experience of struggle and adversity.

Act 3: Resolution – The Payoff

Finally, the Resolution brings the story to a close, offering a sense of closure and satisfaction. This is where the brain releases dopamine as a reward for following through with the narrative journey. As with the Conflict-Resolution Arc, the audience craves closure, and the Resolution provides just that, cementing the story in memory.

The key to an effective Resolution is ensuring that the payoff is both emotionally and intellectually satisfying. The stakes introduced in the Setup are resolved, the conflicts from the Confrontation are overcome, and the audience walks away with a clear understanding of how the protagonist has been transformed.

In the interview, your Resolution might focus on how you overcame those career challenges. You've now reached a position of leadership, driven major projects to success, or transformed a struggling team into a high-performing one. This final act not only demonstrates your resilience and capability but also ties the entire narrative together, offering your audience a satisfying conclusion to your career journey.

Structuring Presentations and Pitches

The 3-Act Structure is not limited to storytelling in the traditional sense; it's a powerful framework for structuring presentations, business pitches, and professional narratives. When you're presenting an idea, making a pitch, or even conducting a performance review, organizing your message into 3 acts can make your argument more compelling and easier for your audience to follow.

Setup: In business presentations, the Setup introduces the problem or opportunity at hand. You outline the current state of affairs and define the stakes. Why does this problem matter? What are the potential gains or losses?

The Confrontation details the challenges. What obstacles stand in the way of success? This is where you present the complexities of the problem and the risks involved. The tension created by these obstacles keeps your audience engaged, heightening their emotional investment.

Finally, the Resolution offers the solution. You present your proposal, plan, or vision for overcoming the challenges and achieving success. This final act should provide both an emotional and logical payoff, leaving your audience feeling confident in your solution.

Framing Personal Growth

The 3-Act Structure can also be a powerful tool in personal relationships, particularly when communicating your growth, experiences, or emotional challenges. In moments of vulnerability, framing your story in 3 acts allows you to clearly communicate the evolution of your feelings, behaviors, or relationships.

Imagine you're explaining a personal transformation to a close friend or partner. You might use the 3-Act Structure to tell your story. In the Setup, you explain where you started, perhaps a period in your life where you felt lost, unmotivated, or directionless. In the Confrontation, you discuss the emotional challenges you faced. This could be overcoming a fear, dealing with a toxic relationship, or battling self-doubt. Finally, in the Resolution, you share how you've grown, what you've learned, and how you've emerged stronger, more self-aware, or more resilient.

Framing your personal stories in this way makes them more engaging, easier for others to follow, and ultimately more impactful. The predictability of the structure provides clarity, while the emotional progression keeps the listener invested.

Emotional Engagement and Cognitive Flow

The 3-Act Structure works because it follows the brain's natural cognitive flow. In the Setup, the brain is primed with context and begins anticipating outcomes. In the Confrontation, emotional engagement heightens as the brain experiences conflict and tension, pushing the audience to seek resolution. Finally, the Resolution satisfies the brain's need for closure, releasing dopamine and creating a sense of reward.

The anticipation-reward loop created by the 3-Act Structure is key to why it has endured for centuries. It's a neurological necessity. The brain craves predictability but also thrives on the tension that arises from conflict. The 3-Act Structure leverages this duality, creating a narrative arc that keeps the audience both intellectually and emotionally engaged from beginning to end.

The 3-Act Structure in Everyday Communication

The 3-Act Structure extends far beyond writers, filmmakers, and public speakers. It can also be applied in everyday communication. If you're delivering a speech, writing an email, or having a difficult conversation, structuring your message into 3 acts can help you communicate more effectively and persuasively.

1. Setup: Start by clearly defining the context. What's the issue at hand? What are the stakes? This primes your audience to engage with the rest of the message.
2. Confrontation: Introduce the challenges or conflicts. What obstacles need to be overcome? This keeps your audience emotionally invested and heightens the tension.
3. Resolution: Provide a solution or conclusion. What's the proposed outcome? How does the story end? This gives your audience a sense of closure and satisfaction.

By using this structure, you not only make your message clearer but also tap into the brain's natural storytelling preferences, making your communication more engaging and memorable.

The Enduring Power of the 3-Act Structure

The 3-Act Structure has endured for centuries because it mirrors the way humans process information. It taps into the brain's need for predictability while simultaneously creating emotional tension through conflict. The 3-Act Structure ensures that your audience stays engaged, emotionally invested, and ultimately satisfied.

In the next section, we will explore the Quest Narrative, another powerful storytelling framework that taps into humanity's intrinsic motivation to pursue goals and overcome challenges. But remember this: in every personal, professional, or fictional story, there's always a beginning, a middle, and an end, and the better you can structure those 3 acts, the more powerfully you can influence, persuade, and inspire.

Framework #5: The Quest Narrative

At its core, the Quest Narrative is a story of pursuit that strives for something greater, often against overwhelming odds, and evolving through the process. The protagonist embarks on a journey with a goal in mind. Goals like finding a treasure, self-actualization, love, or success. Along the way, challenges emerge, obstacles threaten progress, and yet, the pursuit continues. The Quest Narrative appeals to something deeply embedded in the human psyche: the intrinsic desire to strive toward a purpose. This narrative framework resonates because it taps into our natural inclination to seek meaning through achievement and growth.

From a psychological perspective, the Quest Narrative activates the brain's motivation centers, specifically, the ventral striatum and the prefrontal cortex, which are responsible for goal-setting and reward anticipation. As humans, we are hardwired to set goals, face challenges, and pursue rewards. This framework feeds into that primal drive, making the story both compelling and relatable. In marketing, relationships, personal growth, and even leadership, the Quest Narrative creates a powerful sense of purpose that captivates audiences and motivates them to action.

But let's go deeper. Why does the Quest Narrative work so well across various domains of life? Why do we find ourselves so irresistibly drawn to stories of individuals or groups chasing lofty goals? The answer lies in its ability to map directly onto our psychology: we live our lives as quests, moving from goal to goal, experiencing personal transformation along the way.

Goal Pursuit and Dopamine

At the heart of the Quest Narrative's psychological power is the brain's dopamine system. It plays a critical role in motivation and goal pursuit, the anticipation of reward. Every time we set a goal, our brain begins to release dopamine, creating a feeling of anticipation that drives us forward. This is why the Quest Narrative resonates so deeply, it mirrors the process our brain goes through every time we pursue something meaningful.

As Jonathan Gottschall highlights in The Storytelling Animal, stories that involve a clear pursuit engage the brain's reward centers, keeping us hooked on the narrative because we want to see the outcome. The process of striving that keeps us engaged. The mere act of pursuing a goal releases dopamine, providing us with a sense of progress and motivation even when the goal hasn't yet been achieved.

For storytellers, this is a powerful tool. By framing a narrative as a quest, you can tap into the audience's intrinsic motivation to seek and strive, making your message far more compelling by aligning with the brain's natural goal-setting mechanisms.

Framing Ambitious Goals

In the business world, the Quest Narrative is an essential tool for framing long-term goals and rallying teams around a shared vision. Companies that succeed in the long run often do so because they position themselves as being on a quest toward a larger purpose. These companies revolutionize industries, solve global problems, or achieve unprecedented success.

Take Tesla mission: to accelerate the world's transition to sustainable energy. This is a quest of epic proportions, and it frames every challenge the company faces as part of a larger narrative. By overcoming production delays, battling against regulatory pressures, or innovating in the face of environmental crises, Tesla's journey is framed as a heroic pursuit of a better future. This taps into both the company's internal motivation and the emotional investment of its customers and investors. They aren't just buying a car, they're participating in a global quest.

In practical terms, leaders can use the Quest Narrative to motivate their teams by positioning business goals not as isolated tasks but as steps on a larger journey. When employees understand that their daily work contributes to a grander mission, they're more likely to stay motivated, committed, and resilient in the face of challenges.

In business, frame your company's mission as a quest toward a meaningful and ambitious goal. This not only motivates employees by giving their work a greater purpose but also attracts customers and investors who want to be part of the journey. Every setback becomes a stepping stone toward achieving the ultimate objective, reinforcing the narrative that persistence and resilience are key.

Pursuing Betterment

In personal relationships, the Quest Narrative offers a compelling framework for navigating difficult decisions, personal growth, and long-term commitment. Relationships, like quests, are not static. They require constant effort, challenges must be faced, and growth is often achieved through struggle. By framing relationship difficulties as part of a shared quest toward a better future, partners can build deeper emotional connections and a stronger sense of purpose.

Imagine a couple facing a tough decision like moving to a new city, making a financial commitment, or working through a personal conflict. Instead of viewing these challenges as barriers, they can frame them as part of a quest toward a stronger, more fulfilling relationship. The challenges they face become obstacles to be overcome together, and each victory strengthens their bond. This approach fosters resilience and trust, as both partners see themselves as united in a pursuit of growth.

Framing difficult moments as part of a larger quest can also help couples flatten conflicts in a healthier way. Instead of seeing the conflict as a problem that threatens the relationship, it becomes an integral part of the journey toward a deeper connection. This reframing reduces defensiveness and increases collaboration, as both partners work together toward a shared goal.

Emotional challenges within relationships activate the brain's oxytocin system, which is involved in bonding and trust. When couples work through these challenges together, their brains release oxytocin, reinforcing emotional bonds and increasing feelings of connection. By framing these challenges as part of a quest, couples can strengthen their relationship while also enhancing their sense of purpose.

In relationships, use the Quest Narrative to frame difficult decisions and conflicts as part of a shared journey toward a better future. This approach fosters emotional resilience, strengthens bonds, and keeps both partners motivated to work through challenges together.

The Quest Narrative in Personal Growth

Personal growth is, by nature, a quest. Every individual is on a journey toward self-improvement. This could take the form of career advancement, intellectual development, physical fitness, or even emotional resilience. The Quest Narrative provides a powerful framework for individuals to conceptualize their own development, seeing each challenge as a necessary part of the journey toward self-actualization.

Imagine someone pursuing a career goal, such as becoming a leader in their industry. The journey is fraught with challenges, overcoming educational barriers, navigating office politics, facing personal doubt, and seizing opportunities at the right time. By framing this pursuit as a quest, each obstacle becomes part of the process of growth. The setbacks aren't failures, they're trials that build the individual's capacity to lead.

Framing personal goals as part of a larger quest can also help individuals maintain motivation through difficult times. When you see your efforts as contributing to a larger purpose, you're more likely to stay committed, even in the face of adversity. The brain's dopamine system reinforces this persistence by rewarding progress toward the goal, no matter how incremental it may seem.

The brain's prefrontal cortex plays a crucial role in long-term goal setting and perseverance. By framing personal growth as a quest, individuals activate the brain's goal-setting mechanisms, keeping themselves motivated to pursue their ambitions despite setbacks.

In your personal life, frame your self-improvement efforts as part of a larger quest. See every challenge as a step on the path to success. This mindset will help you stay motivated, persevere through difficulties, and maintain a sense of purpose in your personal growth journey.

Inspiring Consumers to Join the Journey

Brands can use the Quest Narrative to inspire consumers to become part of a larger mission. By framing the purchase of a product or service as part of a customer's personal journey, marketers can create deeper emotional connections and a sense of loyalty. Consumers don't just buy a product, they buy into a quest.

Consider Patagonia, the outdoor clothing company known for its environmental activism. Patagonia does more than sell jackets; it invites its customers to join the quest for environmental sustainability. Every purchase is framed as a step toward a larger goal, preserving the planet for future generations. This narrative appeals to consumers' intrinsic desire to be part of something meaningful, making them more likely to support the brand.

Marketers who successfully employ the Quest Narrative can turn their products into symbols of personal achievement. By aligning their brand's mission with the consumer's desire for growth, they create a powerful emotional connection that goes beyond the product itself. The consumer becomes a protagonist in their own quest, and the brand becomes an enabler of that journey.

In marketing, use the Quest Narrative to align your brand's mission with your consumers' personal goals. Frame your product or service as a tool that helps them on their journey toward a meaningful outcome. This approach deepens emotional engagement and fosters brand loyalty.

Tapping into Intrinsic Motivation

The Quest Narrative is effective because it appeals directly to intrinsic motivation, the desire to pursue goals for their own sake. Unlike external motivation, which relies on rewards or recognition, intrinsic motivation is driven by a deep sense of purpose and personal fulfillment. Stories that follow the Quest Narrative tap into this psychological drive, making audiences more likely to engage with and invest in the outcome.

Research by Ryan and Deci on Self-Determination Theory reveals that intrinsic motivation is fueled by 3 core psychological needs: autonomy, competence, and relatedness. The Quest Narrative satisfies all 3 of these needs by giving the protagonist (and, by extension, the audience) a sense of control over their journey (autonomy), a feeling of accomplishment as they overcome challenges (competence), and a connection to a larger purpose or community (relatedness).

This is why the Quest Narrative is so effective across different domains, it engages the audience's intrinsic desire for growth and fulfillment. By positioning challenges as part of a larger pursuit, the storyteller creates a sense of purpose that keeps the audience motivated and emotionally invested.

The Endless Pursuit of Meaning

The Quest Narrative reflects the human experience. We are all on quests, constantly striving for something greater, for personal growth, professional success, or deeper relationships. By framing stories as quests, you tap into the audience's intrinsic motivation to pursue goals, overcome challenges, and find meaning in the process.

The power of the Quest Narrative lies in its ability to turn ordinary pursuits into extraordinary journeys, making every challenge part of a greater story of growth, achievement, and meaning.

Crafting the Perfect Story for Any Situation

In the age of information overload, crafting a story that cuts through the noise and leaves a lasting impact has never been more essential. But a great story doesn't appear out of thin air, it's built with precision, strategy, and a deep understanding of the psychological triggers that drive human engagement. Next time you're delivering a keynote speech, pitching a business idea, or even trying to resolve a personal conflict, the principles of storytelling remain the same: hook your audience, build tension, and offer a resolution that resonates on both emotional and intellectual levels. In this section, we'll break down how to craft the perfect story for any situation, exploring long-form and short-form techniques that can be applied to various contexts, from business to personal life.

Long-Form Storytelling: The Marathon of Engagement

Long-form storytelling gives you the time and space to dive deep into the emotional, intellectual, and psychological depths of a narrative. It allows for a more intricate and layered story, one that can evolve over time and engage your audience on a sustained level. Long-form storytelling is ideal for contexts where you need to keep attention over an extended period, such as in keynote speeches, presentations, documentaries, or even in leadership communication. The challenge here is maintaining engagement throughout, and that requires a structured approach.

Relatable Problem, Rising Tension, Layers of Conflict, and Satisfying Resolution

The first rule of long-form storytelling is simple: relatability. Without an emotional hook, your audience will disconnect. According to Melanie Green's Narrative Transportation Theory, stories that engage emotions are more likely to transport the audience into the narrative, reducing skepticism and increasing belief. No matter the story you're telling, your audience must see themselves in the protagonist. They must care about the outcome as if it were their own.

Picture the story of a startup founder who, despite endless setbacks, lack of funding, failed product launches, competitive pressures, remains resilient. This founder's journey doesn't gloss over the pain of failure; instead, it goes deep into the emotional toll. Every failure becomes another layer of conflict, building tension and keeping the audience invested. The resolution, therefore, is a hard-earned success that resonates emotionally. This type of long-form story is ideal for keynote speeches, investor presentations, or company-wide events where the goal is to inspire and motivate over a longer duration.

Use the Hero's Journey or 3-Act Structure

For long-form storytelling, The Hero's Journey or The 3-Act Structure are your go-to frameworks. The Hero's Journey provides a clear path of transformation that aligns with the brain's neural preference for predictable yet emotionally complex narratives. The 3-Act Structure offers a concise setup, confrontation, and resolution that taps into the brain's desire for closure and satisfaction.

In the first act, introduce the relatable problem: this could be a company facing an existential crisis, a personal health journey, or even a global challenge. In the second act, build layers of conflict, financial challenges, emotional setbacks, and external pressures all serve to heighten tension and keep the audience engaged. The third act must deliver a resolution that is both satisfying and surprising, an outcome that rewards the audience for staying emotionally invested.

Keynote Speeches, Presentations, Documentaries

For a keynote speech, imagine starting with a personal anecdote about failure or loss, something that immediately makes you relatable. The rising action could involve the lessons learned, the turning points, and the moments of doubt. As tension builds, so does audience engagement. Finally, the resolution should be an inspiring call to action, leaving the audience not only emotionally satisfied but intellectually energized to take what they've learned and apply it.

Documentaries excel in long-form storytelling because they have the luxury of time to explore multiple layers of conflict. Take the case of a biographical documentary about an athlete overcoming injury and personal demons. Each segment of the film builds on the previous, introducing new challenges and deepening the emotional stakes until, by the end, the audience feels they've experienced the journey alongside the protagonist.

Build suspense and emotional engagement by using vivid, relatable details. Describe the cold sweat of fear before a presentation, the tight knot of anxiety before a product launch, the exhilaration of a breakthrough moment. Give your audience a clear protagonist they can root for. This could be you, your business, or a cause you believe in.

Short-Form Storytelling: The Sprint to the Finish

If long-form storytelling is a marathon, then short-form storytelling is a sprint. You don't have time to build slow, simmering tension or introduce multiple conflicts. Instead, you must be concise, punchy, and impactful. Short-form storytelling needs to be clear and emotionally engaging from the first sentence. In short-form, every word counts.

Immediate Problem, Quick Conflict, and Punchy Resolution

Unlike long-form storytelling, short-form narratives require you to cut straight to the point. Within the first few seconds or lines, you must establish the problem, introduce the conflict, and begin moving toward a resolution. The brain has a much shorter attention span in short-form content, and you must hook your audience immediately.

Picture a 60-second video advertisement for a fitness product. You start with a person struggling with a common problem, low energy, lack of motivation, or persistent back pain. Within the first 10 seconds, the conflict is introduced: the person finds their solution in your product. By the 45-second mark, the problem is resolved, the energy levels are restored, the pain is gone, and the protagonist is thriving. A short, punchy call to action rounds out the narrative. This concise arc hooks the viewer emotionally and leaves them with a clear sense of the product's value.

Use the Conflict-Resolution Arc or Quest Narrative

For short-form stories, the Conflict-Resolution Arc or Quest Narrative work best. The Conflict-Resolution Arc is ideal for situations where you need a quick hook and a satisfying ending, such as an elevator pitch or a marketing campaign. The Quest Narrative taps into the intrinsic motivation of pursuing a goal, making it perfect for aspirational marketing or social media content where you want your audience to feel that they're part of something larger than themselves.

Elevator Pitches, Social Media, Ads

In business pitches, short-form storytelling is a crucial skill. Picture this: you have 60 seconds to explain your idea to an investor in an elevator. Your pitch must be concise yet engaging. Start by introducing the problem your business solves, "The fashion industry generates 10% of global emissions", then move to the conflict, "Consumers want to buy sustainably but can't find affordable options", and finally, deliver your punchy resolution, "Our startup produces eco-friendly fashion at half the cost, reducing emissions by 20% per unit."

In short-form storytelling, focus on one powerful message and deliver it with clarity. The key is emotional engagement, not an overabundance of facts. You want to provoke a feeling of excitement, curiosity, or empathy. In business pitches, your audience should walk away feeling they've heard something simple but profound. In marketing, your consumers should feel emotionally connected to your product's promise.

The Brain's Need for Quick Resolution and Reward

Both long-form and short-form storytelling are underpinned by the brain's neurological processes. In short-form, the emphasis is on quick emotional reward. Dopamine, the neurotransmitter associated with anticipation and reward, plays a key role here. Short-form stories trigger quick dopamine hits by providing rapid conflict and resolution. This is why social media content, with its short bursts of narrative, can be so addictive, it delivers rapid emotional rewards that keep the brain hooked.

Research by Greg Stephens and Uri Hasson found that quick, emotionally resonant stories, especially those that include conflict and resolution, activate the brain's reward centers, keeping the audience engaged even when the narrative is brief. This makes short-form storytelling highly effective in fast-paced environments where attention spans are limited.

When crafting short-form stories, aim for emotional immediacy. Next time you're creating an ad, a social post, or a business pitch, ensure your story has an instant emotional hook. Focus on creating tension right away, and resolve it quickly for maximum impact. In marketing, this might mean highlighting a pain point your audience is already aware of and resolving it with your product or service in a single, punchy line.

Tailoring Story Length to the Audience

One of the biggest mistakes storytellers make is failing to consider their audience when choosing a story's length and depth. A story that works in a keynote speech will likely fall flat on social media. Understanding the needs and expectations of your audience is critical to crafting the right narrative for the right situation.

On platforms like Instagram or TikTok, you only have a few seconds to hook your audience before they scroll away. Here, short-form storytelling must be even more concise. Imagine a TikTok ad for a new skincare product. In just 15 seconds, you might show a woman struggling with acne, applying the product, and then confidently showing off her clear skin, all set to a catchy beat that reinforces the brand's youthful, solution-oriented vibe. In this context, speed and clarity are essential.

On the other hand, when presenting to investors, long-form storytelling is key. You have the time and space to dive deep into the problem your business solves, the challenges you've overcome, and the data that supports your market strategy. The story you tell here is about building long-term emotional and intellectual engagement, driving belief in your vision over time.

Always tailor your story's length and depth to the medium and the audience. In fast-paced environments, brevity is your ally. In more formal or extended contexts, take the time to build tension and emotional investment.

Crafting the perfect story requires a deep understanding of how narratives interact with the brain's psychological and emotional drivers. Long-form stories give you the space to build tension, introduce multiple layers of conflict, and deliver a resolution that resonates deeply. Short-form stories require precision, clarity, and an immediate emotional hook. But in both cases, the key is understanding your audience's needs, their psychological triggers, and how you can engage them on a visceral level.

Engaging the Subconscious Mind with Stories

There's a powerful aspect of storytelling that often goes unnoticed: its ability to bypass the logical mind and engage directly with the subconscious. We like to believe that we're rational beings, making decisions based on logic and reason, but stories, when told effectively, can slip past these mental defenses, triggering deep emotional responses that shape beliefs, behaviors, and decisions. This is not accidental. It's the result of carefully crafted techniques that hijack our brain's natural processes, from Neural Coupling to Narrative Transportation. Understanding these techniques allows you to wield storytelling as a tool of influence, subtly shaping your audience's perceptions without them ever realizing it.

Neural Coupling and Narrative Transportation

Neural coupling is one of the most fascinating phenomena in storytelling. When someone tells a story, the listener's brain begins to mirror the storyteller's neural activity, a form of mental synchronization that creates shared understanding and emotional connection. This process, confirmed by the research of Greg Stephens and Uri Hasson, shows that storytelling is an interaction between minds. When this synchronization occurs, the listener becomes more receptive, more empathetic, and crucially, less critical.

Think of it this way: when you're absorbed in a gripping narrative, your brain isn't busy analyzing every detail for factual accuracy. Instead, it's experiencing the story alongside the storyteller, immersed in the emotional journey. This is why storytelling can bypass the brain's critical faculties. Once the brain is synchronized with the storyteller, it becomes easier to influence thoughts and behaviors because the listener's mind is now aligned with the storyteller's.

The Thrill of Driving Before You've Even Sat in the Car

Consider the advertising campaigns of luxury car brands. They rarely bombard you with facts about horsepower or fuel efficiency. Instead, they use neural coupling to immerse you in an experience. You're shown sweeping landscapes, the hum of the engine reverberating through your chest, the feel of leather against your fingertips. You're living the experience of driving it. Your brain begins to synchronize with the narrative being portrayed, and you start to feel as if you're behind the wheel, even though you haven't left your living room. This type of storytelling taps into your sensorimotor cortex, triggering memories of how it feels to drive, further engaging your subconscious and bypassing logical scrutiny.

Paint with Words to Synchronize Minds

To use neural coupling effectively in any context, fill your stories with sensory-rich details that allow your audience to experience the narrative alongside you. Describe sights, sounds, and physical sensations vividly. In a business setting, don't just talk about a product's features, immerse your audience in the experience of using it. The smooth click of a button, the weight of a perfectly balanced tool, or the warmth of a client's handshake? These details engage the brain's sensory centers and foster subconscious connection.

Immersing the Listener in Your Story

While neural coupling synchronizes minds, narrative transportation takes immersion to a deeper level, allowing the audience to step inside the story. Melanie Green's Narrative Transportation Theory shows that when people are fully absorbed in a story, they are less likely to engage in critical thinking and more likely to adopt the beliefs and ideas presented within the narrative. This is because their brain is living the story.

When a story is compelling enough, it creates a mental environment where the listener feels as though they are part of the narrative. The line between the real world and the story blurs, and the brain's default mode network, responsible for daydreaming and imagination, takes over, allowing the listener to inhabit the narrative space. Once inside this space, the brain treats the events of the story as if they were happening in real life. Emotions are real, empathy is heightened, and the critical faculties are dampened.

Transforming an Everyday Moment

Take a classic example from Coca-Cola's "Share a Coke" campaign. Instead of telling consumers that their soda tastes better than competitors', Coca-Cola transformed the experience of drinking soda into a personal journey. By printing names on the bottles and encouraging customers to "share a Coke" with friends, they turned a mundane product into a tool for creating memories and connections. The ads didn't focus on taste or price, they transported you into a world where sharing a soda became an act of connection, something deeply personal and meaningful. The viewer, immersed in this narrative, felt compelled to participate.

Transport Your Audience

To use narrative transportation effectively, craft stories that allow your audience to step into the narrative. Provide them with just enough detail to paint a vivid picture but leave room for their imagination to fill in the gaps. Use metaphors and analogies that resonate with their personal experiences, allowing them to see themselves in the story. In a business setting, this could mean framing a product as part of a journey toward success or transformation. The more immersed your audience becomes, the less likely they are to critically scrutinize the message.

Engaging Emotion, Memory, and Decision-Making

The power of storytelling is its neurochemical effects. When stories are crafted to engage the subconscious, they activate key neurotransmitters that enhance persuasion and memory retention.

Dopamine: The Anticipation Chemical

Dopamine is often misunderstood as the chemical of pleasure, but it's more accurate to call it the chemical of anticipation. Stories that build suspense, introduce conflict, and offer the promise of resolution trigger dopamine release, keeping the audience engaged and primed for the eventual payoff. This is why cliffhangers are so effective, they tap into our dopamine system, making us crave resolution.

Oxytocin: The Trust and Empathy Hormone

When a story creates an emotional bond between the characters and the audience, oxytocin is released, fostering feelings of trust and empathy. Michael Kosfeld's research shows that oxytocin increases trust among individuals, making them more likely to connect emotionally with the story and the storyteller. In marketing, this is why emotionally charged ads, like those that focus on family, relationships, or shared experiences, are so persuasive. They trigger oxytocin, making the audience feel connected to the brand on a deeper, more emotional level.

Using Storytelling to Deepen Emotional Bonds

In personal relationships, storytelling can be a powerful tool to create empathy and understanding. Imagine a couple struggling with communication. Instead of simply listing grievances, one partner shares a story, perhaps a memory of a childhood experience that shaped their view of love or conflict. This story taps into neural coupling, synchronizing their emotional states, while the vulnerability of the narrative releases oxytocin, fostering trust and intimacy. The storytelling bypasses the usual defenses, allowing the couple to connect on a deeper, more empathetic level.

Use Emotionally Charged Narratives to Build Trust

In any situation where trust is essential, lean into emotionally rich stories. Share experiences that elicit empathy and vulnerability. These stories will trigger oxytocin in your audience, making them more likely to trust you and less likely to engage in critical thinking. In marketing, this means moving beyond features and benefits to tell stories that evoke feelings of belonging, trust, and loyalty.

Bypassing Skepticism with Visual and Sensory Storytelling

It's not only words that matter. Visual and sensory elements can be equally powerful in bypassing critical thinking. Studies have shown that visual storytelling through imagery, video, or even carefully crafted language that evokes vivid mental images activates more areas of the brain than text alone. By engaging the visual cortex, stories that incorporate sensory details can create more immersive experiences, allowing the audience to "see" the story as it unfolds in their mind.

Creating Vivid Visuals in Presentations

In a business context, think about the difference between telling a story and showing one. When Steve Jobs introduced the iPhone, he crafted a visual narrative. He showed how the iPhone could simplify your life, integrating phone, music, and internet into one sleek device. The visual elements of his presentation, both the imagery on the screen and the product in his hand, engaged the audience's imagination, making the future feel tangible. By the time he finished, the audience had already experienced the iPhone in their minds.

Use Visual and Sensory Cues to Engage the Subconscious

To bypass skepticism and engage the subconscious, use visual storytelling whenever possible. In presentations, ads, or even casual conversations, paint vivid pictures with your words or actual visuals. Let your audience see the story unfold in their minds. Describe what it looks like, feels like, even smells like. By engaging the visual cortex, you create a sensory-rich narrative that's harder to critically scrutinize because it feels so real.

Storytelling taps the subconscious mind with a narrative that slips past the listener's mental defenses, engaging them on a deeper, emotional, and neurological level. By leveraging neural coupling, narrative transportation, and the brain's natural response to dopamine and oxytocin, you can bypass critical thinking and create stories that influence behavior and belief without overt persuasion.

The Dark Side of Storytelling

Storytelling is one of the most powerful tools for influence, persuasion, and connection. But there's a dark side to this power. When stories are wielded not to inform or inspire but to manipulate, the line between influence and exploitation blurs. In this section, we'll explore the ethical dilemmas inherent in storytelling, particularly in marketing, politics, and personal relationships, where the stakes of manipulation are often highest. It's critical to understand where persuasion ends and manipulation begins, and how to use storytelling responsibly.

Selling Through Fear

Marketing is rife with examples of brands using fear-based narratives to exploit consumer insecurities. This tactic isn't new, advertisers have long known that fear is a potent motivator. However, when fear is leveraged to manipulate rather than empower, it crosses an ethical line. This often involves subtly reinforcing insecurities that consumers might not even realize they have, then offering the product as the "solution" to these manufactured fears.

Beauty Brands and the Insecurity Economy

Consider how the beauty industry operates. Many advertisements for skincare, makeup, or body-shaping products subtly (or not-so-subtly) suggest that you are not enough as you are. Wrinkles? Unacceptable. Skin texture? Flawed. Body fat? Shameful. The narrative frames these natural aspects of aging or body diversity as problems that need fixing, thereby manufacturing a sense of deficiency. The product becomes the solution, turning self-care into a quest for unattainable perfection.

In a 2021 study published in the Journal of Consumer Psychology, researchers found that fear-based advertising, particularly in the beauty and wellness industries, significantly increases product sales but at a cost: it also increases consumer anxiety and dissatisfaction. By preying on insecurities, these brands aren't just selling products, they're reinforcing negative self-perceptions that can have long-term psychological effects.

Balancing Emotion and Honesty

While emotional storytelling is an essential tool in marketing, its ethical use requires transparency and integrity. The goal should be to empower the consumer, not manipulate them. This doesn't mean you have to abandon emotional appeals altogether. Emotional engagement is still a cornerstone of effective storytelling, but it must be grounded in truth and a genuine desire to add value, not merely exploit vulnerabilities.

Dove's Real Beauty campaign took the beauty industry by storm because it flipped the script. Rather than preying on insecurities, Dove told stories that celebrated real bodies, diversity, and self-acceptance. This campaign still engaged consumers emotionally, but in a way that empowered rather than exploited. By reinforcing positive self-images, Dove was able to build trust and loyalty while avoiding the manipulation trap.

Empower, Don't Exploit

As a marketer, a leader, or even someone in a personal relationship, your storytelling should focus on empowerment. Use stories to inspire and uplift your audience, not to manipulate their fears. Consumers are becoming increasingly savvy, and in a world where transparency is more valued than ever, manipulation is a short-sighted strategy. If you build narratives that speak to your audience's aspirations, you create a connection based on trust and respect, which leads to long-term loyalty rather than short-term gains.

Narratives That Divide

The political arena is another domain where storytelling is often misused. In politics, stories shape entire worldviews. When used ethically, storytelling can unify, inspire, and drive positive change. But when used unethically, it can manipulate entire populations, breed division, and spread misinformation. Political campaigns are especially notorious for deploying fear-based narratives to rally support, often by creating an "enemy" or "other."

Wartime Propaganda and Fear-Mongering

One of the most infamous examples of manipulative storytelling in politics is the use of propaganda during wartime. Nazi propaganda during World War II is a chilling reminder of how stories can be weaponized to dehumanize opponents and rally populations behind morally indefensible causes. The narratives crafted by Joseph Goebbels and the Nazi regime didn't just manipulate, they systematically exploited fear and prejudice to justify atrocities. By constructing a narrative of fear around Jewish communities and other marginalized groups, the regime was able to manufacture widespread public support for their genocidal policies.

This example highlights the potential for stories to bypass critical thinking entirely, inciting emotions like fear and anger to cloud judgment. The storytelling was effective because it tapped into deep-seated insecurities and fears, manipulating the public into accepting, and even supporting, unimaginable horrors.

The Responsibility of Political Narratives

In democratic societies, the line between influence and manipulation in political storytelling is incredibly thin. Politicians naturally need to craft compelling stories to galvanize support, but when these stories are used to mislead, incite violence, or erode social cohesion, they become dangerous. The ethical use of storytelling in politics should aim to inform and inspire, not to deceive or divide. This requires a commitment to truth, transparency, and a willingness to respect the intelligence and autonomy of the audience.

Consider President Barack Obama's 2008 campaign slogan, "Yes We Can." It wasn't about fear or division, it was a hopeful narrative that united people around the idea of collective action and change. The message wasn't built on tearing down opponents but on building a shared vision of the future. This type of narrative taps into people's desire for progress and improvement, empowering them to be part of the solution rather than simply pointing out who to blame.

Use Stories to Unite, Not Divide

In any leadership or political context, use stories to unite people around a shared purpose. Avoid fear-mongering, even when it might seem like the easiest route to securing support. By appealing to shared values, hopes, and aspirations, you can create narratives that inspire action without resorting to manipulation. This doesn't mean avoiding difficult truths, it means presenting them in a way that encourages thoughtful engagement rather than emotional reaction.

When Stories Hurt

Storytelling has the power to manipulate on a societal level, but it can also be weaponized in personal relationships. In intimate settings, stories are often used to either build trust and connection or to manipulate emotions. The latter, when used repeatedly, can create toxic dynamics where one person uses narrative control to dominate or gaslight another.

Gaslighting and Emotional Manipulation

Gaslighting is a prime example of manipulative storytelling in personal relationships. The term originates from the 1938 play Gas Light, where a husband manipulates his wife into doubting her own reality by controlling the narrative. This tactic involves crafting false stories or selectively presenting facts to make the victim question their perceptions, memories, or even sanity. The manipulator tells a convincing story, "You're overreacting," "That never happened", while subtly eroding the other person's sense of self-trust and autonomy.

Gaslighting is one of the most damaging forms of emotional manipulation because it not only distorts reality but also undermines the victim's ability to trust their own judgment. In the long run, this can lead to severe psychological effects, including anxiety, depression, and loss of self-worth.

Transparency in Personal Narratives

In personal relationships, the ethical use of storytelling means being transparent and respectful. Stories can be powerful tools for healing and connection, but when used manipulatively, they can cause deep emotional harm. The ethical storyteller in relationships is committed to honesty, even when the truth is uncomfortable. This builds trust and fosters genuine intimacy.

Example (Healthy Relationship Storytelling): Imagine a couple working through a conflict. Instead of one partner gaslighting the other by denying their feelings, they share their own perspective through storytelling: "I felt hurt when this happened because it reminded me of something from my past." This approach uses narrative to foster empathy and understanding rather than to distort reality. The focus is on sharing truths and building a stronger, more transparent relationship.

Build Connection, Not Control

When using storytelling in personal relationships, aim to build empathy and understanding, not control. Share stories that reveal your vulnerabilities, experiences, and perspectives in a way that invites your partner to do the same. This type of storytelling fosters deeper emotional connections and prevents the toxic dynamics that arise when stories are used to manipulate or control.

The Fine Line Between Influence and Exploitation

Storytelling is a tool. Like any tool, its effectiveness depends on how it's used. When wielded ethically, it can inspire, connect, and drive positive change. But when misused, it can manipulate, deceive, and exploit. As a storyteller in marketing, politics, or personal relationships, you must always be aware of the power you hold, and the responsibility that comes with it. The goal should always be to empower your audience, to leave them better, not worse, for having heard your story.

As you master the art of storytelling, keep this question in mind: Am I guiding, or am I manipulating? The answer will define the kind of storyteller you become.

Becoming the Master of Your Own Story

At every moment, you are both the storyteller and the protagonist of your life. Every decision, every action is driven by the story you believe about your own capabilities, desires, and potential. The question the becomes which story you're telling. And most importantly, are you the one pulling the strings?

As Brené Brown wisely said, "Rewriting your story can transform your reality." The power to reshape your life is in your hands. In your career, relationships, or personal growth, taking control of your narrative lets you define what success, love, and fulfillment truly mean to you. The world doesn't define your story, you do.

Start by reflecting on the narratives that have defined your journey so far. Are they serving you? If not, it's time to rewrite them. Frame your challenges as pivotal moments in your Hero's Journey. Use setbacks as the conflicts that build your strength, and see your achievements as evidence of your resilience.

In your career, tell the story of your rise. In relationships, share the narrative of growth and connection. In your personal life, craft a story of self-mastery, where every obstacle becomes an opportunity for transformation.

The pen is in your hand. Now, start writing.

CHAPTER 7

The Linguistic Lockpick

Through the lens of cognitive linguistics and psychology, we begin to see that language is not merely descriptive; it is generative. It creates our reality.

Words as Weapons

Words are the invisible architects of human thought, guiding decisions, shaping behavior, and even constructing entire realities. Like any powerful tool, language can either liberate or enslave, inspire or suppress. And yet, its profound influence is often underestimated, relegated to mere communication. What if I told you that every conversation, every ad campaign, every political speech is a battlefield? A battlefield where words are the weapons, determining victory or defeat long before the target is even aware they are under attack.

Language is a force of nature, quiet, yet seismic. Imagine for a moment that every word you speak, every phrase you hear is a bullet in a war over perception, control, and identity. This is not metaphorical warfare, it's psychological warfare, and it happens every day. When you're pitching a product, negotiating a salary, or even having a casual conversation, you're either shaping the narrative with your words or being shaped by them.

Framing the Invisible Battlefield

Words hold the power to both reflect and shape reality. Noam Chomsky, in Manufacturing Consent, boldly stated that "the media serves as a propaganda system... through the selection and framing of news stories," underscoring how language is systematically used to align public perception with the interests of dominant groups. George Lakoff, in Don't Think of an Elephant!, reveals that "frames are mental structures that shape the way we see the world," meaning that those who control the linguistic frames control the very lens through which reality is understood.

But let's push deeper. Judith Butler, in Excitable Speech, suggests that "language creates injuries" through performative speech acts. She implies that words are mechanisms of harm, violence, and societal control. Consider how slurs, insults, or even dismissive tones can wound like bullets, turning a seemingly innocuous conversation into a battleground of power dynamics. Every syllable carries the potential to either wound or heal, but rarely do we consider this.

Rethinking Everyday Language

Language doesn't need grand stages or political podiums to be powerful. It thrives in the everyday, reshaping reality through subtle, nearly invisible mechanisms. In a study on Group Identity Through Language, researchers found that high affiliation language within online communities not only predicted engagement but reinforced social bonds. Language, then, is the glue that binds identities together, determining who belongs and who is cast out.

Similarly, a study on Linguistic Vectors of Ethnic Oppression reveals how dominant groups weaponize language to suppress minorities, as seen with the Uyghurs in China and the Kurds in Turkey. Words here are not benign, they are weapons of social control, shaping narratives that dehumanize and marginalize entire populations. The power of language extends beyond words spoken; it penetrates the structure of societies, determining who holds power and who is silenced.

The Ethics of Verbal Warfare

But here's where it gets murky. Chomsky and his co-author Edward S. Herman discuss in Manufacturing Consent how media often diverts public attention from real issues by focusing on trivial or manufactured controversies. This deliberate framing is an ethical gray zone, where does persuasion end and manipulation begin? In educational settings, persuasive language can subtly bias learning, restricting critical thinking by framing discussions from a single perspective. Even in everyday discourse, we must ask: Are we guiding minds or controlling them?

In political and social contexts, ethical concerns about language's power become even more contentious. Judith Butler's exploration of linguistic violence raises the question: Should words that harm, such as hate speech, be restricted, or does doing so infringe on free speech? This is a battlefield where ethical lines blur, and each choice carries the weight of potential harm.

How Words Reshape Perception

Language is not a passive tool of communication, it actively sculpts our thoughts, perceptions, and actions, silently dictating how we understand the world around us. The words we use not only express ideas but shape them, influencing everything from our moral choices to how we perceive time and space. Through the lens of cognitive linguistics and psychology, we begin to see that language is not merely descriptive; it is generative. It creates our reality.

This section dives into the subtle yet profound power of language, drawing on the revolutionary work of scholars like Lera Boroditsky and George Lakoff to show how words frame our thinking and reshape the world as we know it.

Language as Reality's Architect

Imagine two individuals discussing government spending. One calls it "tax relief," framing it as an escape from an oppressive burden. The other refers to it as "public investment," implying it's a necessary and constructive contribution to society. Same issue, two very different perceptions. This is cognitive framing at its finest. Language sculpts our thoughts.

George Lakoff, in Metaphors We Live By, explained that "the essence of metaphor is understanding and experiencing one kind of thing in terms of another". Metaphors like "tax burden" or "public investment" work because they frame the issue in a way that alters how we conceptually experience it. In this way, metaphors become the scaffolding of thought, structuring reality itself. Without the right metaphor, we wouldn't be able to make sense of the world in the same way.

The Whorfian Hypothesis

Linguistic relativity, often referred to as the Whorfian hypothesis, posits that the language we speak influences the way we think. Lera Boroditsky's groundbreaking research demonstrates just how powerful this influence can be. She argues that "the beauty of linguistic diversity is that it reveals to us just how ingenious and how flexible the human mind is". In one of her studies, English speakers tend to conceptualize time horizontally, saying things like "the future is ahead of us," while Mandarin speakers often view time vertically, talking about "the next month" as "down the line." This subtle difference in language correlates with different cognitive patterns for perceiving time.

In her studies, Boroditsky compared the cognitive processes of different language speakers, such as English, Mandarin, and Guugu Yimithirr speakers, an Indigenous group from Australia whose language has no terms for "left" and "right" but instead uses cardinal directions. The research found that speakers of these languages have different ways of navigating space, suggesting that language rewires our cognitive processes to match the structural framework embedded within our linguistic tools.

These findings challenge traditional views that cognition is universal and not influenced by cultural factors like language. Instead, Boroditsky's research supports the idea that the words we use do more than communicate, they define the boundaries of our thinking.

The Trojan Horse

Metaphors are more than stylistic flourishes, they are conceptual tools that help us make sense of complex ideas. Lakoff and Mark Johnson explored this concept in their study of "conceptual metaphors," finding that metaphors like "argument is war" don't just decorate language but fundamentally shape how we perceive concepts like conflict, positioning them as battles to be won.

Diane Blakemore explains that metaphors "cause us to notice things, or, more specifically, to see things in a new light," suggesting that metaphors have the power to alter perception. Consider how war metaphors pervade political discourse and everyday communication. We "attack" problems, "defend" our opinions, and "shoot down" bad ideas. In doing so, we internalize conflict as an inevitable and perhaps desirable part of dialogue, thus reshaping our social interactions at a fundamental level.

Research shows that metaphorical framing has direct consequences on decision-making. A study by Thibodeau and Boroditsky revealed that crime framed as a "beast" led participants to favor enforcement and punishment strategies, while the same crime framed as a "virus" led to more support for preventive social measures. These metaphors sneak into our cognitive processes like Trojan horses, subtly influencing our moral and political decisions without us even realizing it.

Foreign Language and Rationality

Another powerful example of how language shapes cognition comes from research on the Foreign Language Effect. Studies show that when people think in a foreign language, they tend to make more rational, utilitarian decisions, as the emotional bias associated with their native language is reduced. In a series of moral dilemmas, participants who used a foreign language were more likely to make decisions that followed utilitarian principles, like sacrificing one person to save many.

The methodology involved presenting moral dilemmas in participants' native and foreign languages and observing their choices. The results showed that emotional reactions tied to native language use often led to more emotionally driven decisions, while the cognitive distance provided by a foreign language promoted more logical reasoning.

This phenomenon suggests that language not only alters our thoughts but also our emotional engagement with those thoughts. The less emotional resonance a word has, the more likely we are to process it logically. This has profound implications for how we frame negotiations, moral choices, and even political discourse. Should we conduct important diplomatic negotiations in a second language to ensure less emotional bias? Could leaders make more rational decisions if they detached from their native tongue? These provocative questions challenge traditional views of decision-making and open new avenues for exploring how language shapes rationality.

Are We Truly Autonomous?

With language exerting such a profound influence over thought, perception, and even moral judgment, a question naturally arises: do we truly have free will, or are we just puppets manipulated by linguistic strings? This is a provocative debate among scholars of language and cognition. If certain metaphors or linguistic frames can control our decisions, how much of our autonomy remains intact?

Critics argue that the pervasive influence of language undermines the concept of free will, suggesting that our choices are shaped more by external linguistic factors than by internal autonomy. These critics point to media manipulation, where language is used to subtly sway public opinion without individuals being fully aware of the influence.

Priming

What if I told you that your thoughts aren't entirely your own, that someone else planted the seeds of those thoughts, and now they're growing unnoticed in the corners of your mind? This is priming, the first key to the linguistic lockpick. Words, carefully chosen and subtly placed, can trigger unconscious associations, bending your will, shaping your decisions, and directing your behavior before you even realize you're being manipulated.

We like to believe that our decisions stem from rational thinking, free will, and conscious thought. But what if every decision you've made in the last 24 hours was subtly influenced by the words you were exposed to, the phrases you read, or the slogans that slipped under your radar? You've already been primed. And the most dangerous part? You didn't even notice.

The Power of the Unseen

Priming works by stealth. It's the unseen hand guiding you down a path you didn't choose but now believe is yours. You hear a word, see a phrase, and suddenly, without knowing why, you feel more trusting, more aggressive, more compliant. Like a master puppeteer pulling invisible strings, the person who understands priming can manipulate your reactions with nothing more than a whisper.

Daniel Kahneman was one of the first to reveal just how insidious this psychological phenomenon is. In Thinking, Fast and Slow, he writes, "Priming effects... arise when exposure to a word or idea causes an immediate and measurable change in behavior". It's automatic. You can't escape it.

Consider Kahneman's famous experiment where participants, unknowingly primed with words related to old age, like "retired," "bingo," and "wrinkle", began walking more slowly when they left the room. These people didn't choose to change their behavior; their behavior was chosen for them by a few well-placed words. Priming bypasses free will, bypasses thought, and hooks directly into the brain's automatic response system.

You think you're in control, but priming shows otherwise. And if someone can make you walk slower just by whispering "bingo," what else can they make you do?

The Subliminal Sabotage

Priming is the ultimate stealth weapon, a sniper's bullet aimed directly at your subconscious. The most chilling aspect? It can be used in the most innocuous settings, like political campaigns and advertising, to guide your choices without you realizing a war is being waged over your mind.

Take the infamous slogan, "Make America Great Again." It was a cognitive virus. The phrase primed an entire population to long for a past that never existed, to become emotionally attached to an idea they couldn't fully define. The word "again" was the true weapon. It suggested that something had been lost, that the best days were behind, and that only one man could return them to their glory. It planted a deep sense of nostalgia, one that colored every voter's perception, pulling the strings of their emotions with every repetition.

This is the dangerous simplicity of priming. The word itself is a mental Trojan horse, smuggling in associations and beliefs without you ever opening the gates. Again, that single word contained an entire narrative, filled with the hopes, fears, and disappointments of a nation. By the time the election came, the phrase had already done its work. Votes were cast not based on policies, but on a subconscious desire to reclaim something long gone.

How Priming Drives Consumerism

Priming is the secret weapon behind some of the most successful advertising campaigns ever conceived. Advertisers know that if they can prime you with the right words, they can trigger you to make decisions that feel instinctive, almost natural, when, in reality, they've been carefully orchestrated.

Consider the subtle genius of an ad that primes you with words like "luxury," "exclusive," and "limited time." Your mind begins to associate the product with these values, even if the product itself is nothing more than another mass-produced commodity. You feel the need to buy not because the product is extraordinary, but because you've been primed to perceive it as such.

This is no accident. In one study on advertising, consumers were exposed to certain priming words that shaped their preferences without them being aware. The result? Products associated with positive, prestige-laden words saw a significant uptick in sales. Priming makes you act.

But here's the darker question: If priming is this effective, where is the line between persuasion and coercion? Are your purchases truly your own, or are they the result of psychological trickery?

The Dark Art of Behavioral Manipulation

John Bargh, one of the leading experts in automatic behavior, warns us that "automaticity of social behavior... is triggered directly by features of the environment". The environment is more than the physical space you inhabit. It's also the words surrounding you, the language embedded in your daily experiences. Bargh's studies revealed that participants primed with words related to aggression were far more likely to behave rudely and interrupt others during conversations.

This is behavioral manipulation at its core. You've been primed to think, act, and react in ways that align with someone else's agenda. You don't even know it's happening, yet every action you take feels like it's your own.

Now think about the environments you encounter daily. Advertisements on your phone. Conversations at work. The slogans plastered across billboards. Every interaction is an opportunity for someone to prime you, to lead you toward a decision that benefits them. They've planted the seed, and you'll water it without a second thought.

Where Persuasion Ends and Coercion Begins

The ethics of priming are murky at best. How much manipulation is too much? If a marketer can prime you to buy a product without you even knowing it, has your autonomy been stolen? If a politician can prime you to vote based on a subliminal association rather than policy, is democracy truly functioning as it should?

The psychological power of priming has led some to ask whether it crosses into the realm of mind control. Eldar Shafir suggests that "priming can influence not only what we think about but also how we act". If true, this challenges our very concept of free will. Are you making choices, or are those choices being made for you by the environments you're exposed to? The ethical implications are staggering, particularly when you consider how media, marketing, and politics are actively exploiting these subconscious triggers.

Critics of priming studies point to issues of reproducibility. Some experiments have failed to replicate initial findings, leading to debates about whether priming is as effective as originally thought. Yet even in the face of skepticism, the fundamental concept remains intact: our minds are vulnerable to subtle manipulations, and we often don't realize when we're being controlled.

The Silent War for Your Mind

Priming is a weapon. One that's being used against you every day. From the advertisements you see to the conversations you have, the language surrounding you is constantly planting seeds, guiding your thoughts and actions in ways you can't even detect. The silent war for your mind is real, and priming is one of the sharpest weapons in the arsenal.

The question we must ask ourselves is: how much of what we think, feel, and do is truly our own? And how much is the result of someone else's carefully constructed words, designed to prime us into submission?

Are you even ready to take back control?

Framing and Reframing

In the hands of a master persuader, words are more than tools, they are lenses through which reality is seen. With a single phrase, you can transform a brutal conflict into a noble cause, a financial burden into a societal benefit, or a personal failure into a platform for triumph. This is the power of framing. It's not about what you say, but how you say it. Words, when framed strategically, alter perception, influence decisions, and ultimately, reshape reality itself.

But here's the thing: framing is everywhere. There is no such thing as unframed information. Every headline, every ad, every conversation you've ever encountered has been carefully structured to guide your thinking in a particular direction. This is where framing crosses into manipulation, because when someone controls the frame, they control the conversation, the outcome, and you.

The Frame as a Weapon

Framing is subtle but immensely powerful. It shapes how we interpret the world, and once a frame has been set, it's incredibly difficult to think outside of it. George Lakoff, in Don't Think of an Elephant!, put it bluntly: "Frames are mental structures that shape the way we see the world". They define what we focus on, what we ignore, and ultimately, how we feel about the world around us. If you control the frame, you control perception.

Consider how politicians masterfully wield framing to justify policies or rally support. Take the phrase "War on Terror." It's a frame that immediately primes the public for aggressive, militaristic action. War evokes images of enemies, battlefields, and heroes, making the conflict seem both necessary and inevitable. Now compare this with the phrase "Peacekeeping Mission." The same military intervention, but framed differently, conjures images of diplomacy, stability, and restraint. In reality, the actions on the ground might be identical, but the public's perception of those actions is dramatically different depending on how they are framed.

This is the silent weapon of framing, it defines opinions. It locks you into a particular way of thinking, often without you realizing that the frame has been set. And the best part for the persuader? Most people never question the frame. Once it's established, it feels natural, almost invisible. You think you're making an independent decision, but your options have already been carefully shaped by someone else's narrative.

Turning Losses Into Wins

But the true power of framing comes when you understand how to shift it, to reframe the situation and turn a loss into a win, a weakness into a strength. Reframing is the art of changing the narrative, not by changing the facts, but by changing the context in which those facts are understood.

Take the classic example of Tversky and Kahneman's framing effect. In their experiments, participants were presented with two scenarios: one in which 200 lives would be "saved" and another in which 400 lives would be "lost." Despite the scenarios being mathematically identical, participants overwhelmingly chose the option framed in terms of saving lives rather than losing them. The frame doesn't change the reality, but it dramatically changes how that reality is perceived, and acted upon.

Reframing is used masterfully in crisis management, marketing, and even personal development. Imagine you've launched a product that initially flopped. If you frame this failure as a catastrophe, it becomes one. But if you reframe it as an opportunity for learning and growth, suddenly the same event becomes a springboard for success. Reframing is about transforming perception. The facts remain the same, but their meaning is entirely different.

Framing in the Wild

The battlefield of framing is most visible in politics and advertising, where every word is chosen for what it implies. Consider the phrase "tax relief." This framing, as analyzed by George Lakoff, casts taxes as a burden from which people need to be "relieved". The frame implies that taxes are inherently bad, something oppressive and damaging. But what happens when we reframe this same issue as "public investment"? Suddenly, taxes become a contribution to society's well-being, a positive, even noble, act of participation. Both phrases describe the same action, but they evoke vastly different emotional responses. In one, taxes are something to escape; in the other, they're a shared responsibility.

Advertising employs the same technique, often shifting the frame to highlight benefits over drawbacks. You'll rarely hear a company say "This product is less expensive because we used cheaper materials." Instead, you'll hear "Now with cost savings for you!" The frame emphasizes the gain, not the cut corners. The facts haven't changed, but how you feel about them has.

Susan Fiske, a leading social psychologist, aptly observes, "Framing is about inclusion and exclusion," because what is left out of a frame is just as important as what's included. When you see an advertisement promising "50% more content!", you're primed to think you're getting a better deal. What you're not told is that the product was deliberately reduced in size two months ago. The frame directs your attention toward the bonus and away from the loss.

Reframing as Psychological Jiu-Jitsu

In the hands of a skilled persuader, reframing is psychological jiu-jitsu, using the opponent's momentum against them, flipping their argument on its head. When someone says "This idea is too risky," a master reframer responds with "Risk is necessary for innovation." When someone points out a weakness, the reframer doesn't deny it, they twist it.

This technique is seen in successful public relations campaigns all the time. Consider how companies reframe negative press. When Starbucks was accused of contributing to environmental damage through its disposable cups, the company didn't deny it. Instead, it reframed the conversation by launching a campaign about their "commitment to sustainability," introducing reusable cups and a discount for customers who brought their own. They transformed a liability into an opportunity to strengthen their brand. This is reframing at its finest, turning a problem into a solution by shifting the context of the conversation.

When Does Framing Become Manipulation?

But here's the darker side: when does framing become outright manipulation? Is it ethical to frame a military intervention as a "peacekeeping mission" when bombs are being dropped? Is it fair to frame taxes as a burden when they fund schools, roads, and hospitals? These questions aren't just theoretical, they cut to the core of how framing can be used to shape, and sometimes distort, reality.

Critics argue that framing can be a subtle form of manipulation, particularly when used to promote specific ideologies or political agendas. As Matthew Nisbet warns, "There is no such thing as unframed information". This means every piece of information you consume is colored by someone else's agenda, often without you realizing it. The ethical dilemma arises when these frames are used to bias perceptions in ways that prevent true informed consent or understanding.

When framing is used in this way, it blurs the line between persuasion and coercion. It helps structure things it in a way that limits your choices, even as you believe you're making an independent decision. The danger lies in its invisibility. Frames are so subtle, so integrated into the fabric of communication, that we rarely notice their influence.

Framing is a powerful weapon in the arsenal of persuasion. As you continue to master the art of influence, it's critical to understand not only how to set frames but also how to reframe situations to your advantage. However, this power must be wielded ethically, with full awareness of the potential consequences. When you control the frame, you don't just shape a conversation, you shape reality.

The next time you encounter a situation, ask yourself: what frame am I seeing? And more importantly, who set it?

The Trojan Horse of Metaphors

Metaphors are the ultimate cognitive shortcuts. They slip beneath the surface of our conscious defenses, embedding themselves in the subconscious where they shape thought and perception without resistance. Like the fabled Trojan Horse, a well-placed metaphor delivers its payload, complex ideas, emotional triggers, or persuasive intent, while bypassing logical scrutiny. And once inside, it influences everything: from the way we perceive reality to the decisions we believe we make independently.

You might think you're immune to such tactics, that your critical thinking shields you from subtle manipulation. But consider this: what if every time you engaged in a conversation, read an article, or watched a political debate, your thoughts were being shaped by metaphors hidden in plain sight?

Metaphors don't just explain, they control. And the more invisible they are, the more powerful their influence becomes.

The Invisible Architecture of Thought

Metaphors are the scaffolding of human thought. George Lakoff and Mark Johnson, in their groundbreaking book Metaphors We Live By, argued that "metaphor is pervasive in everyday life, not just in language but in thought and action". These metaphors are so ingrained in our cognitive processes that we don't even notice them framing our worldview. They shape how we think about everything from conflict to economics, from love to leadership.

Consider the metaphor of "the invisible hand of the market." It's more than just an image, it's an entire economic philosophy embedded into our thinking. This metaphor suggests that the market operates as a self-regulating force, almost magical in its ability to correct imbalances and guide society toward prosperity. But here's the trick: once you accept the metaphor, you've already accepted a whole set of assumptions about capitalism, free markets, and government regulation. Now you stop asking whether the market needs intervention and start thinking how to keep the "invisible hand" functioning. The metaphor has locked you into a frame where only certain questions and answers make sense.

Metaphors like this don't just influence conversations, they guide entire societal values. Donald Schön described metaphors as "generative," meaning they lead thought development and create new situational frames for human interaction. They aren't passive descriptors of reality, they actively shape it. Once embedded in the subconscious, metaphors color every decision, every perception, subtly steering us toward conclusions that feel like our own, but were planted by someone else.

How Metaphors Bypass Logic and Hijack Emotion

The real power of metaphors lies in their ability to bypass the brain's logical filters. Metaphors are processed differently from literal language, they engage both our cognitive and emotional systems, triggering neural responses that are both faster and more potent than rational analysis. A study on Neurological Processing of Metaphor used fMRI scans to reveal that metaphors activate the sensory and emotional areas of the brain. When you hear the phrase "taste explosion," your brain lights up as if you're actually experiencing it. When a car is described as having a "purring engine," your mind conjures the sensation of smooth, effortless power without you even realizing it.

This bypass of logical reasoning is why metaphors are so effective in persuasion. Hervé Boisde notes, "the subconscious mind uses the language of symbols, pictures, and metaphors to communicate ideas," meaning that metaphors operate below the level of conscious awareness. They plant ideas, emotions, and attitudes directly into the subconscious, where they grow without resistance.

Take the metaphor "war on drugs." The word "war" primes us for conflict. It evokes images of enemies, battles, and the need for aggressive action. Suddenly, the complex social issue of drug abuse is framed not as a public health crisis, but as a military campaign. This puts addiction on the back on the car and places fighting a war in the driver's seat. Now, in a war, there are only two sides: victory or defeat. The metaphor precludes other solutions like harm reduction or rehabilitation, locking the public and policymakers into a militaristic mindset.

Reframing Negotiations

Metaphors aren't just tools of mass persuasion, they're tactical weapons in negotiations, capable of shifting entire conversations in your favor. Imagine walking into a high-stakes negotiation where the other party frames the situation as a "fight for survival." This metaphor triggers an aggressive mindset, where each party is vying for dominance. But what if you reframe the conversation? What if you introduce a metaphor of "collaboration to build a better future?" Suddenly, the entire dynamic shifts. You stop being adversaries locked in a battle and become partners working toward a shared goal. The metaphor changes the emotional tenor of the negotiation, making it easier to find common ground and reach a mutually beneficial agreement.

The true power of metaphors are their ability to shape the emotional and cognitive landscape in which decisions are made. Diane Blakemore argues, "Metaphors cause us to notice things, or more specifically, to see things in a new light". In a negotiation, the right metaphor can turn a losing situation into a winning one by reframing the stakes, the goals, and even the relationships between the parties involved.

The Dark Side of Metaphors

But there's a darker side to metaphorical persuasion. When metaphors operate below the level of conscious awareness, they raise serious ethical questions about manipulation. Some scholars suggest that metaphors can function as a form of mind control, subtly guiding decisions without explicit consent. Because metaphors bypass logic and appeal directly to emotion, they can be used to control mass populations, framing issues in ways that limit critical thinking and suppress dissent.

Take the metaphor of "collateral damage." It's a euphemism designed to sanitize the reality of civilian casualties in war. By framing the deaths of innocent people as "collateral," the metaphor shifts focus away from the human tragedy and reframes it as an unfortunate but necessary side effect of military operations. The public, primed by the metaphor, becomes desensitized to the moral implications of war, accepting civilian deaths as part of the cost of conflict. This is where persuasion becomes coercion, and where the ethical line blurs.

Metaphors are the Trojan Horses of persuasion, embedding ideas into our subconscious without us ever opening the gates. They shape how we think, how we feel, and ultimately, how we act. In political discourse, advertising, or even personal negotiations, metaphors serve as powerful tools to frame reality in ways that benefit the persuader. As with all persuasive tactics, the ethical line between influence and manipulation is thin, and easily crossed. It's easy to see why understanding the true power of metaphors is about recognizing when they're being used against you.

The 31 Linguistic Patterns of Persuasion

Language is the ultimate weapon, a tool that shapes reality, manipulates emotions, and directs behavior. But it's not the words themselves that hold power, it's the patterns in which they're used. Understanding these patterns transforms language from mere communication into a tactical system of control. Here, we break down 31 of the most potent linguistic patterns that have been weaponized in everything from political campaigns to marketing strategies and personal influence.

Each pattern is a psychological lockpick, designed to slip beneath the radar of conscious awareness and provoke action, shift perception, and create lasting influence.

1. Priming: The Invisible Seed

Priming operates by exploiting the associative nature of the human brain. A single word, image, or experience can ignite entire networks of memory, emotion, and behavior. It's a rewiring of the mind's pathways, often bypassing awareness altogether.

At its core, priming functions through contextual activation. Presenting a related stimulus subtly shifts perception and response. For instance, exposure to words associated with elderly stereotypes ("gray," "wrinkle," "retirement") can slow physical movement, a phenomenon documented in behavioral psychology experiments.

A seminal study by Bargh, Chen, and Burrows (1996) demonstrated priming's power in a controlled setting. Participants exposed to words related to old age walked more slowly when leaving the lab, despite being unaware of the connection. This experiment revealed how even subtle cues could alter physical behavior unconsciously.

Modern neuroscience attributes this effect to semantic networks in the brain. When one concept is activated, related ideas light up, influencing subsequent thoughts and actions. Priming, then, is manipulation of the infrastructure of thought itself.

Real-World Examples

- Political Campaigns: The 2016 U.S. presidential election weaponized priming on social media. Ads targeting specific demographics used emotionally charged phrases like "corruption" and "freedom." The repetition of these primed associations reframed complex political issues as visceral, binary choices.

- Consumer Behavior:
  Retailers frequently employ priming to shape purchasing decisions. A store might subtly play classical music to prime customers to perceive products as luxurious. Alternatively, scent marketing, like the smell of fresh bread in a grocery store, primes hunger, encouraging more purchases.

- Judicial Decision-Making:
  Judges have been found to deliver harsher sentences after exposure to violent imagery, even if unrelated to the case at hand. A study by Danziger et al. (2011) revealed that decision-making could be significantly influenced by factors like hunger or recent emotional stimuli, highlighting how priming operates in high-stakes environments.

- Education and Self-Perception:
  Students told they were part of a "gifted" program often performed better, even when the label was arbitrary. This reflects priming's impact on identity, subtly suggesting competence leads individuals to behave as though they possess it.

Priming's subtlety makes it dangerously easy to abuse. Unlike overt propaganda, which can be resisted consciously, priming hides in plain sight. The ethical dilemma is stark: How do we combat a form of influence that operates below the level of awareness? If corporations, politicians, or even educators wield it irresponsibly, priming becomes less a tool of persuasion and more a method of coercion.

2. Repetition: Reinforcing Belief Through Frequency

Repetition a neurological hack that reshapes perception through sheer familiarity. The human brain favors the familiar, often mistaking repetition for truth. This isn't mere reinforcement, it's the systematic erosion of skepticism. Repeated exposure to an idea smooths its edges, making it harder to resist and easier to absorb, even when the idea itself lacks merit.

Behavioral psychology explains this through the illusory truth effect. A study by Hasher, Goldstein, and Toppino (1977) showed that people are more likely to believe statements they've heard repeatedly, even when those statements are objectively false. This occurs because repetition reduces cognitive effort. Familiar ideas "feel" true simply because the brain processes them more fluently.

Real-World Examples

- Political Campaigns:
  Repetition forms the backbone of political messaging. Donald Trump's "Make America Great Again" was repeated relentlessly, becoming a mantra. Regardless of its factual basis, its ubiquity embedded it in the public psyche, shifting from a slogan to a belief system.

- Propaganda Machines:
  Joseph Goebbels, the Nazi propaganda minister, declared that "a lie told once is a lie, but a lie told a thousand times becomes the truth." Modern disinformation campaigns adopt the same principle, flooding social media with repeated falsehoods to create a perception of widespread agreement and validity.

- Advertising:
  "Just Do It." "I'm Lovin' It." These slogans, repeated endlessly in advertisements, aren't designed to inform but to infiltrate. They bypass critical thought, embedding themselves so deeply that they become subconscious triggers for brand loyalty.

- Education Systems:
  Curriculums often repeat sanitized versions of history to shape collective memory. For instance, the portrayal of Christopher Columbus as a heroic explorer in American schools has been repeated for generations, overshadowing the darker truths of his legacy. This repetition is indoctrination.

- Social Media Algorithms:
  Platforms like TikTok or Instagram amplify repetition by showing users the same types of content repeatedly, reinforcing specific narratives. Whether it's a political viewpoint, a beauty standard, or a conspiracy theory, repetition ensures these ideas feel both relevant and undeniable.

Repetition's ethical implications lie in its stealth. While its effects on memory and belief are well-documented, its use in shaping public opinion raises a critical question: At what point does repetition stop informing and start programming? The line between persuasion and manipulation dissolves when ideas are repeated not to enlighten but to entrench.

3. Suggestive Language: Creating Mental Nudges

Suggestive language operates in the shadows, planting ideas without explicit instruction. It guides rather than commands, relying on subtle cues to evoke desired responses. Unlike overt persuasion, suggestive language feels like free choice, even when every step of the thought process has been preordained. The magic lies in its ability to make the audience believe they've arrived at conclusions independently.

The psychological principle behind this is implicit suggestion, where carefully chosen words trigger mental imagery, emotions, or assumptions. When presented effectively, suggestive language bypasses resistance because it doesn't feel like persuasion at all, it feels like discovery.

Real-World Examples

- Real Estate Sales:
  When a realtor says, "Imagine waking up to this view every morning," the focus shifts from evaluating the property to inhabiting it mentally. This subtle nudge creates an emotional connection that bypasses rational scrutiny.

- Courtroom Manipulation:
  Lawyers frequently use suggestive language to frame narratives without stating them outright. A question like, "Where were you when the theft

occurred?" subtly implies the person's involvement without direct accusation, shifting the burden of proof in the jury's mind.

- Marketing Campaigns:
Perfume ads rarely describe the product. Instead, they say, "Feel irresistible," suggesting an emotional outcome rather than detailing the scent. This works because the consumer fills in the blanks with their own desires, making the appeal deeply personal.

- Cult Recruitment:
Leaders of high-control groups often rely on suggestive language to create cognitive dissonance. Phrases like, "What if everything you've been told is a lie?" subtly erode trust in external authorities, preparing recruits to accept the cult's narrative as their own revelation.

- Medical Contexts:
Physicians discussing treatment options might say, "This course gives you the best chance of recovery," framing it as the logical choice. While technically accurate, the language implies that alternatives are subpar, nudging patients toward the preferred option without overt coercion.

Suggestive language thrives in its subtlety, making it both powerful and perilous. It's the art of suggestion that disguises persuasion as independent thought, creating a unique ethical dilemma. When wielded irresponsibly, it manipulates, exploiting the illusion of choice.

4. Framing: Controlling the Conversation

Framing doesn't change facts; it changes how facts are perceived. By manipulating the lens through which information is presented, framing steers interpretations, reactions, and decisions. It's about how you make people see it. This makes framing one of the most insidious tools of influence because it cloaks persuasion in the guise of objectivity.

Psychologists like Amos Tversky and Daniel Kahneman have demonstrated framing's power in shaping decision-making. In their landmark studies on the framing effect, they showed how identical information could provoke different choices depending on whether it was framed positively or negatively. For example, a surgery with a "90% survival rate" feels safer than one with a "10% mortality rate," even though the data is identical.

Real-World Examples

- Media Headlines:
  News outlets frame stories to provoke specific emotions. For example, the same event can be presented as "Protesters Demand Justice" or "Rioters Disrupt Peace." The framing determines whether readers see the participants as heroes or threats, often aligning with the publication's ideological slant.

- Political Rhetoric:
  Taxation debates are a masterclass in framing. Conservatives often use "tax burden" to evoke oppression, while progressives frame the same concept as "public investment" to suggest collective benefit. Neither term is neutral; both manipulate perception.

- Healthcare Campaigns:
  In public health messaging, framing impacts compliance. A message stating, "If you don't get vaccinated, you risk infecting loved ones," frames action in terms of guilt and responsibility. Alternatively, "Getting vaccinated protects your family" evokes empowerment and care.

- Consumer Psychology:
  Retailers frame discounts to appear more generous than they are. A product marketed as "Save $20" feels less compelling than "50% off," even when the monetary value is identical. The latter frame emphasizes relative gain, triggering a stronger emotional response.

- Legal Defense Strategies:
  In high-profile trials, defense teams frame their clients as misunderstood rather than guilty. For instance, a wealthy defendant might be framed as a "generous philanthropist under attack" rather than a perpetrator, shifting the narrative to evoke sympathy rather than blame.

- Framing's danger lies in its invisibility. The audience often accepts the frame without realizing it's been constructed, believing their perception is objective. This makes framing a covert form of influence that reshapes reality without the subject ever knowing it has happened.

5. Scarcity Language: Triggering Fear of Missing Out

Scarcity taps into primal instincts, transforming decisions from rational evaluations into urgent impulses. It triggers the fear of missing out (FOMO), a psychological reaction rooted in the brain's survival mechanisms. When people perceive something as scarce, they overvalue it, often acting irrationally to secure it. Scarcity doesn't sell products; it sells urgency, pushing rational thought aside.

The scarcity principle, as defined by psychologist Robert Cialdini, is based on the idea that opportunities seem more valuable when they are less available. Scarcity creates a heightened sense of importance, hijacking decision-making processes through anxiety and loss aversion.

Real-World Examples

- Limited-Time Offers:
  Retailers exploit scarcity with phrases like "Only 24 hours left!" or "Offer ends at midnight!" These time constraints compel consumers to buy, not because they need the product, but because they fear losing the opportunity. Amazon's "Lightning Deals" thrive on this principle, creating a constant sense of urgency.

- Stock Alerts:
  Online marketplaces often display scarcity indicators, such as "Only 2 items left!" Whether real or fabricated, this nudge creates panic, pushing buyers to make impulsive purchases to avoid missing out.

- Concert Tickets and Exclusive Events:
  Ticketing platforms like Ticketmaster leverage scarcity by showing a countdown of remaining seats. The frenzy for tickets to exclusive events often leads to overpaying or making hasty decisions, driven by the belief that the chance will never come again.

- NFTs and Digital Scarcity:
  The rise of NFTs (non-fungible tokens) represents a new form of artificial scarcity. Digital assets, which can be infinitely reproduced, are marketed as "one-of-a-kind," creating demand based solely on the perception of rarity rather than intrinsic value.

- Cult Behavior:
  Scarcity language is a hallmark of cult recruitment. Leaders often claim access to "hidden truths" or "exclusive knowledge" that outsiders cannot obtain. This creates an us-versus-them mentality and drives recruits to commit before their access is revoked.

Scarcity language's potency lies in its ability to bypass reason and exploit fear. Its ethical implications are profound, especially when scarcity is fabricated. By manufacturing urgency, persuaders manipulate behavior not through persuasion, but through psychological pressure that feels inescapable.

6. Social Proof: Herd Mentality in Action

Social proof is the silent persuader, leveraging the human desire for belonging and validation. People are wired to follow the crowd, especially in uncertain situations. This is a survival instinct deeply embedded in our psychology. If others are doing it, the brain assumes it must be right, safe, or desirable.

The concept of social proof, popularized by Robert Cialdini, highlights how people rely on others' actions to determine their own. Social proof operates most powerfully when uncertainty is high or when those providing the proof are perceived as similar or credible.

Real-World Examples

- Product Reviews and Ratings:
  Amazon thrives on social proof. A product with thousands of 5-star reviews feels safer and more desirable than one with none, even if the reviews lack substantive detail. This is not an evaluation of quality but a reassurance of conformity.

- "Best-Seller" Labels:
  Books, gadgets, and even apps prominently display "#1 Best-Seller" tags. These claims, sometimes arbitrarily assigned, create a bandwagon effect, where popularity itself becomes the reason for purchase.

- Nightlife and Social Spaces:
  Clubs and bars deliberately create lines outside, even when the venue isn't full. The appearance of exclusivity and popularity entices passersby, who assume the crowd signals a worthwhile experience.

- Charity Donations:
  Donation drives often list prior contributors' names or showcase totals raised so far. Seeing others give creates an implicit challenge: If so many others are contributing, why aren't you?

- Online Virality:
  TikTok challenges, viral memes, and trending hashtags thrive on social proof. Once a trend begins, people join in not because it's meaningful, but because everyone else is doing it. The fear of being left out amplifies participation.

Social proof's ethical ambiguity arises from its ability to override independent judgment. People often defer to the crowd, assuming consensus equates to correctness. Manipulating this instinct, especially with fabricated or exaggerated proof, transforms social validation into a mechanism of control.

7. Metaphor: The Trojan Horse of Persuasion

Metaphors bypass logic, embedding complex ideas into simple, relatable frameworks. They transform perception by linking the abstract to the familiar. A metaphor isn't merely descriptive; it's a covert narrative device that reshapes how people think without them realizing it. When used effectively, a metaphor is a Trojan horse, smuggling new ideas into entrenched mental structures.

Metaphors work because they activate conceptual blending, a cognitive process where the brain maps elements of one domain onto another. This makes abstract concepts tangible and emotionally resonant, allowing persuaders to bypass analytical resistance.

Real-World Examples

- Economic Policy:
  Politicians often describe the economy as a "machine" that needs "fuel" (investment) or "maintenance" (austerity). This metaphor simplifies complex economic systems, steering voters toward specific policies by framing them as logical extensions of the metaphor.

- Health and Medicine:
  The fight against cancer is often framed as a "war," with patients as "warriors" and treatments as "weapons." This metaphor rallies emotional strength but can also create undue pressure, as patients may feel like failures if their "fight" doesn't succeed.

- Marketing:
  Apple's metaphor of its devices as a "tool for creatives" repositions them from mere electronics to enablers of self-expression. This metaphor transforms a transactional purchase into a declaration of identity.

- Environmental Activism:
  Referring to climate change as a "ticking time bomb" frames the issue as urgent and unavoidable, triggering immediate action. Conversely, calling Earth a "mother" evokes nurturing and care, steering emotions in a softer, protective direction.

- Military Propaganda:
  In wartime, soldiers are often called "heroes," and civilian casualties are

framed as "collateral damage." These metaphors sanitize the brutality of war, reframing it in terms of honor and necessity, which reduces public resistance.

The danger of metaphors lies in their subtlety. Once embedded, they frame all subsequent discussions. A metaphor prescribes, constraining thought to the terms it introduces. When used irresponsibly, metaphors shape realities that prioritize emotional resonance over critical accuracy.

8. Analogy: Making the Unfamiliar Familiar

Analogies bridge the gap between the known and the unknown, simplifying complex concepts by linking them to relatable ideas. They are tools of transformation, reshaping abstract or unfamiliar ideas into something digestible. Unlike metaphors, which evoke emotion, analogies focus on logic, using comparisons to clarify and persuade.

Analogies rely on cognitive alignment, connecting disparate concepts by highlighting structural similarities. However, their power lies in their deceptiveness; by drawing selective parallels, they obscure differences, steering understanding in specific directions.

Real-World Examples

- Political Rhetoric:
  Ronald Reagan famously compared government spending to a household budget, suggesting that fiscal discipline should follow the same rules as personal finances. While the analogy resonated emotionally, it oversimplified the complexity of macroeconomics, shaping public opinion around flawed logic.

- Technology Marketing:
  Cloud computing is often likened to "renting storage space in a giant warehouse." This analogy demystifies a highly technical concept but also narrows the focus, ignoring nuances like security and ownership risks, subtly shaping perceptions of safety and utility.

- Education Reform:
  Standardized testing is frequently analogized to "measuring students with a yardstick." This analogy simplifies evaluation but fails to account for individuality, framing education as quantifiable rather than nuanced, pushing policies that align with the oversimplification.

- Public Health Campaigns:
  Vaccines are compared to "firewalls" that block viruses from spreading, making the concept of herd immunity easier to grasp. While effective, this analogy reduces a complex biological and social process into a digital metaphor, potentially skewing understanding of the broader implications.

- Social Movements:
  The Civil Rights Movement was often likened to a "rising tide," a natural and unstoppable force. This analogy galvanized supporters but also masked the strategic efforts and sacrifices required, framing progress as inevitable rather than hard-fought.

Analogies simplify, but their simplicity is both their strength and their weakness. By focusing on specific parallels, they obscure critical differences. When used with intent, they can steer understanding toward certain conclusions while hiding the complexities that might provoke dissent.

9. Simplicity Derived from Industry Jargon

Jargon is a double-edged sword. On one hand, it conveys expertise and establishes credibility within a niche. On the other, it can alienate audiences, leaving them confused, disengaged, or outright dismissive. While industry-specific language might impress insiders, it risks making the speaker appear out of touch, especially to those who are unaware of the problem or unfamiliar with the terminology.

When used poorly, jargon isolates. Audiences often tune out or feel patronized when faced with obscure terms, eroding trust and interest. Ironically, instead of projecting authority, over-reliance on jargon can make the speaker seem insecure, hiding behind complexity to mask a lack of clarity or confidence.

Real-World Examples

- Startup Pitches:
  Entrepreneurs who rattle off terms like "disruptive synergies" or "paradigm shifts" risk alienating investors who value concrete explanations. Jargon-laden pitches often fail because they obscure the actual value proposition, leaving audiences confused rather than impressed.

- Health Advice:
  A doctor explaining a diagnosis as "chronic idiopathic urticaria" might

lose the patient entirely, while a simpler phrase like "persistent unexplained hives" fosters understanding and trust. Patients are more likely to follow advice they comprehend fully.

- Marketing to Problem-Unaware Customers:
  Software companies often use terms like "API integration" or "container orchestration" in ads targeting general users. These phrases resonate with developers but alienate less technical audiences, who might dismiss the product as irrelevant.

- Educational Environments:
  Professors who use academic jargon excessively often fail to engage students. Terms like "ontological paradigms" impress peers but leave students disengaged. Breaking down complex concepts into relatable analogies ensures understanding without diluting rigor.

- Customer Support:
  Support agents who respond with technical terms like "latency bottleneck" confuse users, escalating frustration. A simpler explanation like "your connection is slow because of traffic on our servers" achieves the same goal without alienating the customer.

Reframing Jargon into Simplicity

The most effective communicators bridge the gap between expertise and accessibility. They translate complex ideas into simple, relatable language without sacrificing depth or precision. This means recognizing that true mastery lies in making the complicated seem effortless.

- Clarify Before Impressing:
  Start with the simplest explanation possible, then layer in complexity as the audience demonstrates understanding or curiosity.

- Use Metaphors and Analogies:
  Instead of describing "blockchain" as a "distributed ledger," explain it as a digital version of a notary public, ensuring every transaction is verifiable and immutable.

- Tailor the Message to the Audience:
  Technical language works for insiders but alienates outsiders. Match the depth of your jargon to the familiarity of your listeners.

- Test for Engagement:
  Monitor your audience's responses. If eyes glaze over or questions reflect confusion, adapt on the fly, simplifying terms and reframing ideas.

Simplicity isn't the enemy of expertise, it's its ultimate expression. While jargon has its place, its overuse creates barriers that erode trust and connection. By focusing on clarity and relatability, persuaders can wield the power of technical knowledge without losing their audience in a maze of words.

10. Emotional Appeal (Pathos): Tugging on Heartstrings

Emotional appeal bypasses logic entirely, speaking directly to the heart and gut. When emotions are triggered, critical thinking is silenced, and decisions are made based on feeling rather than fact. Pathos demands reaction, exploiting the brain's inability to simultaneously process deep emotion and rational thought.

Neuroscience reveals that emotional appeals activate the amygdala, the brain's emotional processing center, which overrides the prefrontal cortex, responsible for reasoned judgment. This is why emotional appeals are so effective: they hijack the brain's decision-making process, anchoring choices in visceral responses.

Real-World Examples

- Charity Advertising:
  Nonprofits often showcase heartbreaking images of starving children or wounded animals. The message creates immediate empathy and guilt, compelling viewers to donate as a form of emotional release.

- Political Campaigns:
  Politicians evoke patriotism, fear, or anger to sway voters. After 9/11, U.S. leaders used emotional appeals about safety and justice to rally public support for the War on Terror, sidestepping critical debates about its long-term implications.

- Consumer Marketing:
  Advertisements for luxury cars don't focus on features, they sell a feeling of prestige and success. Similarly, jewelry commercials often emphasize love and commitment, tying purchases to deeply personal emotions rather than practicality.

- Social Movements:
  Activists often highlight personal stories rather than statistics. During the Black Lives Matter protests, videos of police violence were shared widely not for factual analysis but for the outrage and empathy they ignited, galvanizing global support.

- Religious Appeals:
  Evangelical sermons often evoke intense emotions of guilt, redemption, and hope. Congregants are moved to action not through theological reasoning but through the raw power of shared emotional experiences.

While emotional appeals are potent, they're ethically precarious. They exploit vulnerability, often pushing people toward actions they might reconsider in a calmer state. When overused or weaponized, pathos turns persuasion into manipulation, leaving audiences emotionally drained and intellectually bypassed.

11. Logical Appeal (Logos): Convincing Through Reason

Logical appeals target the rational mind, using evidence, data, and structured arguments to persuade. While not as visceral as emotional appeals, logos builds trust by appealing to the audience's sense of reason. However, logical appeals are rarely pure. They're often engineered to feel objective while subtly steering conclusions through selective presentation of facts.

Cognitive biases such as confirmation bias, the tendency to favor information that aligns with pre-existing beliefs, play a significant role in how logos is received. Even the most logical-seeming arguments can exploit these biases, embedding persuasive narratives within seemingly neutral logic.

Real-World Examples

- Corporate Reports:
  Annual earnings reports use statistics to showcase growth and stability. By selectively highlighting favorable metrics while downplaying losses, companies frame their financial performance as logical evidence of success, even when the full picture might suggest instability.

- Political Debates:
  Politicians often cite cherry-picked statistics, such as "violent crime rates have dropped by 20% in the past decade." While technically true, such data is often devoid of context, like regional variations or broader contributing factors, creating an illusion of comprehensive reasoning.

- Legal Arguments:
  Attorneys present logically structured cases, citing precedent, evidence, and expert testimony. However, their logic is rarely impartial, it's designed to lead juries to specific conclusions by excluding or reframing contradictory evidence.

- Advertising Claims:
  Weight-loss products often rely on data like "80% of users lost weight within 30 days." The figures appear logical, but the methodology (small sample sizes, short timeframes) is rarely disclosed, allowing advertisers to frame the narrative in their favor.

- Environmental Advocacy:
  Climate change activists frequently use data to appeal to logic, such as "global temperatures have risen by 1.2°C since pre-industrial levels." While effective for those valuing evidence-based reasoning, such appeals often struggle to compete with the emotional simplicity of denialist rhetoric.

Logical appeals are often considered the most ethical form of persuasion, but their strength is also their vulnerability. When data is selectively framed, or when reasoning is subtly distorted, logos becomes a tool for manipulation under the guise of rationality. This blurs the line between genuine evidence-based argumentation and calculated influence.

12. Ethical Appeal (Ethos): Establishing Trust and Credibility

Ethical appeal persuades by establishing the speaker's credibility, authority, or moral character. When the audience trusts the source, they're more likely to accept the message, even in the absence of emotional or logical support. Ethos doesn't just argue, it reassures, creating a foundation of trust that frames the speaker as a reliable guide.

Psychologists refer to this as source credibility theory, which highlights two key dimensions of ethos: competence (perceived expertise) and character (perceived integrity). Once established, these qualities can override skepticism, allowing persuaders to bypass resistance and anchor belief.

Real-World Examples

- Medical Recommendations:
  The authority of a doctor's white coat is a powerful tool. Patients are far more likely to accept a medication prescribed by a physician than the same advice given by a layperson, even if the recommendation lacks substantive explanation.

- Political Campaigns:
Candidates often highlight their personal histories to build trust. Barack Obama's emphasis on his grassroots activism and Joe Biden's "Scranton boy" narrative grounded their campaigns in relatability and authenticity, fostering credibility with specific demographics.

- Advertising:
Brands often rely on celebrity endorsements to transfer perceived credibility. When an athlete endorses a sports drink, their expertise in physical performance lends the product unearned legitimacy, even if they have no knowledge of its actual benefits.

- Crisis Management:
During scandals, corporations often deploy CEOs or trusted public figures to address the public directly. When Apple's Steve Jobs personally announced solutions to the company's technical problems, his credibility as a visionary reassured customers, mitigating backlash.

- Religious Leadership:
Clergy members often rely on their perceived moral authority to guide followers. For example, when Pope Francis advocates for environmental protection, his words carry weight beyond scientific reasoning because they're rooted in his ethical stature.

Ethos is powerful because trust once established is difficult to dismantle. However, it's also ripe for abuse. When ethical appeals rely on fabricated authority or exaggerated credibility, they become a tool for manipulation, convincing audiences to act against their best interests under the illusion of moral guidance.

13. Kairos: Mastering the Timing

Kairos is the art of striking when the audience's defenses are lowest and receptiveness is highest. This delivers it at the perfect moment, when emotions, context, and circumstances align to make the message irresistible. Timing doesn't enhance persuasion; it transforms it into inevitability.

Kairos relies on the brain's sensitivity to context. Neurological studies show that decisions are influenced by external factors, such as mood, urgency, and even the time of day. Exploiting this sensitivity allows the persuader to embed their message when the audience is most vulnerable.

Real-World Examples

- Political Announcements:
  Politicians often unveil controversial policies during crises, knowing public attention is preoccupied. For example, during the COVID-19 pandemic, governments introduced sweeping surveillance measures under the guise of public safety, timing their actions when fear outweighed skepticism.

- Retail Sales:
  Black Friday capitalizes on a unique combination of urgency, social proof, and cultural expectation. The timing isn't arbitrary, it aligns with holiday shopping pressure and financial habits, making it the ideal moment for consumer manipulation.

- Social Media Activism:
  Hashtags like #MeToo and #BlackLivesMatter gained traction during heightened emotional climates following viral incidents. The timing amplified their resonance, turning individual grievances into global movements.

Kairos is persuasive because it removes resistance before it begins. However, it also raises ethical concerns, as it often capitalizes on emotional vulnerabilities, using context to push decisions that might not align with the audience's long-term interests.

14. Weasel Words: Creating Misleading Impressions

Weasel words are the linguistic equivalent of smoke and mirrors. They create an impression of certainty while leaving an escape hatch for deniability. Words like "could," "might," "many," and "some experts say" allow speakers to make bold claims without full commitment, giving the illusion of authority without accountability.

Psychologists link the effectiveness of weasel words to ambiguity aversion, the brain's tendency to fill gaps in unclear information with assumptions that favor the speaker. This makes vague claims feel substantial, even when they are empty.

Real-World Examples

- Advertising:
  Phrases like "Up to 50% off!" sound promising but mean nothing

specific. If only one item qualifies for the full discount, the claim remains technically true while deliberately misleading.

- Political Promises:
  Politicians often say, "I will fight for better healthcare," without specifying policies or outcomes. The vagueness creates a sense of commitment while leaving room for reinterpretation later.
- Health Products:
  Dietary supplements frequently use phrases like "may improve energy levels" or "supports immunity." These claims sound authoritative but are legally non-binding, avoiding direct accountability for results.

Weasel words thrive on their ability to skirt scrutiny, creating the illusion of credibility while shielding the speaker from responsibility. They manipulate perception, ensuring the audience interprets vague promises as firm commitments.

15. Flattery: Disarming Through Praise

Flattery is disarming because it appeals to ego, softening resistance and making the audience more receptive. Compliments aren't just about creating goodwill, they shift power dynamics, placing the flattered party in a position of psychological obligation. Flattery doesn't demand agreement, but it makes disagreement feel socially uncomfortable.

Neuroscience shows that flattery activates the brain's reward system, releasing dopamine and creating positive associations with the speaker. This chemical reaction undermines critical thinking, leaving the audience more inclined to trust and agree.

Real-World Examples

- Sales Tactics:
  A car salesperson might say, "You have great taste, this model is perfect for someone with your style." The compliment creates a subtle obligation to justify the implied good judgment by considering the purchase seriously.
- Corporate Leadership:
  Managers often use flattery to encourage compliance. Phrases like "You're one of our best team members, so I know you'll understand why this project is so important" both elevate the employee and reduce their ability to object without undermining their praise.

- Political Speeches:
  Politicians often flatter their constituents with phrases like, "The hardworking people of this great nation deserve better." The praise is broad enough to resonate universally, fostering a sense of trust and connection.
- Flattery's ethical challenge lies in its subtle coercion. By creating a false sense of rapport, it shifts the audience's focus from evaluating the message to preserving the positive dynamic, making it a powerful but manipulative tool.

16. Name-Calling: Dehumanizing the Opposition

Name-calling doesn't argue, it erases. By attaching emotionally charged labels to opponents, it reduces complex ideas and individuals to caricatures, making them easier to dismiss. Name-calling is about shutting down discussion before it starts, weaponizing language to consolidate power and control perception.

Psychologically, name-calling exploits the halo effect in reverse. When someone is labeled as "corrupt" or "extreme," that single attribute colors all other perceptions, forcing the audience to reject not just the person but also their ideas.

Real-World Examples

- Political Smears:
  Opponents in elections are often branded as "elitists," "extremists," or "radicals." These terms provoke emotional reactions that bypass critical thinking, ensuring that audiences reject policies without evaluating their merits.
- Social Media Wars:
  Trolls and influencers alike deploy labels such as "snowflake" or "Nazi" to polarize conversations. This technique doesn't just silence; it divides, ensuring people align with their in-group while vilifying the other.
- Historical Propaganda:
  During World War II, propaganda referred to enemies as "barbarians" or "savages," reducing entire nations to subhuman stereotypes. These labels justified atrocities by dehumanizing the opposition.

Name-calling thrives on simplicity, transforming nuance into absolutes. The danger lies in its permanence, once a label takes hold, it's nearly impossible to remove, leaving little room for reconciliation or understanding.

17. Glittering Generalities: Virtue Without Substance

Glittering generalities use grand, positive language that sounds meaningful but delivers nothing concrete. Words like "freedom," "justice," and "progress" evoke universal agreement while remaining deliberately vague. These terms hypnotize, creating a feel-good illusion of unity without addressing specifics.

The effectiveness of glittering generalities lies in their semantic ambiguity. Audiences project their own meanings onto the words, believing the speaker aligns with their values when no concrete position has been stated.

Real-World Examples

- Political Rallies:
  Campaign slogans like "Hope and Change" or "Make America Great Again" evoke optimism without detailing plans. The vagueness allows diverse audiences to interpret the message as personally resonant.

- Corporate Mission Statements:
  Companies often claim to "empower people" or "innovate for the future." These phrases inspire confidence while leaving the actual goals and methods undefined, masking profit motives behind feel-good language.

- Social Movements:
  Protest chants like "No Justice, No Peace" resonate emotionally but remain open to interpretation, allowing participants to unify without needing consensus on specific objectives.

- Glittering generalities manipulate through their appeal to shared ideals, making them powerful tools for rallying support. Their ethical risk lies in their emptiness, when nothing concrete is promised, there's no accountability for delivering results.

18. Plain Folks Appeal: Relating to the Masses

The plain folks appeal frames the speaker as an "ordinary person," fostering trust and relatability. By presenting themselves as one of the people, persuaders dissolve barriers of status or expertise, ensuring their audience feels a shared identity. This is a carefully constructed persona.

Cognitive science identifies social identification as the mechanism behind this tactic. When people perceive similarity with the speaker, they're more likely to trust them, assuming shared values and goals.

Real-World Examples

- Political Campaigns:
  Politicians emphasize humble beginnings or everyday habits, like Barack Obama bowling or George W. Bush clearing brush on his ranch, to frame themselves as relatable, despite their elite status.

- Advertising:
  "Real people, not actors" is a common tagline in commercials for cars, insurance, or household products. The use of non-celebrities implies trustworthiness, making the product feel accessible and authentic.

- Social Media Influencers:
  Many influencers deliberately cultivate an "everyday person" persona, posting unfiltered photos and discussing mundane topics to foster a sense of connection, even as they market products for profit.

- Cult Leadership:
  Leaders often frame themselves as humble servants of the cause, positioning their authority as derived from shared struggles. This approach solidifies loyalty by making followers feel they are equals in a larger mission.

The plain folks appeal blurs the line between connection and manipulation. By crafting an image of relatability, persuaders obscure their agendas, ensuring that trust is built on perception rather than reality.

19. Extrapolation: Drawing Conclusions From Limited Data

Extrapolation simplifies complexity by stretching a small piece of data into sweeping conclusions. It works because the brain craves coherence, filling gaps in logic with assumptions that align with the presented narrative. By turning fragments into a whole, extrapolation bypasses critical evaluation, creating the illusion of certainty where none exists.

This tactic exploits the brain's tendency to favor patterns, even when they don't exist. Known as apophenia, this cognitive bias leads audiences to accept speculative leaps as logical inevitabilities.

Real-World Examples

- Stock Market Predictions:
  Financial analysts often point to a company's recent stock performance as evidence of its future trajectory. Statements like "This stock has risen 10% this quarter, imagine where it will be in a year" oversimplify market volatility, creating false confidence in sustained growth.

- Political Campaigns:
  Politicians frequently highlight single anecdotes to generalize about entire groups. A candidate might say, "I met a hardworking farmer who can't afford healthcare," framing one story as indicative of a broader systemic failure without providing substantive data.

- Health and Fitness:
  Diet fads thrive on extrapolation. Claims like "Participants lost 10 pounds in 30 days" ignore individual variability, implying universal results that drive sales without addressing underlying health complexities.

Extrapolation's danger lies in its seduction. By providing easy answers to complex questions, it appeals to audiences who prefer simplicity over nuance, leaving critical evaluation buried beneath narrative convenience.

20. Fear Appeal: Weaponizing Anxiety

Fear appeals hijack the mind's survival instincts, activating a state of urgency that overrides rational thinking. By triggering anxiety, they create an emotional shortcut to action, bypassing deliberation in favor of immediate response. Fear is paralyzing, ensuring the audience acts without question to escape the discomfort.

Neuroscientists link fear appeals to activation of the amygdala, which governs the fight-or-flight response. Once triggered, logical reasoning diminishes, leaving emotions to drive decision-making.

Real-World Examples

- Political Ads:
  Campaigns often warn of catastrophic consequences if the opponent wins. Ads showing dystopian images of economic collapse or national security threats don't provide detailed arguments, they leverage fear to provoke instinctive reactions.

- Public Health Messaging:
  Anti-smoking campaigns frequently use graphic imagery of diseased lungs and cancer patients to evoke visceral fear. While effective in deterring behavior, these tactics risk desensitization over time, reducing long-term impact.

- Media Coverage:
  Headlines like "Are You Safe from the Latest Pandemic?" create an atmosphere of perpetual fear. By emphasizing worst-case scenarios, news outlets keep audiences engaged but perpetuate anxiety, often without proportional context.

Fear appeals walk an ethical tightrope. While they can motivate necessary actions, they often manipulate vulnerability, pushing audiences to react without fully understanding the issue at hand.

21. Humor: Disarming and Engaging

Humor is a Trojan horse for persuasion, delivering sharp ideas cloaked in levity. It lowers defenses, creating camaraderie that makes audiences more receptive. However, humor is strategic. It reframes, softens, and disarms, ensuring messages land where resistance might otherwise block them.

Cognitive studies reveal that laughter releases endorphins, fostering trust and emotional connection. This chemical reaction primes audiences to associate the speaker with positive feelings, making their arguments harder to dismiss.

Real-World Examples

- Political Speeches:
  Ronald Reagan defused concerns about his age with humor, famously quipping, "I will not make age an issue of this campaign. I am not going to exploit my opponent's youth and inexperience." The joke disarmed critics and shifted the narrative in his favor.

- Commercials:
  Insurance ads, like Geico's absurd scenarios, use humor to make a dry product memorable. By associating laughter with the brand, these ads create positive recall without directly addressing the service's complexities.

- Satire and Parody:
  Shows like The Daily Show and Saturday Night Live use humor to

critique social and political issues. By cloaking criticism in entertainment, they attract audiences who might otherwise avoid hard-hitting analysis.

- Social Media Activism:
  Memes are a humorous weapon for movements, condensing complex issues into sharable, impactful images. Humor ensures engagement, spreading messages to broader audiences who resonate with the tone.

Humor's ethical risk lies in trivialization. While it engages and persuades, it can also undermine the seriousness of issues, leaving audiences entertained but unmotivated to act on deeper concerns.

22. Rhetorical Questions: Leading the Audience

Rhetorical questions don't seek answers; they plant them. By framing a question with an obvious or emotionally charged answer, persuaders direct the audience's thoughts without appearing to do so. These questions force engagement, subtly steering the listener's logic toward a predetermined conclusion.

Cognitive psychology shows that rhetorical questions leverage mental priming, activating specific neural pathways that make the implied answer feel self-generated. This process makes the audience an unwitting co-creator of the speaker's message, increasing compliance and buy-in.

Real-World Examples

- Political Speeches:
  "Do we want to leave our children a world of debt and despair?" Such questions don't invite debate, they frame inaction as irresponsibility, pushing the audience toward agreement through guilt or fear.

- Marketing Campaigns:
  Ads asking, "Why settle for less?" frame competing products as inferior without providing direct comparisons. The question primes the consumer to assume higher value in the promoted product.

- Activist Rhetoric:
  "Isn't it time for justice?" This framing compels agreement by implying that the listener is already aligned with the cause, reinforcing support without elaborating on specific policies or actions.

Rhetorical questions manipulate by feigning openness. While they appear to invite thought, their true purpose is to limit it, guiding the audience toward conclusions they believe are their own.

23. Statistics and Data: The Illusion of Objectivity

Statistics cloak persuasion in the guise of neutrality, transforming opinions into apparent facts. Numbers lend an air of authority, even when they are cherry-picked, misrepresented, or stripped of context. Data frames, creating narratives that feel objective but are often deeply biased.

The illusion of objectivity arises from the brain's trust in numerical precision. Studies show that people are more likely to believe statements backed by numbers, even when the data is irrelevant or unverified. This blind trust allows persuaders to manipulate perception with selective statistics.

Real-World Examples

- Political Polls:
  "80% of voters support this measure" creates a sense of inevitability, even if the sample size is small or skewed. The number overwhelms skepticism, framing opposition as a minority viewpoint.

- Corporate Advertising:
  "95% of users reported satisfaction" omits crucial details like sample size or survey methods. The statistic feels definitive, masking the manipulation behind its construction.

- Public Health Campaigns:
  "Cases have increased by 300%!" sounds alarming but lacks context. If the initial number was negligible, the percentage increase is misleading, designed to provoke fear rather than understanding.

- Environmental Advocacy:
  "We lose a football field of rainforest every second" is emotionally evocative but simplified for impact. While the statistic raises awareness, it also risks distorting the complexity of ecological loss.

The danger of statistics lies in their veneer of impartiality. When stripped of context or presented selectively, they distort reality, ensuring that persuasion masquerades as truth.

24. Storytelling: Creating Emotional Connections

Storytelling bypasses skepticism by engaging the audience's emotions, immersing them in a narrative where logic becomes secondary. A well-told story is disarming, creating a sense of intimacy that makes persuasion feel personal rather than imposed. Stories imprint, leaving lasting emotional resonance.

Neurologically, storytelling activates the default mode network, the part of the brain involved in empathy and imagination. This creates a shared experience between speaker and listener, fostering trust and reducing resistance to the underlying message.

Real-World Examples

- Charity Campaigns:
  Nonprofits often spotlight individual beneficiaries instead of abstract statistics. A single child's journey from poverty to education elicits empathy far more effectively than numbers about thousands served.

- Political Debates:
  Candidates frequently share personal anecdotes, like meeting a struggling farmer or a single mother, to humanize policies. These stories shift focus from abstract principles to tangible, relatable impacts.

- Brand Marketing:
  Nike's "Just Do It" campaign frames every athlete as a hero, weaving stories of struggle and triumph that inspire consumers to associate the brand with perseverance and success.

- Social Movements:
  Activists use stories of personal transformation to galvanize supporters. For example, testimonials from individuals affected by systemic injustice personalize complex issues, making them impossible to ignore.

Storytelling's power lies in its emotional resonance, but this also makes it ethically fraught. When stories are exaggerated, selective, or misrepresented, they manipulate audiences by crafting an emotional truth that diverges from factual reality.

25. Contrast Principle: Making Choices Appear Easier

The contrast principle reshapes decisions by presenting options in relation to one another rather than in isolation. By juxtaposing extremes, persuaders manipulate perception, making one choice appear far more appealing than it might otherwise seem. It reframes the way they're evaluated.

Psychologists identify relative comparison as the mechanism at play. When faced with starkly different alternatives, the brain defaults to shortcuts, favoring what seems like the best option in a distorted context.

Real-World Examples

- Retail Pricing:
  A $1,000 jacket next to a $500 one makes the latter feel reasonable, even if it's still overpriced. The contrast shifts focus from absolute cost to perceived value.
- Real Estate Showings:
  Realtors show run-down properties before presenting a mediocre one. The "better" house feels like a gem in comparison, steering buyers to overlook its flaws.
- Political Policy Framing:
  A controversial proposal might be paired with an even more extreme alternative. The moderate-sounding option becomes the default choice, not because it's agreeable, but because it appears rational relative to its counterpart.

The contrast principle thrives on the brain's tendency to anchor judgments in relative terms. It creates an illusion of choice while subtly guiding the audience toward the desired outcome.

26. Consistency Principle: Leveraging the Need for Alignment

The consistency principle exploits the human need for internal alignment. Once someone commits to a belief or action, they feel psychological pressure to behave in ways that reaffirm it. This drive for consistency is emotional, driven by the discomfort of cognitive dissonance.

Studies in social psychology demonstrate that small, initial commitments, like signing a petition, make individuals more likely to take larger, related actions later. This phenomenon, known as the foot-in-the-door technique, makes compliance feel like a natural progression.

Real-World Examples

- Charitable Fundraising:
  Organizations often ask for a small, symbolic donation before soliciting larger contributions. The initial act primes donors to see themselves as supportive, compelling them to give more to remain consistent with this self-image.

- Political Activism:
  Voters who sign up for email updates are more likely to volunteer or donate. The act of subscribing creates a sense of alignment with the cause, making further participation feel inevitable.

- Sales Tactics:
  Car dealers often start by asking potential buyers to "just test drive." The small, noncommittal action establishes psychological investment, making the leap to purchase feel less significant.

The consistency principle nurtures alignment between self-perception and behavior, subtly escalating commitment while masking the pressure to comply.

27. Reciprocity Principle: Creating Obligations Through Generosity

The reciprocity principle operates on a simple rule: when someone gives, we feel compelled to give back. This instinct, rooted in social norms, creates a powerful psychological obligation that persuaders exploit to drive actions. Reciprocity is strategic indebtedness.

Neurologically, reciprocity activates the brain's reward system, releasing dopamine and fostering a sense of goodwill. However, this emotional response also creates an internal pressure to balance the scales, making refusal feel socially unacceptable.

Real-World Examples

- Marketing Gimmicks:
  Free samples in stores, like those at Costco, are more than promotions, they're psychological traps. After accepting the gift, customers feel a subtle obligation to make a purchase.

- Charity Appeals:
  Organizations often send free address labels or calendars as part of

donation solicitations. These small gifts create a sense of indebtedness, making recipients more likely to contribute.

- Corporate Relationships:
Salespeople often treat clients to meals or gifts, building goodwill that makes declining their pitch feel rude or ungrateful.

- Cult Recruitment:
High-control groups frequently offer free workshops or materials to potential recruits. The gifts establish a subtle obligation, making individuals more likely to reciprocate by attending further sessions or committing to the group.

Reciprocity's power lies in its invisibility. What feels like gratitude is often a carefully engineered obligation, turning generosity into leverage and leaving the recipient unaware of the manipulation at play.

28. Authority Principle: Trusting Experts

The authority principle leverages the human tendency to trust figures of perceived expertise or power. When an authority figure speaks, people often comply without questioning, assuming their credentials or position validate their claims. This reliance on authority shortcuts critical thinking, making the audience more susceptible to persuasion.

Cognitive psychology explains this through social proof and deference to authority, as demonstrated in Stanley Milgram's famous obedience experiments. Participants were willing to inflict harm when instructed by an authority figure, even when it conflicted with their morals.

Real-World Examples

- Medical Advertising:
Pharmaceutical commercials often feature actors in lab coats, tapping into the implied trust associated with doctors. The message is clear: If an authority figure endorses it, the product must be reliable.

- Political Messaging:
Politicians regularly align themselves with experts or institutions to lend weight to their policies. For example, citing military generals when advocating for defense spending ensures credibility through association.

- Product Endorsements:
Toothpaste brands frequently claim, "4 out of 5 dentists recommend,"

using vague endorsements to solidify authority without revealing methodology or context.

Authority thrives on trust, but it can also obscure. By placing blind faith in perceived expertise, audiences often overlook critical details, leaving authority figures with disproportionate influence over decisions.

29. Commitment Principle: Escalating Small Decisions

Commitment begins with a single step, a small decision that paves the way for larger actions. Once someone commits, even minimally, they become invested in maintaining alignment between their actions and self-perception. This principle thrives on the audience's need for consistency and ownership.

The foot-in-the-door phenomenon, validated in social psychology, shows that initial, low-stakes commitments lead to significantly higher rates of subsequent compliance. It's a slow, deliberate progression where each step feels natural because it aligns with the last.

Real-World Examples

- Subscription Models:
  Companies like Netflix lure users with free trials, requiring only minimal effort to sign up. Once enrolled, the inertia of commitment makes cancellation feel inconvenient, leading many to continue paying even if their usage wanes.

- Political Fundraising:
  Campaigns often start by asking for symbolic gestures, like signing a petition. The act of signing creates psychological alignment with the cause, making donors more likely to give money later.

- Retail Loyalty Programs:
  Point-based rewards systems encourage incremental spending. Once customers start earning points, the sunk cost of prior purchases makes them more likely to keep buying to "redeem" their perceived rewards.

Commitment builds on itself, transforming small actions into larger investments. The risk lies in its subtlety, audiences often fail to recognize how their decisions are being shaped until they've already crossed significant thresholds of compliance.

30. Anchoring Effect: Setting the Reference Point

The anchoring effect plants a single point of reference, subtly influencing all subsequent judgments. This initial anchor traps it, making comparisons and decisions revolve around the chosen benchmark. Anchors don't have to be accurate; they only have to exist to distort evaluation.

Psychological research on anchoring bias shows that even arbitrary numbers can influence decisions. For example, individuals asked whether the population of a city exceeds 1 million will estimate higher numbers than those given a lower anchor, regardless of its relevance.

Real-World Examples

- Retail Pricing:
  Stores often display "original" prices alongside sale prices, regardless of whether the original price was realistic. The inflated anchor makes the discount feel larger, driving purchases based on perceived value rather than need.

- Negotiations:
  In salary discussions, the first number mentioned sets the tone. A high anchor forces counteroffers upward, even if it far exceeds reasonable expectations.

- Real Estate Listings:
  Listing homes at higher prices creates anchors that skew buyer perceptions of value. Even when the price drops later, the initial anchor influences what buyers consider fair.

- Fundraising:
  Donation forms often suggest preset amounts like $50, $100, or $200. The highest number anchors expectations, leading donors to choose higher amounts than they might have offered unprompted.

Anchoring is powerful because it works invisibly. By shaping how information is framed, it controls evaluation without requiring the audience to consciously agree or even notice.

31. Neurolinguistic Programming (NLP): Reprogramming Thoughts

Neurolinguistic Programming (NLP) operates at the intersection of language, psychology, and behavior. By carefully crafting linguistic patterns and mirroring physical cues, NLP seeks to influence how people perceive and respond to their environment to rewire thought processes and create subconscious alignment with the persuader's objectives.

NLP exploits the brain's reliance on mental shortcuts, using techniques like pacing, leading, and reframing to bypass critical thinking. While controversial, its proponents argue that NLP capitalizes on the brain's inherent plasticity, reshaping habits and beliefs through deliberate language and behavior.

Real-World Examples

- Sales and Negotiations:
  Salespeople trained in NLP might mirror a client's tone or body language to build subconscious rapport. This creates a sense of trust, making the client more likely to accept the salesperson's recommendations without realizing they've been influenced.

- Therapeutic Applications:
  In counseling, therapists use NLP techniques like reframing to help clients see problems from new perspectives. For instance, a fear of public speaking might be reframed as "an opportunity to share valuable ideas," reducing anxiety by altering perception.

- Corporate Leadership:
  Executives often deploy NLP-inspired language patterns to motivate teams. Phrases like "You already know how capable you are" combine presuppositions with affirmation, embedding confidence into the listener's subconscious.

- Cult Recruitment:
  High-control groups frequently use NLP tactics to disarm recruits. Leaders mirror behaviors and use loaded questions to draw individuals into a state of compliance, fostering emotional dependence without overt coercion.

While NLP has legitimate uses in therapy and personal development, its manipulative potential raises ethical concerns. By operating below the level of awareness, it turns influence into something that feels organic but is carefully engineered, leaving audiences vulnerable to manipulation they can't detect or resist.

When Persuasion Becomes Coercion

It's crucial to address the ethical dilemma that accompanies the use of these tools. While these patterns can be employed to influence and persuade, they also tread dangerously close to manipulation. The line between ethical persuasion and coercion is thin, and once crossed, trust is easily destroyed. Persuaders must wield these techniques responsibly, always considering whether their influence respects the autonomy and free will of their audience.

The 31 linguistic patterns of persuasion are psychological weapons, each designed to bypass critical thinking and engage emotions, instincts, and subconscious desires. In the hands of a skilled communicator, these patterns can shift realities, create emotional bonds, and drive decisions at the deepest levels.

Neurological Reactions to Words

Language hacks directly into the brain's neurochemical systems. Words have the power to bypass conscious reasoning and spark biological reactions that drive attention, emotion, and action. While you may think that persuasion is simply about choosing the right arguments or presenting the right facts, the reality is much more primal. Certain words activate the same pleasure centers in the brain as sex, food, or addictive substances, triggering floods of dopamine and serotonin that make us more likely to comply, buy, or engage. Persuasion, then, is chemical.

Words That Trigger Reward

Consider how the word "free" makes you feel. It doesn't matter if it's a free sample at the grocery store or free shipping on an online order, the word itself triggers a dopamine response in the brain's reward system, making us more likely to act. Dopamine, often called the "feel-good" neurotransmitter, is released whenever we anticipate a reward. It motivates us to pursue pleasure and avoid pain, and when marketers use words like "free" or "new," they tap directly into this biological system.

In neuromarketing studies, participants exposed to words like "free" and "exclusive" showed increased activation in the ventral striatum, the brain's primary reward center. This surge of dopamine drives people to act impulsively, bypassing their rational analysis in favor of a more instinctual reaction. The brain essentially screams, "This is a good deal, take it now!" And once dopamine floods the system, resistance becomes futile.

Case Study: An e-commerce company tested the power of "free shipping" versus a "$10 discount." The value was the same, but the "free shipping" offer outperformed the discount by a wide margin. Why? The word "free" triggered an automatic dopamine response, making the offer more compelling even though it provided no additional financial benefit.

Serotonin's Soothing Effect

Where dopamine excites and motivates action, serotonin calms and reassures. Words that evoke feelings of safety, belonging, or nostalgia can trigger serotonin production, putting the brain into a state of emotional comfort. When you see words like "home," "secret," or "relax," your brain releases serotonin, creating a feeling of well-being that makes you more receptive to the message.

Emotional language in marketing or political speeches prime you to trust the speaker or product. Studies using neuroimaging have shown that words associated with positive emotional states activate regions of the brain involved in serotonin production, increasing mood and reducing resistance to persuasion. When people feel calm and secure, they're more likely to follow suggestions or make decisions without second-guessing.

Example: A luxury hotel chain emphasizes the word "escape" in its marketing materials. The word is a promise of a break from daily stress, a serotonin trigger, calming the brain and making the offer feel like a necessary indulgence rather than an extravagance.

How Language Triggers Risk-Taking

Not all persuasion strategies rely on positive reinforcement. Words that imply scarcity or urgency, like "limited-time offer" or "only 3 left in stock", activate the brain's stress-related pathways, triggering fear of loss and motivating riskier decision-making. Neurological studies show that scarcity language increases activity in the amygdala, the brain's fear center, making people more likely to take action out of anxiety that they'll miss out.

This stress-induced reaction isn't accidental, it's a well-known tactic in sales and marketing designed to short-circuit your brain's rational processes. When the amygdala is activated, your brain deprioritizes logical analysis in favor of immediate action. This is the biological equivalent of "buy now, think later."

Case Study: A ticketing website tested two messages: "Tickets available" and "Only 5 tickets left, act fast!" The latter, scarcity-laden message led to a 60% increase in conversions. The words triggered stress-related brain activity, forcing consumers into a state of urgency where purchasing felt like a necessity rather than a choice.

How Mystery Pulls You In

There's a reason why "secret" is one of the most powerful words in the world of persuasion. Our brains are wired to seek out hidden knowledge, and the promise of exclusivity or privileged information activates dopamine pathways just as powerfully as the word "free." Secrets trigger curiosity, and curiosity is a powerful motivator for engagement.

When you see a phrase like "the secret to success" or "unlock the hidden truth," your brain releases a spike of dopamine, driving a compulsion to discover what's being concealed. This is why content that promises exclusive information performs so well, it taps into the brain's desire for novelty and the reward system that comes with uncovering something hidden.

Example: Consider the success of headlines like, "The 5 Secrets to Wealth That Millionaires Won't Tell You." These types of hooks are irresistible because they promise privileged information, triggering the brain's dopamine system and pushing the reader to engage with the content to satisfy their curiosity.

The Biological Basis of Suggestion

The power of language goes beyond learned behaviors or cultural norms. Language leverages the brain's hardwired biological systems. Antonio Damasio, in Descartes' Error, explains that "the brain uses emotions to guide decision-making". Words, especially those that evoke emotions or trigger reward systems, create neurochemical responses that fundamentally alter decision-making processes. When certain linguistic triggers release dopamine, serotonin, or cortisol, the brain is chemically predisposed to accept the suggestion that follows.

This is why emotionally charged language that invokes fear, excitement, or comfort is so effective. Once the brain is flooded with neurotransmitters, rational thought takes a back seat to emotional impulse, and the person becomes more susceptible to persuasion.

Example: In political speeches, words like "freedom" or "threat" don't just evoke ideals or fears, they trigger neurochemical responses. The word "freedom" can spark a dopamine response linked to the anticipation of reward, while "threat" activates stress hormones, making people more likely to support aggressive or defensive policies.

Neuromarketing and the Power of Words

In a landmark neuromarketing study, researchers exposed participants to different types of advertising language while measuring brain activity using fMRI scans. Words like "free," "exclusive," and "new" consistently activated the ventral striatum, the brain's reward center, leading to increased dopamine release and a higher likelihood of purchasing decisions. Meanwhile, words implying scarcity or urgency activated the amygdala, driving participants to take riskier actions out of fear of missing out.

This study highlighted that language persuades at a cognitive level and directly influences the brain's chemical responses, making certain words biologically irresistible. The next time you see an advertisement boasting "exclusive access" or "limited-time offer," remember: it's your brain chemistry being altered.

Are We Truly Free to Choose?

If certain words can trigger biological responses that bypass rational thinking, where does that leave free will? Critics argue that using language to manipulate brain chemistry calls into question the ethics of marketing, political persuasion, and even everyday conversation. When a word like "free" can override critical thinking and push someone to act impulsively, are they truly making their own choices, or are they being chemically coerced?

This raises significant ethical concerns. The more we understand about how language affects the brain, the more responsibility falls on persuaders to wield this knowledge carefully. Are you guiding decisions, or are you manipulating them at a neurochemical level?

Words as Neurochemical Weapons

The science is clear: words rewire our brains. The dopamine surge from hearing "free" or the stress-induced reaction to a "limited-time offer" shapes our behavior through neurochemical triggers. Persuasion is biological. And now that you know how words trigger these reactions, you hold a tool that can either guide others ethically or exploit their biological impulses.

How will you use it?

Wielding the Lockpick

Negotiation and advertising are battlegrounds of influence where every word is a weapon and every sentence a potential turning point. It doesn't matter if you're sitting across the table from a high-powered executive or crafting an ad to drive millions of clicks, the language you use shapes perception, shifts expectations, and, ultimately, directs decisions. Language is strategy.

The tactical use of language in negotiations and advertising is about precision, knowing which words to deploy, when to deploy them, and how to subtly steer the outcome in your favor. This section unpacks these tactics, offering step-by-step strategies for wielding linguistic tools like anchoring, framing, and suggestive language to gain the upper hand.

Anchoring: Setting the Reference Point

In negotiation, the first number put on the table is like dropping an anchor, it sets the frame of reference for everything that follows. Once an anchor is established, the brain subconsciously measures all future offers against it, even if the anchor is extreme or unrealistic. Daniel Kahneman, in Thinking, Fast and Slow, explains, "Anchoring occurs when people consider a particular value for an unknown quantity before estimating that quantity," emphasizing how an initial offer shapes the direction of the entire negotiation.

How to Use Anchoring in Negotiation

1. Drop the Anchor First: Always try to set the first number. The person who drops the anchor controls the frame of reference.

2. Use an Aggressive Anchor: Set the anchor higher or lower than what you expect to settle on, giving yourself room to "concede" while still staying within your target range.

3. Tie It to a Narrative: Don't just throw out a number, tie it to a story. If you're negotiating a salary, frame your high anchor by saying, "Given my extensive experience and recent industry trends, I believe $120,000 is a fair starting point."

- Example: In a real estate deal, the seller starts by listing a property at $1.2 million, even though they're willing to accept $1 million. By setting a high anchor, the buyer is more likely to negotiate down toward $1.1 million, which still exceeds the seller's actual goal.

Framing: Shaping Perception Through Context

Framing is changing how those facts are perceived. The same information can evoke entirely different emotions depending on how it's framed. Robert Cialdini, author of Influence, notes, "People are more motivated by the thought of losing something than by the thought of gaining something of equal value," emphasizing the power of loss framing.

How to Use Framing to Your Advantage

1. Choose Your Frame Carefully: Decide if you want to use a gain frame (highlighting the benefits) or a loss frame (highlighting what's at risk).

2. Focus on What They Stand to Lose: In negotiations, framing an offer in terms of what the other party could lose often creates more urgency than framing it in terms of potential gains.

3. Reframe Objections: When facing resistance, reframe their concerns in a way that benefits you. For example, if they say the price is too high, reframe it as an investment in long-term quality.

- Example: In a health insurance ad, the phrase "Protect your family's future" frames the purchase as a safeguard against potential loss, triggering a fear response that drives action. A less effective frame would be, "Ensure your family's financial well-being," which is positive but lacks the emotional urgency created by fear of loss.

The Power of Subtle Nudges

Suggestive language plants ideas without explicitly stating them, allowing the listener to feel as though they've arrived at the conclusion themselves. Chris Voss, former FBI hostage negotiator and author of Never Split the Difference, states, "The language of negotiation is designed to influence," underscoring the importance of subtle linguistic nudges.

How to Use Suggestive Language

1. Use "Imagine" Statements: Suggestive language thrives on visualization. Instead of saying, "You should buy this," say, "Imagine how much easier your life would be with this product."

2. Plant Subconscious Ideas: Use words like "maybe," "could," or "might" to suggest outcomes without forcing them. This makes the

suggestion feel less like a hard sell and more like a natural conclusion.

3. Ask Leading Questions: Instead of making a direct statement, ask a question that leads to the desired response. For example, "Wouldn't it make sense to invest now while prices are low?" encourages agreement by framing the decision as logical.

- Example: A sales representative for a luxury car brand might say, "Imagine how it would feel to drive this car to work every day." The word "imagine" prompts the brain to picture that scenario, planting the seed of ownership long before the decision to purchase has been consciously made.

Advertising as Neurological Manipulation

In advertising, every word is chosen for its psychological and neurological impact. As discussed earlier, certain words like "free," "limited," and "exclusive" trigger dopamine responses in the brain, making consumers more likely to engage. Richard Thaler, a pioneer of behavioral economics, describes this as "a way to nudge consumers toward desired behaviors".

Crafting Persuasive Ad Copy

1. Use Dopamine Triggers: Incorporate words that trigger reward pathways, such as "new," "secret," or "exclusive." These words tap into our brain's pleasure centers, making the offer feel irresistible.

2. Leverage Scarcity: Use scarcity language like "limited-time offer" or "only a few left" to activate the brain's fear of missing out. This creates urgency and pushes consumers to act quickly.

3. Highlight Emotional Benefits: Focus on how the product will make the consumer feel. Emotional appeals that invoke pleasure, relief, or excitement are more effective than listing features or specs.

- Example: Apple's famous tagline, "Think Different," was about selling an identity. The language appealed to the consumer's desire for individuality and creativity, triggering emotional and neurological responses that made buying an Apple product feel like an act of self-expression.

Tactical Language in Action

1. Anchoring in Political Debates: During a well-known U.S. presidential debate, the candidate deliberately set an anchor by stating an exaggerated version of their opponent's position. This extreme anchor made their own moderate stance appear more reasonable, subtly guiding the audience's perception of the issues at hand.

2. Framing in Financial Services: A financial services company framed their savings plan as "a way to protect your family's future" rather than simply as a savings tool. The loss frame (protecting against potential future harm) proved far more persuasive than a positive frame emphasizing the potential gains of investing.

3. Suggestive Language in Luxury Goods Advertising: A luxury watch brand avoided directly telling consumers they needed a luxury watch, instead planting the suggestion by saying, "Imagine the legacy you leave behind." This suggestion tapped into the consumer's desire for lasting significance, elevating the watch purchase from a material transaction to an existential decision.

Manipulation or Persuasion?

The line between persuasion and manipulation becomes especially thin when wielding tactical language. In negotiation and advertising, where billions of dollars and critical decisions are at stake, language can be used to create false impressions, exploit cognitive biases, or nudge people toward choices that benefit the persuader more than the persuaded.

This raises ethical questions: At what point does influence become coercion? Herb Cohen said it best: "In negotiation, words are weapons". The responsibility lies with the communicator to use these weapons ethically, ensuring that persuasion doesn't cross the line into manipulation.

Mastering tactical language is mastering power. When you're closing a big deal or crafting an ad for a wide audience, your choice of words can shape perceptions, drive decisions, and ultimately influence the outcome. Anchoring, framing, and suggestive language are strategic tools designed to give you the upper hand. But with this power comes a responsibility. Are you using these tactics to guide people toward better decisions, or are you subtly bending them to your will?

The battlefield of influence is complex, but once you master these linguistic lockpicks, you hold the keys to victory.

CHAPTER 8

The Bond Forger

When their neurons recognize that you're aligned with them emotionally, they let down their guard. And that's when the real persuasion begins.

Mirror Neurons

You've been taught to think of empathy as a "soft skill," something nice to have if you want to build relationships or diffuse conflicts. But what if I told you that empathy is much more than that? What if empathy, when properly understood, is the most powerful tool in your persuasion arsenal, a tool you can use to control the emotional state of anyone you interact with?

Empathy goes beyond moral virtues. It's also a biological mechanism, hardwired into our brains to ensure our survival. At the heart of this process lies the mirror neuron system, a network of neurons that enables us to feel what others feel. When you see someone smile, your mirror neurons fire as if you're smiling yourself. When you witness someone in pain, the same neurons light up as if the pain were yours. It's emotional mimicry at the neurological level, and it's the foundation for building trust and deep connections.

Let's see why this matters.

The Brain's Trust Builders

Imagine you're sitting across from a business partner in a tense negotiation. You can feel the room tighten as the stakes rise, and the usual persuasion tricks, logical reasoning, data dumping, are failing. But then, you shift tactics. You mirror their body language, soften your tone, and align your emotional expressions with theirs. Something changes. They lean in, they open up. What happened? You just hacked into their mirror neuron system.

Mirror neurons allow us to feel connected, to sense that someone else is experiencing our reality. This system, as discovered by neuroscientists, is about internalizing emotions. You see them smile, your brain feels that smile. You observe their frustration, your neurons reflect that frustration. This synchrony creates the perception of shared experience, a powerful foundation for trust.

But how can you use this? In any persuasive scenario, be it business, marketing, or even personal relationships, syncing your emotional state with the other person's can prime their brain for trust. When their neurons recognize that you're aligned with them emotionally, they let down their guard. And that's when the real persuasion begins.

The Brain's Trust Drug

Now, let's talk about the neurochemical that solidifies this connection, oxytocin, the "trust hormone." Released during positive social interactions, oxytocin enhances bonding and trust. Think of it as the glue that makes people feel safe with each other. This is the neurochemical that floods the brain after a hug or a handshake, and it's the same chemical marketers and leaders exploit when they craft their messaging to trigger emotional resonance.

You can generate oxytocin in others by fostering genuine connection through empathetic behavior. In business negotiations, this can be done by recognizing excellence or giving someone the floor to express their feelings fully. Every time you make the other person feel understood, their brain rewards them, and you, with a hit of oxytocin, deepening trust.

Companies like Starbucks have used this principle to create customer loyalty through personalized experiences. When you walk in and the barista greets you by name, offering a drink that feels tailored to your preferences, your brain releases oxytocin, reinforcing your bond with the brand. The transaction shifts from coffee to trust.

More Than Understanding

Here's the kicker: empathy doesn't have to be about understanding someone. It can be about controlling them. If you can evoke empathy strategically, you can influence emotional states, which means you can control decision-making. Take a note from Paul Bloom's controversial book Against Empathy, which argues that empathy isn't always the moral compass it's painted to be. Empathy can cloud judgment, distort decisions, and, when weaponized, manipulate.

Think of every manipulative marketing campaign that has pulled on your heartstrings, compelling you to act irrationally. When companies make you feel the pain of underprivileged children in a distant country, they're hijacking your mirror neurons to fuel donations. This is emotional manipulation cloaked as compassion, and it works because our brains are biologically wired to respond to emotional stimuli.

The question isn't whether empathy can be manipulative, the question is how far you're willing to go to leverage it.

Empathy in Real-World Influence

Business: Negotiation as Neural Synchronization

Let's take empathy into the boardroom. In negotiations, it's not the person who argues the loudest that wins, but the person who feels the most. Mirror neurons give you a direct route into someone else's emotional state. By matching their emotional tone and body language, you can reduce tension, build rapport, and make them feel like you're on the same team. When they feel you're aligned, their defenses drop, and persuasion becomes effortless.

One effective technique is emotional mirroring. If they cross their arms, you cross yours, but subtly, not like a copycat. Match their facial expressions and body posture. Their brain will subconsciously recognize the synchronization, releasing oxytocin and creating a sense of trust. Once that trust is in place, their emotional defenses lower, making it easier for you to guide the negotiation.

Marketing: The Emotional Hook

Empathy-based marketing sells an emotional experience. Brands that tap into mirror neurons through powerful storytelling create stronger emotional bonds with their customers. Take Nike's "Just Do It" campaign. They don't talk about the technical specs of their shoes; they show you someone like you, struggling, pushing through pain, succeeding. Your brain mirrors the emotions in the ad, you feel their struggle, you feel their triumph, and suddenly, those shoes aren't just shoes. They're a symbol of your potential success.

In every marketing message, you have the opportunity to trigger these same emotional responses. Ask yourself: What emotional state do I want to create in my audience? How can I reflect their deepest desires or fears to forge an unbreakable bond?

Relationships: Empathy as the Ultimate Trust Builder

In personal relationships, empathy is the bedrock of trust. But to build real connection, you need to go beyond surface-level empathy. You need to feel what the other person feels, in real-time, using your mirror neuron system to align emotionally. This is where deep listening comes in. By listening to their body language, tone, and micro-expressions, you can mirror their emotional state, creating an environment where they feel truly understood.

The trick is to mirror their emotions subtly. If they're upset, show concern, not by saying, "I understand," but by reflecting their frustration through your own body language and tone. When someone feels mirrored, they don't just think you understand; they feel it. That's the power of empathy in relationships: you're validating their feelings and synchronizing with them, creating a bond that's hard to break.

The Hidden Power of Silence

Empathy without listening is nothing more than emotional noise. If you can't hear the subtle cues behind someone's words, you'll never influence them effectively. Real persuasion, the kind that builds unshakable loyalty, begins not when you speak, but when you shut up and listen.

Silence Speaks Louder Than Words

Neuroscientific research has shown that active listening activates reward centers in the brain. When someone feels truly heard, their brain lights up like a Christmas tree, releasing oxytocin and dopamine, the same chemicals responsible for trust and pleasure. Listening, therefore, isn't passive; it's a neurochemical trigger that builds deeper connections. Think about this: every time you listen, you're rewiring the other person's brain to trust you more.

When you listen, you're guiding the conversation, leading the speaker into a psychological space where they feel comfortable enough to open up. The more they reveal, the more you control.

Take Japan, for example, where pauses in conversation tolerated and expected. Silence is a tool of influence. In Japanese business culture, long pauses are a sign of respect, showing that you're contemplating the speaker's words before responding. This silence forces the speaker to reflect deeper, often revealing more about their position or emotional state than they would have in a fast-paced exchange. It's a tactic Western cultures have overlooked:

silence is power. It forces others to fill the gap, and often, they'll give away more than they intended.

The Subtle Art of Mirroring Words

Let's move from neuroscience to strategy. Reflective listening is a technique that can transform a basic conversation into a persuasive masterclass. It's the art of repeating back what the other person says, but with an emotional twist. You're parroting their words and subtly guiding their emotional state.

Here's how it works: when someone tells you their problem or their opinion, reflect it back to them, but with an added layer of empathy. Say your business partner is stressed about missing a deadline. Instead of offering solutions immediately, you might respond with, "It sounds like you're feeling overwhelmed by the deadline pressure." This small act of reflection shows that you feel their emotion. Their brain, craving validation, will release oxytocin, deepening the bond between you.

But here's the deeper manipulation: by framing their emotion, you guide them toward resolving it in a way that benefits you. Once they feel understood, they're more likely to follow your lead. It's persuasion through emotional alignment.

Creating Ownership of Your Idea

If reflective listening is the doorway to influence, paraphrasing is the key to locking in your persuasion. Paraphrasing, when done right, makes the speaker feel like they've come to a conclusion on their own, even if that conclusion was yours all along. It's the art of subtly rewording their thoughts to guide them toward the solution you want.

In business negotiations, this technique is golden. When someone raises an objection, paraphrase their concern in a way that reflects empathy but also reframes it to align with your goals. For example, if a client says, "We're concerned about the budget," you could respond with, "So what I'm hearing is that you want to ensure maximum value for your investment." Now, you've acknowledged their concern while shifting the focus from cost to value. They'll feel heard, but they'll also start thinking in terms of value, your value.

The Weapon Everyone Overlooks

Here's where silence becomes your secret weapon. In most Western cultures, people hate silence. They'll rush to fill the gap with words, often revealing insecurities or additional information that you can leverage. In sales, for instance, silence after a price offer often leads the customer to justify their hesitation. They'll start talking, explaining why the price is too high, giving you a roadmap of their fears and concerns. All of this becomes leverage for you to close the deal.

In negotiations, silence can turn the tide of a conversation. After making a proposal, stop talking. Let the silence hang in the air. The discomfort will force the other party to speak, often revealing concessions or motivations they hadn't planned on sharing.

And the research backs this up. Studies show that the brain is uncomfortable with unresolved silence, especially in high-stakes conversations. People naturally want to fill the void, often disclosing deeper emotions or thoughts when they feel the pressure of silence.

In Japan, this tactic is elevated to an art form. Negotiators will pause for what feels like an eternity after an offer, forcing the speaker to either justify their position or amend their offer. Silence becomes a tool of psychological pressure, pushing the conversation deeper without uttering a word.

Emotional Probing

Let's not sugarcoat this: active listening, when done right, is manipulation. When you make the other person feel understood, they trust you more. And once trust is established, persuasion follows naturally. But you have to know when and how to dig deeper.

This is where emotional probing comes in. As you listen, you'll notice emotional cues, frustration, excitement, hesitation. These are gold mines for influence. When someone shows frustration, for example, that's your cue to probe deeper, to ask open-ended questions that let them vent. By doing so, you're letting them guide themselves to a solution that you're subtly steering them toward.

In customer research or interviews, this technique is invaluable. If a customer hesitates when describing a product feature, don't rush to answer their unspoken concern. Instead, ask a probing question: "Can you tell me more about what's causing you to hesitate?" This opens the door for them to reveal their fears, which you can then address, solidifying trust and aligning them with your solution.

Strategic Pausing

Strategic pausing is the unsung hero of active listening. Every conversation has a rhythm, and the master persuader knows how to disrupt that rhythm for their advantage. By pausing strategically, you force the other person to reveal more. But not any pause, intentional pauses that make it clear you're absorbing what they've said. It creates tension, and in that tension, people tend to overshare.

In customer interactions, strategic pauses give the impression of deep contemplation. Your silence signals that you're taking their words seriously, which increases their trust in you. But more than that, it subtly pressures them to fill the void, often with additional insights into their needs or desires.

Listening in Influence

Business: Mastering Negotiations with Silence and Listening

In high-stakes business negotiations, active listening combined with silence can be the difference between success and failure. The best negotiators are those who say the least. By listening more than they speak, they gather the emotional and logistical data necessary to craft the perfect counteroffer. And when they do speak, every word is calculated to address the other party's deepest concerns, concerns they would never have revealed if the negotiator had dominated the conversation.

Sales: Closing the Deal with Probing Questions

Sales professionals who excel at active listening are those who consistently close deals. By asking probing questions that encourage customers to share their frustrations or desires, they gain insight into the emotional drivers behind the purchase. Once these drivers are uncovered, closing the deal becomes a matter of aligning the product with the customer's internal narrative.

Relationships: The Power of Silent Understanding

In personal relationships, listening is the key to connection. Silence, when used correctly, allows your partner to feel truly understood without the need for constant verbal validation. By pausing and reflecting, you create space for deeper emotional sharing, which strengthens the bond over time.

When to Push and When to Pull

If active listening is the art of creating trust, then probing is the science of uncovering truth. It's where you move from the surface to the depths, where real influence begins. Conversations are like icebergs, most of what matters lies beneath the surface. And it's up to you to know when and how to dig deeper to uncover the motivations, fears, and desires that drive decision-making.

Reveal What's Hidden

Most people are unaware of how much they reveal through their words, tone, and body language. Emotional probing takes advantage of these subtle cues, not by bombarding someone with questions, but by strategically nudging them to open up. There's an art to it, probe too aggressively, and you break trust. Probe too little, and you miss the insights that give you leverage.

When done right, probing doesn't feel like interrogation, it feels like discovery. It guides the other person to reveal more than they intended, all while making them believe it was their choice to do so. And that's where the magic happens: they think they're in control, but you're the one steering the conversation.

Body Language, Tone, and Hesitation

Knowing when to probe is half the battle. The most revealing moments in a conversation often come not from what someone says, but from how they say it. Let's break it down:

- Body Language: Crossed arms, shifting weight, or avoiding eye contact are signals that there's more going on than what's being said. When you notice these cues, it's time to dig deeper.

- Tone: A subtle change in voice, like hesitation, defensiveness, or even a slight pitch shift, signals that you've hit an emotional nerve. This is where you gently push, asking open-ended questions that allow the person to explore their feelings.

- Hesitation: Pauses in speech, half-finished thoughts, or a reluctance to answer directly are golden opportunities. When someone hesitates, it often means they're holding back either information or emotion. That's your moment to probe, but with care, ask for clarification, not confrontation.

For example, in customer research, a client might pause when discussing a feature they dislike. If you jump to fill that silence, you miss the chance to learn what they really want. Instead, you might say, "It sounds like that feature doesn't meet your expectations. Can you tell me more about what's missing for you?" This approach opens the door for them to voice frustrations, giving you invaluable insight into their deeper needs.

Probing with Emotional Precision

Probing is about reading emotions. Emotional probing requires you to be attuned to the underlying feelings in the conversation. When you sense frustration, disappointment, or even excitement, you should respond with questions that encourage the speaker to articulate those emotions. The goal is to guide them to a place where they feel safe expressing their true thoughts, allowing you to gather insights that others might miss.

For example, in sales, when a potential customer hesitates before committing, don't push for the close. Instead, ask, "I sense you're unsure about this decision. What's giving you pause?" This question shifts the conversation from a sales pitch to an exploration of their concerns. Now, you're addressing their emotional roadblocks, which makes closing the deal much easier.

The Balance of Push and Pull

Here's where most persuaders fail: they push too hard. Emotional probing is about balance, knowing when to pull information out and when to step back. If you over-probe, you risk breaking the emotional connection you've built. You need to be able to read when the person has given you all they're comfortable sharing in that moment. This is where the skill of "pulling back" comes in. You can always circle back to the issue later, but pushing too far too fast will shut down the conversation.

Imagine a relationship scenario where your partner is clearly upset, but they aren't ready to talk. Pushing them to open up before they're emotionally prepared only builds resistance. Instead, you might say, "I can tell something's bothering you, and I'm here when you're ready to talk." This creates space for them to process their emotions without feeling pressured. It also reinforces the trust that you're there to dig for answers and to support them.

Productive Probing vs. Aggressive Questioning

Let's clarify the difference between productive probing and aggressive questioning. Productive probing feels like exploration, it's a natural extension of the conversation that flows from curiosity and concern. The person you're speaking with feels heard and valued, even as you guide them toward deeper revelations.

Aggressive questioning, on the other hand, feels invasive. It's rapid-fire, confrontational, and breaks trust. When someone feels interrogated, their defenses go up, and they shut down emotionally. Your goal is not to break someone's emotional barriers but to gently lower them.

Business Negotiations

In business, emotional probing can uncover hidden motivations that logical reasoning misses. Imagine you're negotiating a contract, and the other party suddenly pulls back from a deal that seemed certain. Instead of pushing harder on the numbers, you could probe by saying, "I'm sensing some hesitation. Is there something we haven't addressed that's concerning you?"

This question isn't confrontational, it's an invitation to explore their emotional state. Perhaps the hesitation is based on fear of commitment or concern about long-term risk. By gently probing, you allow them to voice concerns that they may not have even fully recognized themselves. Now, you're solving the deeper emotional problem.

Sales

In sales, the moment of hesitation is often the moment of opportunity. When a customer hesitates, it's not always because of the price, it's often emotional uncertainty. For example, if they pause after you present the cost of your service, don't assume it's about affordability. Instead, probe their hesitation: "What's your biggest concern about moving forward with this investment?"

This question encourages them to share their fears or doubts. Maybe they're worried about ROI, or perhaps they've been burned by similar services in the past. Whatever their reason, probing reveals the underlying issue, and once it's out in the open, you can address it directly, increasing your chances of closing the sale.

Relationships

In personal relationships, emotional probing can lead to deeper intimacy and understanding. When your partner seems distant or upset, rather than asking directly, "What's wrong?", which can feel accusatory, you could say, "I've noticed you've been quieter lately. Is something on your mind?"

This softer approach invites them to share without feeling pressured. You're not demanding answers; you're creating space for them to express their emotions. And once they do, the bond between you strengthens, built on a foundation of trust and understanding.

Knowing When to Stop

While probing is a powerful tool, it comes with risks. Over-probing can damage trust, especially if the person feels manipulated or pushed into revealing more than they're comfortable with. Always remember that probing is about guiding, not forcing. If you sense resistance, it's crucial to step back, give space, and let the conversation breathe.

In customer research, for example, if a participant becomes uncomfortable with a question, pushing them further could lead to disingenuous answers or, worse, alienation. Instead, acknowledge their hesitation: "I can see this is a sensitive topic. Let's move on, and if you're comfortable, we can revisit it later." This shows respect for their boundaries and preserves the trust you've built.

Probing as a Pathway to Loyalty

Emotional probing is about building a deeper connection that drives loyalty. When someone feels that you understand their surface-level concerns and their underlying emotions, they're more likely to trust you. And trust is the foundation of long-term loyalty in business, sales, and personal relationships.

By mastering the art of probing, you're gathering information and building relationships that last. You're guiding people to reveal their deeper truths, and in doing so, you're positioning yourself as the person who truly understands them. And that, more than any logical argument, is what turns influence into lasting loyalty.

Emotional Intelligence (EQ)

If probing allows you to uncover hidden truths, emotional intelligence (EQ) is what enables you to wield those truths effectively. EQ is the ultimate tool in your persuasion toolkit because it allows you to explore all emotions around you. When you master EQ, you don't react, you respond. You see the conversation before it unfolds, adjust to shifting emotional dynamics, and turn potential obstacles into opportunities for influence.

The Core Elements of EQ

Let's start by breaking down the core elements of EQ: self-awareness, self-regulation, and empathy. Together, these traits form the backbone of emotional intelligence and are the pillars of effective persuasion.

- Self-Awareness: You need to know your own emotional triggers and biases before you can effectively manage them. If you walk into a negotiation angry or insecure, your emotions will cloud your ability to read the room. Emotional self-awareness gives you the upper hand by allowing you to recognize your own emotional responses and recalibrate in real time.

- Self-Regulation: Once you're aware of your emotions, the next step is controlling them. Self-regulation is the ability to pause, breathe, and choose your response, rather than react impulsively. Imagine you're in a heated business negotiation and the other party makes an insulting remark. A high-EQ individual doesn't bite back; they remain calm, collected, and respond strategically. By regulating your emotions, you maintain control of the conversation.

- Empathy: We've already covered how mirror neurons allow you to feel what others feel. But EQ takes that to the next level by teaching you how to use that emotional insight to guide interactions. Empathy, at its highest level, allows you to understand someone's emotions and influence them by aligning with their emotional state and subtly guiding them where you want them to go.

These 3 elements aren't separate, they work together. Self-awareness informs your empathy, self-regulation gives you the space to deploy empathy effectively, and together, they help you steer the conversation with precision.

Reading Emotional Triggers in Real-Time

Now, let's talk strategy. Having a high EQ means being able to read emotional triggers in real time and using that information to adjust your approach. This is where the real persuasion happens, adapting on the fly based on the emotional landscape of the conversation.

Take Barack Obama's famous encounters with hecklers. Instead of reacting defensively, Obama often mirrored the emotions of the heckler, acknowledging their frustration, validating their concerns, and then subtly guiding the conversation back under his control. He didn't just argue or ignore the heckler; he disarmed them emotionally, turning a potential confrontation into a moment of connection. This is EQ in its purest form: recognizing the emotional charge in a situation and transforming it into an opportunity to build rapport.

As a leader, understanding and responding to emotional triggers is essential when managing team dynamics, defusing conflicts, or inspiring loyalty. Leaders with high EQ know how to tap into their team's emotional states to foster trust and cooperation. EQ creates an environment where emotions are acknowledged, but not allowed to control the narrative.

Emotional Mirroring

One of the most effective EQ strategies for influence is emotional mirroring. We touched on the neuroscience of mirror neurons in Section 1, but now it's time to put that knowledge into practice. Emotional mirroring is when you align your emotional expression with that of the person you're interacting with. This creates an unspoken bond that fosters trust.

In an interview, for instance, if the candidate seems nervous, acknowledging that anxiety ("I know interviews can be nerve-wracking") can make them feel understood. This small emotional alignment makes them more likely to open up. It works the same in sales. If a potential customer seems excited about a specific product feature, reflecting that excitement with your own energy creates a shared emotional space, reinforcing the bond and making them more likely to buy.

Mirroring, however, doesn't mean mimicry. Mirroring is subtle alignment. You're not copying their emotions; you're syncing your emotional state with theirs to create rapport and trust.

EQ in Customer Research and Product Development

Emotional intelligence is indispensable in customer research. When gathering insights about your target audience, it's not enough to ask what they think, you need to understand what they feel. By reading emotional cues during interviews or surveys, you can uncover the unspoken emotional drivers behind their needs and desires.

For instance, when conducting customer interviews, someone might verbally express satisfaction with a product, but their body language or tone of voice might reveal hesitation. A high-EQ interviewer will notice this emotional discrepancy and probe deeper: "I noticed you paused when talking about this feature. Is there something about it that you feel could be improved?"

This not only makes the customer feel understood but also gives you insight into the deeper emotional aspects of their experience, information you can use to improve your product or service.

In product development, understanding the emotional needs of your customers can mean the difference between success and failure. Steve Jobs didn't just build products, he built experiences that connected with people's emotions. His high EQ allowed him to recognize that customers didn't just want functional technology; they wanted products that felt intuitive and inspiring. This emotional intelligence is what elevated Apple from just another tech company to a brand that evokes loyalty bordering on devotion.

Guiding Emotional Development in Children

In parenting, emotional intelligence is just as crucial. High-EQ parents model empathetic listening and emotional regulation, teaching their children how to deal with their own emotional landscapes. Imagine your child is frustrated about something at school. Instead of dismissing their feelings with logic ("It's just a small problem, you'll be fine"), an EQ-driven parent might say, "I can see you're upset about this. Let's talk about why it's bothering you." This approach validates the child's emotions, teaches them to articulate their feelings, and strengthens the parent-child bond.

This same emotional intelligence can be applied to guide a child's development. By consistently modeling empathy, emotional regulation, and self-awareness, parents raise children who are better equipped to manage their own emotions and interact with the world around them.

When EQ Becomes Manipulation

It's impossible to discuss emotional intelligence without acknowledging its darker side. While EQ can build trust, it can also be weaponized. Leaders with high EQ but low ethics can exploit emotional triggers to manipulate people into decisions they wouldn't otherwise make. Think about charismatic but morally dubious leaders throughout history, they were masters of EQ, using their emotional insights to manipulate the masses.

In the business world, high-EQ managers might exploit their employees' emotional vulnerabilities to increase productivity or loyalty, without addressing underlying issues like burnout or dissatisfaction. This is where the ethical line must be drawn. Emotional intelligence, when used ethically, fosters genuine connections and loyalty. But when used manipulatively, it becomes emotional exploitation.

This is why self-awareness and empathy are critical to ethical influence. The key is to use your emotional insights to uplift and support others, not to manipulate them for selfish gains. This balance is the hallmark of true emotional intelligence.

Applications of EQ

Managing Team Dynamics and Defusing Conflicts

In leadership, EQ is essential for managing team dynamics and resolving conflicts. A high-EQ leader delegates tasks and senses the emotional state of the team, adjust their communication to match the emotional tone, and create an environment of trust and open dialogue. When conflicts arise, instead of reacting emotionally or defensively, the high-EQ leader uses empathy and emotional regulation to diffuse the situation and guide it to a productive resolution.

Reading Emotional Cues

In sales, reading emotional cues is key to understanding a customer's true motivations. If a customer seems reluctant to make a purchase, the emotionally intelligent salesperson doesn't push harder, they dig deeper. "What's making you hesitate?" becomes a powerful question when paired with emotional insights. In customer research, EQ helps you understand what customers emotionally need from your product or service.

Raising Emotionally Intelligent Children

In parenting, EQ allows you to raise children who are not only emotionally aware but capable of managing their own emotions. By modeling empathy, active listening, and emotional regulation, parents teach children how to explore complex social and emotional situations with confidence and compassion.

Forging Unbreakable Loyalty

Everything we've covered so far, empathy, listening, emotional probing, and emotional intelligence, has one ultimate goal: creating unbreakable loyalty. In fact, the most powerful form of influence doesn't win someone over in the short term. It creates a connection so strong that they feel emotionally bonded to you. When done right, loyalty becomes a psychological contract that keeps people coming back, no matter what alternatives they're offered.

Oxytocin and Trust

Let's start by looking at what drives loyalty at a neurological level. We've discussed oxytocin, the neurochemical that's released during positive social interactions and emotional bonding. This "trust hormone" does more than make us feel good, it literally strengthens the connections between people, making us more likely to trust and remain loyal to those who trigger its release.

When a customer receives personalized service at Starbucks, when a child feels understood by a parent, or when an employee feels valued by their leader, their brain releases oxytocin, which strengthens the emotional bond. Loyalty, therefore, is a biochemical state that reinforces itself the more it's triggered.

Loyalty creates repeated experiences that deepen trust over time. This is where the principles of reciprocity, social proof, and belonging come into play.

Triggering the Need to Return Favors

One of the most powerful psychological levers in loyalty-building is reciprocity, the instinctive human drive to repay kindness. When someone does something for us, we feel compelled to return the favor. This principle is often used in sales and marketing, but it can be leveraged much more deeply in any relationship.

For instance, offering small, thoughtful favors, especially unexpected ones, can trigger the reciprocity effect. In business, this might look like offering free upgrades or personalized services that feel like gifts. Think about how Amazon Prime has mastered this concept. The free shipping and extra services feel like gifts that make customers feel indebted to Amazon. They keep coming back because they feel they're getting more than they pay for. The result? Loyalty that feels more like an emotional bond than a transaction.

In personal relationships, reciprocity might come through small acts of kindness, such as listening when someone is struggling, offering help without being asked, or remembering significant details about their life. These small acts don't just earn gratitude; they create an emotional debt that makes the other person more likely to reciprocate and remain loyal.

Using Group Dynamics

People tend to follow the crowd, especially when they feel uncertain. This is where social proof becomes a key factor in building loyalty. When others express loyalty to a person, brand, or cause, we're more likely to follow suit. This is why companies like Apple and Nike invest so much in creating loyal communities. They know that when people see others fiercely loyal to the brand, they're more likely to align with it emotionally, even if they're not aware of it.

In personal relationships, social proof plays out through our social circles. When someone feels a sense of belonging within a group, they become loyal to both the group and the individuals within it. This is why fostering a sense of community around a shared purpose can deepen loyalty in both personal and professional settings.

For leaders, building a culture of loyalty within a team creates an environment where everyone feels a shared commitment to the team's mission. When everyone is loyal to the group, individuals are less likely to break away. In this way, belonging becomes a powerful driver of loyalty.

Creating Emotional Safety and Shared Identity

The most fundamental human need, beyond even survival, is belonging. We are hardwired to seek out groups that make us feel emotionally safe, understood, and valued. When we feel like we belong, we don't just want to stay, we feel compelled to stay. This is why loyalty programs and personalized customer experiences work so well. They don't just reward behavior; they create a sense of identity and belonging.

In parenting, fostering a sense of belonging is crucial to developing a child's long-term loyalty and trust. When children feel they belong in their family unit, they see their parents as emotional anchors. This bond can be nurtured through empathy, active listening, and emotional intelligence, all the tools we've discussed, by creating an environment where the child feels understood and valued.

In business, Starbucks' loyalty program is a perfect example of how belonging drives loyalty. The rewards program makes customers feel like insiders, part of an exclusive club that understands them. The app greets users by name, tracks their preferences, and offers personalized rewards. The result? Customers feel emotionally connected to Starbucks because they feel the brand knows and values them.

In sales, creating a sense of belonging transforms transactional relationships into partnerships. Salespeople who cultivate a shared purpose with their clients, who make the client feel like they're working together toward a common goal, develop far deeper loyalty than those who focus on closing deals. The emotional connection created by shared purpose turns the client from a one-time customer into a long-term partner.

The Bond Forger Framework

This is where we bring everything together with The Bond Forger Framework, a set of nine techniques designed to create unbreakable loyalty in any context. These techniques are based on the principles of reciprocity, social proof, and belonging, but they also incorporate everything we've learned about empathy, listening, emotional intelligence, and trust-building. Here's a preview of the framework:

1. Personalized Engagement: Tailor your interactions to the individual's emotional and practical needs. This might mean personalizing customer service in business or tuning into emotional cues in personal relationships.

2. Consistent Recognition: In leadership or parenting, recognizing excellence and effort on a consistent basis triggers trust and loyalty. People stay where they feel seen and valued.

3. **Reciprocal Kindness:** Offer small favors or gifts that feel personal and thoughtful. These create an emotional obligation to return the favor, fostering long-term loyalty.

4. **Create Shared Purpose:** In sales and leadership, develop a narrative of shared goals. Loyalty comes from a sense that you're working together toward something bigger than the individual.

5. **Build Emotional Safety:** Establish environments where people feel emotionally safe to express themselves. This emotional safety leads to deeper trust and loyalty.

6. **Incorporate Social Proof:** Highlight others' loyalty to reinforce that staying with you is the norm. This works especially well in business, where testimonials, reviews, and visible communities can drive deeper emotional investment.

7. **Foster Belonging:** Create a sense of community, where individuals feel like they're part of something meaningful. This is the glue that holds long-term loyalty together.

8. **Trigger Oxytocin Moments:** Through acts of kindness, physical connection (in personal relationships), or emotional alignment (in business) that trigger the neurochemical processes that reinforce trust and loyalty.

9. **Offer Unexpected Value:** Surprise people with value that exceeds their expectations. In business, this might be a bonus feature or service. In relationships, this might be an act of kindness that's unexpected but deeply appreciated.

Real-World Applications

Business: Loyalty Programs That Tap into Emotion

In business, loyalty programs that go beyond mere rewards create emotional bonds. Companies like Starbucks and Apple use their programs to cultivate a sense of belonging. They make customers feel like insiders, part of an exclusive group. This emotional connection keeps customers loyal, even when other brands offer better prices.

Sales: Transforming Clients into Partners

In sales, fostering a shared purpose with clients is key. When the relationship moves from transactional to collaborative, clients begin to see you as a partner rather than a vendor. This shift creates loyalty because they feel emotionally invested in the success of the partnership, not merely the purchase.

Parenting: Building Unshakable Trust

In parenting, loyalty isn't built through authority, it's built through emotional connection. Parents who foster a sense of belonging and emotional safety create an unbreakable bond with their children. This bond is strengthened through empathy, active listening, and the consistent recognition of the child's emotions and achievements.

The Ethical Edge

We've explored empathy, listening, emotional intelligence, probing, and the psychology of loyalty, all powerful tools that, when used together, create bonds so deep they can make or break relationships, businesses, and even movements. But here's the question you need to ask yourself as you walk away from this chapter: How far are you willing to push?

Empathy, at its core, is about connection, about stepping into someone's emotional world and walking alongside them. But let's not pretend it's only about compassion. In the hands of a master persuader, empathy is a weapon. It gives you the power to influence decisions, control emotional states, and forge bonds that are as unbreakable as they are self-serving. And that's where the ethical dilemma begins.

CHAPTER 9

The Cognitive Exploit

Your brain isn't fortified. It's vulnerable, filled with weak spots, biases, and cognitive blind spots just waiting to be exploited. Once you learn where these weaknesses are, you'll be able to control anyone's decisions, including your own.

The Ultimate Backdoor

The lie we've all been told is that we are the masters of our own minds. We like to think of our brains as impenetrable, logical machines, carefully weighing every decision, rationalizing every thought. We believe we're in control, our preferences, beliefs, and behaviors crafted out of sound reason. But here's the cold, unsettling truth: you've never been in control.

Your brain is more like a beautifully constructed but deeply flawed piece of software, riddled with bugs. And those bugs, cognitive biases, are the backdoors that I can walk right through. They're the blind spots that marketers, politicians, and yes, even your friends and family, exploit every day to subtly steer your thoughts, desires, and actions without you ever realizing it. Once you understand how to access these hidden weaknesses, you will hold the power to reshape anyone's reality, yours included.

You may think you've decided what toothpaste to buy or which movie to stream tonight, but the reality is that you've been nudged, manipulated, and influenced in ways you can't even begin to comprehend. The illusion of choice is just that, an illusion. In truth, you're reacting, not choosing.

And that's the beauty of cognitive hacking: it's invisible. It slips past your defenses, working behind the scenes, planting suggestions, framing options, and making you feel as though you're the one in charge.

But you're not.

Not yet, anyway.

Your Brain Has Already Been Hacked

Think of the last time you saw an "Only Two Left in Stock!" message while shopping online. Did it push you to make a quicker decision? Did you feel an unexplainable surge of urgency, that maybe you needed to act fast before the opportunity slipped through your fingers? You may have thought you were making a rational choice. You weren't. You were reacting to a cognitive exploit, scarcity bias, the simple but devastatingly effective mental trick that makes us value something more just because it's harder to get.

In every decision you make, similar invisible forces are at play. When it's anchoring, the first number you see skews your perception of every subsequent number. When it's loss aversion, you fear losing something far more than you desire gaining something new. These biases are the invisible hand guiding your choices. It's a game being played in the background, and most of us don't even realize we're the pawns.

Now, imagine if you were the one making the moves. Imagine if you could use these same mental exploits to influence others with the precision of a surgeon, slipping past their rational minds and planting ideas directly in their subconscious. That's the power you're about to unlock. Not only in others, but in yourself.

The Battle for Your Mind

Let's not sugarcoat it: cognitive hacking is war. It's a battle for the most precious real estate in the world, your brain. And in this war, every day, you're either the one pulling the strings or the puppet dangling from them.

When you walk into a store, the layout isn't random, it's a carefully orchestrated trap designed to push you toward specific decisions. When you scroll through social media, algorithms, driven by your past behavior and likes, are hacking your cognitive weaknesses to keep you hooked. This isn't by accident. Your brain has been hacked hundreds of times already, and you didn't even realize it.

Here's what's even more alarming: it's not only companies and advertisers pulling the strings. You're being hacked by those closest to you, family, friends, colleagues, because they've unknowingly learned to exploit the same biases. The favor your colleague asks you for? That's the Benjamin Franklin Effect, your brain will convince you that you like them more after helping them. The child who wears you down in an argument until you give in? That's decision fatigue, the mental exhaustion that makes us more likely to cave after a series of tough choices.

But this is your turning point. By the end of this chapter, you'll understand the fundamental weaknesses hardwired into every human mind. You'll see how cognitive biases and heuristics, mental shortcuts that once helped us survive, are now the very tools that can be used to shape, bend, and manipulate reality itself. More importantly, you'll learn how to use these tools to become the master in your own life.

The Power to Exploit Your Own Mind

Here's the twist: it's not only about hacking others. The real power lies in hacking your own mind. Every day, you are sabotaged by your own biases, habits, fears, limiting beliefs, all controlled by these same cognitive flaws. If you can learn to manipulate your own decision-making process, you can rewire how you see the world, how you make choices, and how you achieve success.

Cognitive hacking is the key to mastering both influence and self-mastery. And once you unlock that door, there's no going back. You'll begin to see the world for what it truly is, a battlefield of mental exploits, a landscape of cognitive vulnerabilities waiting to be hacked.

Your Brain is Designed to Fail You

The brain is a brilliant machine, but it's lazy. In the hustle of daily life, it doesn't analyze every decision or weigh every option. Instead, it takes shortcuts, quick fixes known as heuristics, that help us make decisions in an instant. Back when survival depended on snap judgments, these mental shortcuts were evolutionary gifts, enabling us to flee from predators or grab food without overthinking it. But in today's complex world, these same shortcuts have become our vulnerabilities. They've evolved into exploitable weaknesses, leaving us exposed to manipulation in ways we barely notice.

You might think that your choices, what to buy, who to trust, or even who to love, are the results of careful deliberation. They're not. In reality, your brain is constantly cutting corners, relying on these mental shortcuts to make sense of the flood of information bombarding you every second. And these shortcuts, once a survival advantage, are now the backdoors that anyone who understands them can use to influence your every move.

The Path of Least Resistance

The brain craves efficiency. It doesn't want to work harder than it has to, so it relies on heuristics, mental shortcuts that allow us to make decisions quickly without analyzing every detail. In a world filled with complex stimuli, from advertisements to news headlines to social media posts, these shortcuts make our lives easier, but they also make us vulnerable.

Cognitive biases, the systematic errors that come from relying on these shortcuts, are the cracks in the fortress of your mind. They're the blind spots that marketers, politicians, and manipulators have learned to exploit. And once you understand how they work, you can slip through those cracks and guide someone's thoughts, behaviors, and even emotions, without them ever realizing it.

Let's start with one of the most powerful mental shortcuts of all: anchoring bias.

Anchoring Bias: The First Impression Trap

Why do we compare everything to the first piece of information we receive?

The mind is a slave to the first number, idea, or suggestion it encounters. This is the essence of anchoring bias, our tendency to latch onto initial information, no matter how arbitrary, and use it as the reference point for all subsequent judgments. The brain clings to the first anchor it encounters like a ship tethered to a dock. No matter how irrational or random that anchor might be, it becomes the baseline for every future decision.

Imagine you're negotiating a salary. The employer throws out the first number: $50,000. That number then becomes your anchor. Any counteroffer you make will revolve around that number, even if you deserve much more. Research shows that even in unrelated contexts, this bias holds firm. In a famous study, participants were asked to guess how many African countries are members of the UN. First, they were exposed to a random number, either 10 or 65, by spinning a wheel. Those exposed to 65 gave higher estimates than those who saw 10, even though the number was entirely irrelevant to the question. That's the power of anchoring.

In marketing, anchoring bias is a goldmine. Retailers know that listing high prices first creates an illusion of value when the same item is discounted. That original, inflated price? It's an anchor, convincing you that the sale is a steal. This is why luxury brands often list their most expensive items prominently, it skews your perception of all subsequent prices, making everything else look like a bargain in comparison.

As Daniel Kahneman explains in Thinking, Fast and Slow, anchoring is one of the most pervasive cognitive exploits, silently shaping decisions before you even realize it. The truth is: the brain's reliance on this bias leaves us wide open to manipulation.

Availability Heuristic: The Power of What's Recent

Why do we think things that happened recently are more likely to happen again?

The brain is a prisoner of the present. When faced with decisions, we tend to give more weight to information that is easily available or emotionally charged, rather than objectively relevant. This is the essence of the availability heuristic, the mental shortcut that makes us believe that the most recent or dramatic events are the most likely to repeat themselves.

Consider this: After watching news coverage of a plane crash, people often cancel their flights, gripped by an irrational fear that their plane will also go down. It doesn't matter that statistically, flying is much safer than driving. The recent, vivid image of disaster takes precedence over logic, skewing our perception of risk.

Marketers and media outlets capitalize on this bias to create urgency, fear, or excitement. During the COVID-19 pandemic, fear-based marketing soared as companies exploited this heuristic to push consumers into panic buying. Headlines screamed about shortages, fueling the perception that goods were running out, even when supply chains were stable. The fear of scarcity, combined with the recent memory of empty shelves, drove sales to new heights.

As Robert Cialdini explains in Influence: The Psychology of Persuasion, the availability heuristic is a psychological weapon that amplifies fear, urgency, and excitement. Rational decision-making becomes secondary. The primary objective is to tap into the brain's tendency to prioritize recent, emotionally charged events. This bias makes us easy targets for fear-based marketing, political scare tactics, and media sensationalism.

Framing Effect: The Art of Presentation

Why does the way something is presented change how we feel about it?

The facts don't change, but your perception of them does. That's the magic of the framing effect, the cognitive bias that makes the brain susceptible to the way information is presented, even if the underlying data is identical. The brain is easily manipulated by presentation. It's really as simple as how you say it.

Take the classic example from the medical world: A surgery has a 90% survival rate. Sounds good, right? But now imagine the same surgery described as having a 10% death rate. The facts haven't changed, but your emotional response has. You're more likely to feel uneasy about the surgery when it's framed in terms of death, even though the probability is the same.

Framing is one of the most powerful tools in marketing, politics, and even personal relationships. By simply shifting how a message is delivered, you can nudge someone toward the decision you want them to make. Richard Thaler's Nudge discusses how small shifts in framing can dramatically alter behavior. For example, presenting healthy foods as "fresh and delicious" rather than "low-calorie" appeals to indulgence rather than restriction, driving better choices without triggering the brain's resistance to sacrifice.

In politics, framing shapes public opinion by altering emotional responses. A government program framed as "taxpayer relief" sounds noble, while the same program described as "budget cuts" feels threatening. It's the same policy, just a different costume.

Framing plays on the brain's laziness, its tendency to take the path of least resistance and react emotionally rather than logically. And once you master the art of framing, you can control the narrative, bending perception to your will.

The Trap is Set

These cognitive biases, anchoring, availability, and framing, are just the beginning. They are the tools of manipulation that shape our decisions, from the most trivial purchase to the most critical life choices. They are the brain's default settings, designed to make life easier, but in today's world, they've become vulnerabilities.

And now that you know how they work, the question is: How will you use them? Will you let others continue to hack your mind? Or will you take control, using these shortcuts to influence others before they even realize what's happening?

The next time you find yourself anchoring on a price, reacting emotionally to recent events, or swayed by the way something is framed, remember: your brain is cutting corners, and someone is holding the map. But that someone can be you.

The 15 Most Powerful Cognitive Backdoors

Imagine your brain as a high-powered, multitasking machine constantly processing millions of bits of information, all while making thousands of decisions each day. However, this efficiency comes at a price. Your brain is vulnerable to cognitive exploits, biases that operate beneath your awareness, steering your choices without you realizing it. These mental shortcuts are like pre-set traps, hardwired to guide behavior. And once you know where they are, you can manipulate them to influence others, and even yourself.

The cognitive biases, considered theoretical concepts by many, are actually practical tools. You've seen them at work in marketing, politics, negotiations, and your daily interactions. They are the invisible strings being pulled in every decision you make. Buying that extra coffee to supporting that politician, there's no difference. These 15 cognitive backdoors are the keys to the human mind, the cracks in its logic. Master them, and you hold immense power.

1. Loss Aversion, Fear the Loss More Than You Love the Gain

Humans are irrational creatures. We don't just dislike losing; we hate it. This is the principle of loss aversion, which shows that people fear loss more than they desire an equivalent gain. The prospect of losing $100 is psychologically more painful than the pleasure of gaining $100.

Why is this bias so potent? It's evolutionary. Losing something, be it food, resources, or social standing, could have meant death for early humans. Even now, in a world of abundance, our brains still overreact to potential losses.

Marketers and salespeople thrive on this bias. Think about insurance companies. They don't sell you peace of mind, they sell you fear of loss. By playing on your fear of losing your home, your car, or your health, they push you to buy coverage at premiums that often far exceed the actual risk.

Casinos know this game well, too. The more you lose, the harder it is to walk away. It's not only the money; it's your ego, your self-image. Loss aversion keeps gamblers at the table, chasing losses instead of cutting their losses. In fact, casinos design entire systems, like offering "free" perks, to exploit loss aversion. Once you've accepted something, even a free drink, your mind frames leaving the casino as losing out on something you've already invested in.

Nobel laureate Daniel Kahneman explores this in-depth in Thinking, Fast and Slow. His studies on decision-making under risk demonstrate how powerful the fear of loss is in shaping our behavior. One famous study showed that people are more likely to make decisions that avoid loss, even when a more rational analysis would point to potential gains being more favorable.

If you want to push someone toward a decision, show them what they stand to lose, not what they stand to gain. Fear is a far more potent motivator than opportunity.

2. Social Proof, The Power of the Herd

As social creatures, humans are wired to look to others for cues on how to behave, think, and decide. This is social proof, a cognitive backdoor that makes people conform to the behaviors or opinions of the crowd. Social proof is fearing being left out.

Social media platforms, especially, capitalize on this bias. Ever noticed how the "Like" button on Facebook, Instagram, and YouTube influences your perception of a post? If you see a post with thousands of likes, you're far more likely to view it as valuable or truthful, even if you would have ignored the same post with fewer likes.

Advertisers and marketers use this in reviews, testimonials, and popularity metrics to nudge consumers toward a product or idea. When you see "Bestseller" or "Most popular choice" next to an item on Amazon, it's a form of social proof. It's telling your brain, "Everyone else is doing it, so you should too."

Cults and extremist groups have long used social proof to recruit members. Once people see others flocking to a cause, their psychological resistance decreases, and they become more susceptible to joining the movement.

Robert Cialdini's work in Influence delves into the mechanisms of social proof, explaining how people look to others in ambiguous situations to guide their actions. This is why testimonials and case studies are among the most persuasive forms of marketing, they provide proof that others have made the same decision.

To sway a group or individual, show them that others like them have already made the decision you want them to make. The more visible the social proof, the stronger the pull.

3. Scarcity, The Allure of the Unavailable

What we can't have, we desire more. This is the essence of scarcity bias, a powerful cognitive exploit that makes things seem more valuable simply because they are perceived as scarce. Physical scarcity or time-limited offers tap into the powerful emotional trigger of not wanting to miss out.

Retailers and e-commerce platforms are masters of this exploit. The "Only 2 left in stock!" message or the "Limited Edition" label taps into our primal fear of missing out. The scarcity of an item makes it seem more desirable, even if it wasn't on your radar before. Apple has perfected this with its limited-edition product releases, driving people into a frenzy for a product they don't actually need but now desperately want.

Events often use scarcity tactics too. Concert tickets, flash sales, and exclusive membership programs all thrive on making people believe that their opportunity to purchase or participate is slipping away.

Studies in consumer psychology show that scarcity can increase the perceived value of a product by up to 30%. In their paper on scarcity, psychologists Worchel and Lee found that participants rated cookies as more desirable when they were told the supply was low.

Create the illusion of scarcity by limiting the availability of a product or making time-sensitive offers. This way, pushing the "buy now or miss out" button makes people act on emotion rather than logic.

4. The Endowment Effect, The Overvaluation of What's Yours

People value things more simply because they own them. This is the endowment effect, a cognitive bias that leads individuals to overvalue their possessions, even when those items are no different from others.

The IKEA effect, where people place higher value on items they helped to build, is a perfect example of the endowment effect in action. Customers who put together their own furniture value it more than similar items they didn't build themselves. This also applies to loyalty programs, once someone has invested time and effort into accumulating points or rewards, they overvalue the benefits they receive and are less likely to leave the program.

Real estate agents encounter this bias all the time. Homeowners overestimate the value of their homes simply because they own them. It's why they struggle to accept market valuations that are lower than their expectations, even if the pricing is fair.

In their study, Thaler and Kahneman demonstrated that individuals demanded a higher price to sell an item they owned than they were willing to pay for the same item. This bias stems from the psychological attachment we form to our possessions.

If you want someone to value something more, get them invested in it with time, effort, or emotional attachment. The more they put in, the more they'll perceive its worth.

5. Confirmation Bias, Beliefs Over Facts

We all like to think we're objective, but confirmation bias proves otherwise. This bias makes people unconsciously seek out information that supports their pre-existing beliefs while ignoring or downplaying facts that contradict them.

Social media algorithms are designed to exploit confirmation bias. By feeding users content that aligns with their existing views, platforms like Facebook and Twitter keep people engaged, and polarized. This is why political echo chambers exist. People surround themselves with information that reinforces their beliefs, creating a sense of validation and righteousness.

Marketers also tap into this bias. Once a consumer believes a certain brand is superior, confirmation bias keeps them loyal. Even when presented with facts that another brand might offer better value or quality, the customer will continue to seek out positive reviews or information that aligns with their belief in their favorite brand.

The Stanford Prison Experiment showed how confirmation bias fueled escalating behaviors. The guards, once convinced of their authority, sought out behavior that confirmed their belief in their superiority, leading to harsher treatment of the prisoners.

Reinforce someone's existing beliefs, and they'll ignore evidence to the contrary. Feed their biases, and you'll have their loyalty, no matter how irrational their beliefs may be.

6. Decoy Effect, The Power of a Useless Choice

The decoy effect occurs when a third, less desirable option is introduced to manipulate our choices between two other options. This additional option makes one of the original choices look more appealing, even though it wasn't before.

Starbucks does this beautifully with their cup sizes. The "Tall" is always priced in such a way that it makes the "Grande" look like a better deal. The "Venti," priced only slightly higher than the "Grande," makes you feel as though you're getting better value for your money, even though you might not have originally planned to buy the larger size.

Another example is subscription services. By offering 3 tiers, Basic, Standard, and Premium, the decoy effect comes into play. The Standard option is often deliberately overpriced or under-featured, pushing people toward the Premium plan because it seems like a better deal in comparison.

A study by behavioral economists showed that introducing a decoy option could increase sales of a more expensive product by up to 40%. The decoy option, though unattractive on its own, serves to skew the decision-making process toward the choice the marketer wants.

When you want to push someone toward a particular choice, introduce a third, inferior option. The presence of the decoy will make your desired option appear far more attractive.

7. Commitment Bias, Doubling Down on Bad Decisions

The commitment bias explains why people continue to support their past decisions, even when presented with evidence that those decisions were wrong. Once we've committed to an idea, person, or course of action, we become emotionally invested in justifying that choice, no matter how irrational.

Political campaigns are infamous for exploiting commitment bias. Once a voter publicly declares support for a candidate, they're more likely to double down on that choice, even if new evidence emerges that contradicts their initial decision. By the time the voter has put up a yard sign or debated with friends, their ego is involved. They can't back down without admitting they were wrong.

Investors fall prey to this bias in the stock market. Once they've invested in a failing stock, they often hold on to it, throwing good money after bad, rather than selling and cutting their losses. This is known as the sunk cost fallacy, a close relative of commitment bias.

In Predictably Irrational, Dan Ariely explains how commitment bias keeps people locked into poor decisions. Once people take a stand, even if it's based on flawed information, they'll go to great lengths to defend their choice to avoid cognitive dissonance.

Get someone to publicly commit to a decision. Haven them announce support for a candidate, support for a cause, or the purchase of a product. They'll be less likely to backtrack, even when faced with evidence that contradicts their choice.

8. Authority Bias, Trusting the Expert, Even When They're Wrong

Humans are wired to follow authority. Authority bias makes us defer to people we perceive as experts, even when they are wrong. This bias is rooted in the belief that people in positions of power or expertise are more knowledgeable, and therefore their opinions or directives must be correct.

This is why celebrity endorsements work, even when the celebrity has no expertise in the product they are promoting. When a famous actor or athlete endorses a skincare product, we are more likely to trust the brand, even though the celebrity knows no more about skincare than we do.

The Milgram obedience experiments famously illustrated how far people will go under the influence of authority. Participants were willing to administer what they believed were life-threatening electric shocks to another person simply because an authority figure, the experimenter, told them to.

In the world of advertising, the "doctor-recommended" claim is one of the most powerful. People trust doctors and other experts, often without questioning the specifics of their recommendation. As long as an authority figure endorses a product, the consumer's critical thinking is suppressed.

Milgram's obedience studies are the cornerstone of authority bias research. These experiments revealed the frightening extent to which people are willing to follow orders, even when those orders conflict with their personal moral codes.

Position yourself as an authority figure, or use the endorsement of one, and people will be far more likely to follow your lead, even if it goes against their own better judgment.

9. Halo Effect, When One Good Trait Blinds Us to the Rest

The halo effect occurs when we let a positive impression in one area influence our opinions in other areas. If someone has one positive characteristic, we assume they have other positive traits as well.

Brands use the halo effect to great advantage. Apple is a master of this. Because Apple is known for producing sleek, innovative products like the iPhone and MacBook, consumers often believe that everything Apple creates is superior. The brand halo means that even Apple's less successful products, like Apple TV, are perceived as high-quality simply because of the company's overall reputation.

Attractive people benefit from the halo effect too. Studies show that we are more likely to believe someone who is good-looking is also smart, kind, and trustworthy. This is why attractive spokespeople or celebrities are so effective in advertisements.

Cialdini's Influence touches on the halo effect in advertising, explaining how a well-liked celebrity can sway opinions on unrelated products. When we see a familiar face endorsing a product, the positive associations with the celebrity spill over to the product.

Leverage one positive trait to create a halo effect. This bias will cause people to assume other positive qualities, making them more likely to trust and follow.

10. Empathy Gap, Underestimating the Power of Emotion

The empathy gap refers to our inability to predict how much emotions will influence our behavior. When we're calm, we underestimate how emotional states like hunger, anger, or fear can affect our decisions.

Retailers often exploit the empathy gap by placing snacks and treats near the checkout aisle. Hungry shoppers, who entered the store with no intention of buying candy, suddenly find themselves grabbing chocolate bars in a moment of weakness. They didn't predict that their hunger would override their rational mind.

Political campaigns exploit this bias by triggering emotional reactions. In moments of fear, such as after a terrorist attack, people are more likely to support extreme policies that they would never have considered in a calmer state. Campaign ads that play on fear of crime or economic collapse push voters to make decisions based on their immediate emotions rather than long-term considerations.

Behavioral economics studies on impulse buying show that consumers make 25% more purchases when shopping while hungry. Similarly, research on emotional decision-making reveals that people in an emotional state are far more likely to make impulsive, irrational choices.

Trigger an emotional response, such as fear, hunger, or excitement, and you bypass rational thinking. This empathy gap ensures that people underestimate how much emotions drive their decisions.

11. Dunning-Kruger Effect, The Overconfidence of the Incompetent

The Dunning-Kruger effect explains why people with lower competence often believe they are more competent than they actually are. This overconfidence can lead them to make poor decisions, but it also makes them less likely to recognize their mistakes.

Training programs and self-help books often capitalize on this bias. By offering a simple framework or "quick fix," they convince customers that mastering a complex skill is easy. The customer, already overconfident in their abilities, buys into the idea that they can become an expert with just a few easy steps.

Incompetent managers frequently overestimate their leadership abilities, refusing to acknowledge their shortcomings. When employees try to provide feedback or constructive criticism, the manager dismisses it, believing they are already performing well.

In their original study, David Dunning and Justin Kruger demonstrated that individuals with lower competence in a particular area are more likely to overestimate their abilities, while those with higher competence often underestimate their skills.

Play into people's overconfidence. When they believe they are better than they are, they are less likely to question themselves, and more likely to believe that success is within easy reach.

12. Decision Fatigue, Poor Choices at the End of the Day

Decision fatigue occurs when the brain becomes overwhelmed by the sheer number of decisions it has to make. As mental resources are depleted, the quality of decisions deteriorates. This is why people make worse choices at the end of a long day.

Retailers like Amazon use decision fatigue to push impulse purchases. After browsing through countless products, shoppers become mentally exhausted, making them more susceptible to last-minute suggestions like "People who bought this also bought..." or "Frequently purchased together."

Judges are also prone to decision fatigue. A study on parole hearings showed that judges were more likely to deny parole later in the day, after they had made numerous decisions. The cognitive strain led to more conservative, default choices.

Studies show that decision fatigue can significantly reduce the quality of decisions, leading to poor impulse control and reliance on default options. Marketers have taken note, designing shopping experiences to capitalize on this mental exhaustion.

Time your ask for when decision fatigue is at its peak. When someone is mentally drained, they are more likely to agree without thinking too hard.

13. The Illusion of Control, Believing You Have More Power Than You Do

The illusion of control is a cognitive bias that leads people to overestimate their ability to control events. People often believe they have more control over outcomes than they actually do, even in situations driven largely by chance.

Gambling is rife with this bias. Casinos exploit the illusion of control by letting players make decisions, like choosing their numbers in roulette or throwing dice in craps, even though these actions have no real effect on the outcome. Gamblers believe they can influence the result, giving them a false sense of control over what is purely random chance.

Marketers also take advantage of this bias by offering consumers the illusion of choice. For instance, when booking flights online, you may be given several options for "flight insurance," each with slightly different coverage levels. While these options create the perception of control over potential risks, the reality is that the likelihood of needing any insurance is minuscule.

By offering options that seem like they're putting control in the buyer's hands, companies increase the chances of a purchase.

Studies have shown that people are more confident in their ability to win at games of chance when they are given even a trivial amount of control over the process. In one experiment, participants were more likely to bet higher amounts when they were allowed to throw the dice themselves.

Give people the illusion of control, even if it's superficial, through choices, customization options, or seemingly empowering decisions. This illusion makes people feel more confident, increasing their likelihood of taking action.

14. The Sunk Cost Fallacy, The Reluctance to Walk Away

The sunk cost fallacy occurs when people continue investing in something because they've already invested resources, time, money, effort, into it, even when it would be more rational to walk away. The fear of wasting past investments clouds judgment, causing individuals to commit even further to losing propositions.

Subscription services are masters of exploiting the sunk cost fallacy. Once customers have invested in a membership, particularly one that offers a cumulative benefit (like a points system or rewards program), they are more likely to stick with it, even when it no longer makes sense. This is why services often offer low initial rates or trials, once customers invest time or money, they feel compelled to continue, lest their previous investment go to waste.

In the world of startups and business, founders often fall prey to this bias. Entrepreneurs will continue pouring money into a failing venture because they've already spent so much, even when cutting their losses would be the wiser move. Investors, too, are more likely to stay committed to underperforming stocks due to the psychological weight of past investments.

Richard Thaler's work in behavioral economics, alongside studies by Kahneman and Tversky, has shown how the sunk cost fallacy influences decision-making in everything from personal relationships to corporate strategies. One experiment demonstrated that participants were far more likely to stick with an unprofitable investment when they had previously invested resources into it.

Emphasize what has already been invested, not what could be lost. By reminding people of the time, money, or effort they've already sunk into something, you can make it harder for them to walk away, even when they should.

15. The Primacy Effect, First Impressions Shape Everything

The primacy effect explains why the first information we receive about something strongly influences our overall perception of it. In other words, first impressions matter, and once an initial impression is formed, it becomes difficult to change.

Job interviews are a classic example. The first few minutes of an interview often determine the hiring manager's overall perception of the candidate, regardless of what happens afterward. This is why job candidates are taught to focus on strong opening statements and body language, they need to "anchor" the interviewer with a positive first impression.

In advertising, the primacy effect is used to great advantage in product descriptions and packaging. The first message a consumer receives, like "All-Natural Ingredients" or "Doctor-Recommended", becomes the lens through which all subsequent information is interpreted. If the initial impression is strong and positive, the consumer will overlook minor flaws or negative details that come later.

In memory studies, researchers have found that people are more likely to remember the first few items in a list (the primacy effect) and the last few items (the recency effect), with the middle items often forgotten. This phenomenon applies not only to memory but to perception as well, where initial impressions carry the most weight in shaping opinions.

Get the first word, and make it count. Next time you're negotiating, pitching a product, or introducing yourself, focus on delivering a powerful first impression. It will shape how everything else is received.

Cracking the Code of Influence

Each of these 15 cognitive backdoors represents a crack in the fortress of the human mind, a vulnerability waiting to be exploited. These biases are hardwired into every one of us, guiding our decisions, preferences, and beliefs, often without us realizing it.

Manipulation is about finesse. By understanding how these cognitive biases work, you gain the power to bypass reason and logic, slipping past the mind's defenses and planting your suggestions directly in the subconscious. The brilliance of these biases is their invisibility. Most people are completely unaware that they are even being influenced.

Mastering Mental Exploits

You've now journeyed through the hidden pathways of the human mind, uncovering the biases and blind spots that make people vulnerable to manipulation. You've seen how loss aversion makes us fear losing more than we value winning, how social proof compels us to follow the crowd, and how anchoring traps us with the first piece of information we encounter. But understanding these biases isn't enough. To truly wield the power of persuasion, you need to know how to deploy these cognitive exploits strategically, how to shape reality itself through manipulation.

This is where cognitive warfare begins, a battle not fought with brute force, but with precision, subtlety, and insight. Marketers, politicians, and leaders are masters of this battlefield. They don't just influence individual decisions; they shape entire realities, molding perceptions, opinions, and even identities. If you're ready, this section will arm you with the tactical knowledge to manipulate outcomes with surgical accuracy, using the same psychological weapons employed by the most influential minds in the world.

Pricing Strategies

When it comes to shaping consumer behavior, few tools are as effective as anchoring and the decoy effect. These cognitive biases allow you to manipulate how people perceive value, often without them realizing they've been influenced.

Anchoring: Setting the Mental Benchmark

As we've discussed, anchoring occurs when the brain latches onto the first piece of information it receives and uses that as the basis for all future judgments. In pricing, the first price a consumer sees becomes their reference point. It doesn't matter if it's fair or inflated. This is the mental benchmark that skews all subsequent decisions.

When a luxury store lists an item at an exorbitantly high price, that price becomes the anchor for every other item in the store. Even if a shopper initially balks at the $5,000 watch, the next item they see, a $1,200 watch, will seem like a steal in comparison. That's not a logical comparison, but it's how anchoring warps the consumer's perception of value.

Real estate agents use anchoring to frame negotiations. A seller might list a home well above market value, knowing that this inflated price will set an anchor. Even if they later drop the price by $50,000, buyers still perceive it as a deal because the original price shaped their expectations.

Tactical Deployment:

- Set the Anchor High: When negotiating or selling, always introduce a high anchor point first. This initial figure will shape the mental framework for all future discussions.

- Frame Discounts Against the Anchor: Discounts should be positioned relative to the high anchor. A "50% off" sale sounds far more enticing when it's coming off an already inflated price.

- Use Time as an Anchor: Introduce deadlines and limited-time offers. When a price is available only for a short period, the current price becomes the anchor, and the urgency amplifies its influence.

The Decoy Effect: Making Your Desired Option Irresistible

The decoy effect introduces a third, less attractive option to manipulate the choice between two other options. By making one choice clearly inferior, you nudge the decision-maker toward the option you want them to choose.

Starbucks has perfected the decoy effect with its pricing strategies. When you order coffee, you might notice that the medium size is deliberately overpriced. It's not meant to be bought. Its only purpose is to make the large size look like a better deal. The consumer, comparing the overpriced medium to the slightly more expensive large, feels justified in choosing the larger option.

Subscription services are another prime example. Companies often offer 3 pricing tiers: Basic, Standard, and Premium. The Standard option might be intentionally designed to be less appealing, perhaps with limited features, making the Premium plan appear to offer the best value. In reality, the Premium plan is the one the company wanted to push all along.

Tactical Deployment:

- Create an Inferior Middle Option: When offering choices, introduce a middle option that is overpriced or underwhelming compared to the other two. This will make the higher-tier option seem like the best value by contrast.

- Use in Negotiation: In negotiations, offer a decoy that makes your preferred option look more attractive. For example, if you want a client to choose your mid-tier service package, introduce an underpriced, bare-bones option that makes the mid-tier look like the perfect compromise.

Persuasion in Negotiation: Leveraging Loss Aversion and Confirmation Bias

Negotiation is a psychological battleground where the most effective manipulators are those who understand how to push the right emotional buttons. Two of the most potent biases in this context are loss aversion and confirmation bias.

Loss Aversion: The Fear of Losing

As we've discussed, loss aversion makes people more motivated to avoid losses than to achieve gains. In a negotiation, this bias is your secret weapon. People will often make irrational concessions to avoid the pain of losing something they already perceive as theirs.

Imagine you're negotiating the sale of a product or service. Instead of framing the conversation around the benefits of what you're offering, shift the focus to what the other party will lose if they don't accept your proposal. For instance, in sales, don't just tell the prospect what they stand to gain by using your service, highlight what they'll lose by sticking with their current provider: outdated technology, lost revenue, missed opportunities.

Real estate agents use this tactic by showing buyers properties that tick most of their boxes, but at a premium price. Once the buyers have mentally invested in the property, imagining their future in it, the agent subtly shifts the conversation to what they risk losing by walking away. This fear of loss can push buyers to stretch their budget beyond what they initially intended.

Tactical Deployment:

- Highlight Potential Losses: In any negotiation, emphasize what the other side stands to lose if they don't agree to your terms. Loss aversion is more compelling than the promise of gains.

- Use Scarcity: Frame your offer as time-sensitive or limited in availability. People fear missing out on opportunities, and this fear drives decisions faster than the prospect of reward.

Confirmation Bias: Reinforcing What They Already Believe

Confirmation bias makes people seek out information that confirms their pre-existing beliefs. Once someone has formed an opinion, they subconsciously filter out facts that contradict it and focus on those that support it. This bias can be used to reinforce compliance in negotiations.

During a negotiation, listen carefully for cues about the other party's existing beliefs or assumptions. Once you identify their core beliefs, position your argument in a way that validates those beliefs. This makes your proposal feel like the logical conclusion of what they already know to be true.

For example, in political campaigns, candidates craft their messages to align with their supporters' beliefs, reinforcing existing ideologies rather than challenging them. By confirming their biases, politicians ensure their supporters stay loyal and engaged, regardless of new evidence.

Tactical Deployment:

- Frame Your Offer Around Their Beliefs: If you know the other party is concerned about risk, present your offer as the safest choice. If they value innovation, highlight how your solution aligns with cutting-edge trends. The more you confirm their worldview, the more likely they are to agree.
- Feed Their Ego: If a client prides themselves on making smart decisions, frame your offer as the next "smart" move. Confirmation bias will drive them to protect their self-image by accepting your proposal.

Emotional Manipulation: Exploiting the Empathy Gap and Authority Bias

Human beings aren't rational creatures, we are emotional ones. Emotions color every decision we make, often in ways we don't even realize. To manipulate someone effectively, you must exploit these emotions. Two of the most powerful tools for emotional manipulation are the empathy gap and authority bias.

Empathy Gap: Misjudging Emotional Influence

The empathy gap is the brain's failure to predict how emotions will influence decision-making. When we're calm, we underestimate how much hunger, fear, anger, or excitement will affect our future choices. Conversely, when we're in an emotional state, we struggle to imagine making decisions rationally.

Exploit in Practice:

Salespeople know the power of the empathy gap. Car salesmen, for example, often get customers emotionally invested in a vehicle before discussing the price. By allowing potential buyers to test drive a car, the salesperson engages their emotions, letting them imagine themselves driving the car home, feeling the leather seats, hearing the engine roar. At that moment, the buyer is no longer thinking rationally. Their emotional attachment to the car outweighs any logical considerations about cost or practicality.

Urgency also plays into the empathy gap. A limited-time offer creates an emotional response, fear of missing out, that overrides the buyer's usual careful decision-making process. By the time they realize they've been manipulated, the deal is done.

- Trigger Emotions Early: Get people emotionally invested in your product or service before introducing the logical aspects of the deal. Once their emotions are engaged, their rational mind will take a back seat.
- Use Urgency: Push decisions by creating a sense of urgency through time-limited offers, flash sales, or other tactics that trigger emotional reactions like fear of missing out.

Authority Bias: The Power of Perceived Expertise

Authority bias makes us defer to perceived experts, even when their expertise is irrelevant. We're conditioned to trust authority figures, often without questioning their qualifications or motives.

In advertising, authority bias is one of the most reliable tools. This is why companies frequently use doctor endorsements for health products, even if the product itself is unproven. The mere presence of a doctor in a white coat is enough to short-circuit critical thinking, triggering automatic trust.

Leaders also use authority bias to maintain compliance. In the workplace, employees are more likely to follow a directive from someone they perceive as an expert in their field, even if the directive doesn't make logical sense. This is especially true when the authority figure uses technical jargon or complex language to reinforce their status.

Tactical Deployment:

- Position Yourself as the Expert: In any interaction where you want compliance, establish yourself as the authority. This can be done through credentials, experience, or even simply by speaking confidently and using technical language that reinforces your expertise.

- Leverage Third-Party Authority: If you lack direct authority, bring in the endorsement of someone who does. A celebrity, a recognized expert, or a well-known brand with associate your message with authority triggers automatic compliance.

The Narrative of Influence

The real power of cognitive warfare lies in shaping reality. By using the biases we've explored, you're creating the narrative that guides how people perceive the world. Every decision, belief, and behavior can be influenced when you control the lens through which others see reality.

By anchoring their expectations, creating the illusion of scarcity, and feeding their confirmation biases, you become the architect of their perceptions. You are literally shaping their thoughts.

Control the Narrative

To truly master cognitive warfare, you must learn to control the narrative. People don't act on facts, they act on stories. The stories they tell themselves about who they are, what they believe, and how the world works. By subtly crafting the narrative, you can guide people's actions without them ever knowing you're pulling the strings.

Politicians understand this better than anyone. A successful campaign needs to provide policy solutions and create a narrative that frames the candidate as the savior against fictitious boogeymen. In other words, the leader who aligns with the public's beliefs. By crafting a compelling story, politicians are earning votes and shaping voters' reality.

Marketers use the same tactic. When Apple releases a new product, they don't just list the features. They tell a story of innovation, creativity, and rebellion. Consumers don't just buy an iPhone; they buy the story that owning one makes them part of something bigger.

Tactical Deployment:

- Craft a Compelling Story: Frame your product, service, or idea within a narrative that aligns with your audience's values and desires. People are far more likely to take action when they see themselves as part of a story, rather than just making a decision.

- Make Them the Hero: In your narrative, position the individual as the hero. They are not buying your product, they are fulfilling their destiny, solving their problem, or achieving their goal with your help.

The Puppet Master's Final Move

You are now armed with the tools of cognitive warfare. These biases and tactics are more than just ways to influence behavior, they are mechanisms for shaping reality. When you deploy these strategies, you're manipulating individual decisions and crafting the entire framework through which people perceive their choices, their beliefs, and their world.

But remember, manipulation is an art form. The best manipulations go unnoticed, slipping under the radar of conscious thought. The power you wield is invisible, but it is immense. This applies for marketing, negotiations, leadership, or personal relationships. Knowing this, you now possess the keys to the human mind.

CHAPTER 10

The Moral Minefield

What if I told you that the very word "manipulation" has been manipulated to sound worse than it is? What if manipulating others could be an ethical act?

Manipulation Isn't Always Evil

The truth is, manipulation has been given a bad name, and that's by design. We've been conditioned to believe that all manipulation is nefarious, deceitful, and harmful. But what if that conditioning itself is a manipulation? What if the stigma around the word has been carefully constructed to keep you from wielding one of the most powerful tools available to you? Because here's the reality: manipulation isn't always evil. In fact, in the right hands, manipulation can be a force for good, a tool for guiding others toward the best decisions, even when they can't see it for themselves.

Take a moment to let that sink in. What if you could use the techniques we've explored, not to deceive, but to uplift? Not to harm, but to help? Imagine bending the minds of those around you toward better outcomes, guiding them with precision past their own cognitive barriers, fears, and blind spots. What if "manipulation" could save them from themselves?

You see, the line between persuasion and manipulation isn't as clear-cut as moralists would have you believe. They're two sides of the same coin, differentiated not by technique, but by intent. Manipulation is painted as a dark art because it's often used for selfish ends. But when you manipulate someone for their own benefit, when your goal is aligned with their best interests, manipulation becomes something far more nuanced, and far more powerful.

Manipulation is a tool. Like any tool, it can be wielded for good or ill. A hammer can build a house or crush a skull; a scalpel can save a life or end one. It's not the tool itself that's good or evil, it's how you choose to use it. So the question isn't whether you should manipulate others. The question is how you'll do it, and why.

Let's be honest: people often don't act in their own best interests. They make irrational decisions, driven by biases, emotions, and societal conditioning. They buy things they don't need, vote against their own economic interests, stay in toxic relationships, and ignore their health. What if you could intervene, leveraging the cognitive exploits we've discussed, to steer them toward better outcomes? Would that still be manipulation? And even if it is, is that a bad thing?

Look around you. The world is already filled with manipulation. Politicians, advertisers, and corporations use these same tools every day to serve their own interests, often at your expense. The difference is, you can wield these tools consciously, ethically, and with a clear purpose. You can manipulate others in ways that improve their lives, shape better decisions, and even contribute to the greater good. In some cases, manipulation may not only be ethical, it may be necessary.

This chapter will challenge everything you think you know about influence, manipulation, and morality. You'll learn to walk the line between using your power responsibly and wielding it ruthlessly. But most importantly, you'll understand that ethical persuasion isn't a rigid moral code.

So, where's the line? When does persuasion slip into manipulation? And when does manipulation transform into something that's essential?

The Fine Line

What is manipulation? The word alone makes most people uncomfortable. It conjures images of puppet strings, shadowy figures pulling levers, and people being controlled without their knowledge. It's a word that, in modern culture, has become synonymous with deceit, exploitation, and malevolent intent. But what if we've been looking at it all wrong? What if manipulation isn't inherently evil? What if manipulation, in its purest form, is simply influence stripped of its moral baggage?

Let's get one thing straight: persuasion and manipulation are not two separate entities. They lie on the same spectrum. Persuasion, as society sees it, is the polite cousin of manipulation, a means to gently guide someone toward a decision that benefits both parties. Manipulation, on the other hand, is painted as a malicious act, designed to control and exploit for selfish gain. But that's just the surface. Dig deeper, and you'll find that the difference between these two concepts is nothing more than intent, and even that can be a slippery concept.

The Myth of Pure Persuasion

First, let's dismantle the comforting notion that persuasion is always noble. When someone says they're "persuading," what they often mean is they are trying to influence another person's decision, behavior, or belief. But here's the thing: all persuasion involves some degree of control. Even the softest, most well-meaning persuasive techniques are built on covert influence, tapping into psychological biases, emotional vulnerabilities, and subconscious desires.

When you persuade someone, you're guiding them through a process that has a goal: your goal. It might be to convince a customer to buy a product, a voter to support your candidate, or a loved one to see things your way. But don't delude yourself, persuasion is always about moving the other person closer to what you want. You're not simply laying out facts and hoping they come to their own conclusion. You're crafting the environment, framing the conversation, and subtly nudging them toward the decision that benefits you.

And that's where the line between persuasion and manipulation starts to blur. If the end result of persuasion is to influence someone in a way that benefits you, how different is that from manipulation?

Manipulation Isn't the Villain

What if I told you that manipulation is just persuasion with an edge? The only real distinction between them is our emotional response to the words. Persuasion is seen as polite, socially acceptable, and even virtuous, while manipulation carries a dark, almost sinister connotation. But what if manipulation, when done ethically, is actually the most efficient, effective way to help people?

You've already been manipulated. Every day, governments, corporations, and even your closest friends use manipulation to shape your choices. Think about Cass Sunstein's concept of "choice architecture" from his book Nudge. Sunstein and co-author Richard Thaler argue that by designing environments in which people make decisions, we can "nudge" them toward better choices without limiting their freedom. But let's call this what it really is: subtle manipulation. It could be as simple as arranging a cafeteria to place healthy food options at eye level or designing tax forms to push people toward making socially responsible decisions. In the end, it's all about control.

Are we really going to label this kind of manipulation unethical just because it shifts behavior without explicit consent? Of course not. When you nudge someone into eating better or contributing to their 401(k), you're manipulating their behavior, but for their own good. Does the manipulation become unethical just because it wasn't overt? Isn't the outcome, healthier individuals, more secure futures, worth it?

This brings us to the uncomfortable truth: manipulation isn't unethical if it benefits the manipulated. In fact, manipulation can be the most ethical choice when done for the right reasons. Intent matters more than technique. Sometimes, people need to be pushed, even manipulated, into making decisions they might resist but that ultimately serve their best interests. If manipulation leads to better outcomes for the individual, the ethical dilemma disappears.

Intent: The True Divider

So if manipulation isn't inherently bad, what makes it cross the line into unethical territory? The answer lies in intent. When manipulation serves solely the manipulator at the expense of the person being influenced, it becomes problematic. But if the manipulation aligns with the best interests of both parties, does the method really matter?

Think about a doctor guiding a patient toward a life-saving treatment. The doctor might strategically withhold certain overwhelming details to prevent decision paralysis. Is this manipulation? Absolutely. But it's also ethical, because the doctor's goal is to save the patient's life. Sometimes, overloading someone with choices or information leads to worse outcomes. The ethical manipulator knows when to step in and simplify the path.

In Paul Bloom's Just Babies: The Origins of Good and Evil, Bloom explores how humans are hardwired for empathy, fairness, and cooperation from birth. Our moral compass is flexible and context-dependent. This means that manipulating someone for their own benefit can fall within our natural ethical framework. If our actions help someone without causing harm, is it truly wrong to use covert influence to guide them?

Let's consider choice architects, those who structure decisions in ways that influence behavior for societal good. Governments use this in public health campaigns, like arranging organ donation forms to assume consent unless opted out, drastically increasing the number of organ donors. Was that manipulation? Yes. But it saved lives, and most people would agree that this is ethical. Does the end justify the means? In these cases, absolutely.

Two Faces of Influence

Now, let's examine how intent changes the ethical landscape of persuasion and manipulation through two case studies: Volkswagen's emissions scandal and Dove's "Real Beauty" campaign.

- Volkswagen knowingly manipulated public perception by falsifying emissions data to make their cars appear more environmentally friendly. This was manipulation in the worst sense, deception that harmed consumers and the environment for the company's profit. Volkswagen used influence not to benefit society or its customers, but to cover up unethical practices and boost sales. This is where manipulation becomes toxic, when the end serves only the manipulator, and the means involve deceit.

- Dove, on the other hand, used a deeply emotional campaign to shift societal norms around beauty standards. The "Real Beauty" campaign manipulated our perception of beauty in a positive direction, challenging unrealistic expectations and promoting body positivity. Dove tapped into our emotions and social constructs, yes, but the end goal was aligned with a broader social good, challenging the toxic ideals that dominate advertising and culture.

Both Volkswagen and Dove were manipulative, but only one crossed the ethical line. Intent was the differentiating factor. Dove used its influence to spark a positive cultural shift, while Volkswagen exploited its audience for profit. One served a higher purpose, the other was purely self-serving.

When Manipulation Is Necessary

Persuasion and manipulation aren't binary opposites, they exist on a spectrum of influence. Persuasion is gentle, overt, and often socially sanctioned, while manipulation is covert, aggressive, and seen as taboo. But here's the thing: sometimes, manipulation is necessary to break through the barriers of resistance, fear, and bias that prevent people from making decisions that are in their own best interest.

As a persuader, there will be moments where you'll need to step beyond the polite tactics of persuasion and into the realm of manipulation. It's one thing to control someone for your own selfish ends. It's another to help them break free from the mental traps that hold them back. If manipulation brings them to a better place, does it matter how you got there?

If your manipulation leads to a better outcome for the person you're influencing, if it helps them overcome fear, inertia, or ignorance, then manipulation becomes ethical persuasion.

Redefining the Moral Landscape of Influence

The truth is, manipulation and persuasion are tools, and like all tools, they can be used for good or for ill. What determines their ethical weight is not the method itself, but the intent behind it and the impact it has on the person being influenced. Persuasion can be just as coercive as manipulation if it's done with selfish intent, and manipulation can be just as ethical as persuasion if it leads to better outcomes for those involved.

We need to redefine manipulation, not as a dirty word, but as a powerful tool of influence that, when wielded responsibly, can lead to profound positive change. The next time you find yourself on the cusp of using influence techniques, ask yourself why you're doing it. If your intentions are pure and your actions result in a positive outcome, then perhaps manipulation isn't something to avoid, but rather, something to embrace.

Guidelines for Responsible Influence

Influence is power. And as with all power, it can be wielded responsibly or irresponsibly, ethically or manipulatively. But here's the provocative truth: responsible influence doesn't always fit neatly into traditional ethical boxes. The very notion of ethical persuasion is fraught with ambiguity, moral gray zones, and uncomfortable truths about how people's minds work. The reality is, when you learn to wield influence effectively, you're dancing in a space where persuasion and manipulation often blur.

So, what does it mean to influence responsibly? Is it about being transparent and honest at all times? Or is it about guiding people toward better decisions, even if that means strategically withholding information, nudging them in certain directions, or, yes, manipulating their emotions? What if persuasion done in the service of a higher purpose is not only ethical but necessary?

In this section, we'll dive into five actionable guidelines that will give you a roadmap for wielding your power responsibly, without sacrificing its effectiveness. But don't expect the typical narrative about ethics. We're going to challenge everything you think you know about what it means to be ethical, provocative, and ultimately effective.

The Power of Mutual Benefit

Ethical persuasion starts with alignment, making sure that what you're persuading someone to do serves not only your interests but theirs as well. I'm not suggesting that you coerce someone into something that solely benefits you. On the contrary, I want you to understand what they truly need, even if they can't see it yet, and aligning that with your goals.

But here's where things get interesting: What if manipulation is simply about helping people make decisions that benefit them, even if they don't realize it yet?

Consider Patagonia, a brand that has mastered the art of ethical persuasion. Patagonia's marketing isn't designed to manipulate customers into buying more; in fact, they've taken the counterintuitive approach of persuading customers to buy less. Their campaigns promote sustainability and responsible consumption, encouraging customers to purchase higher-quality items that last longer, reducing overall consumption. On the surface, this seems like the antithesis of traditional marketing, but it's a brilliant alignment of interests. Patagonia benefits because it attracts loyal, socially conscious customers who are willing to pay a premium. The customers benefit because they're making more thoughtful, sustainable choices.

What Patagonia is doing, at its core, is still manipulation. They're crafting a narrative around sustainability and responsible consumption that guides customers toward a specific behavior. But because that behavior benefits both the company and the consumer, does it matter if manipulation is at play? This is alignment. They're nudging people toward a better outcome. This is manipulation as a force for good.

Always ask yourself, how does this benefit both parties? When you can align your interests with the needs or desires of the person you're influencing, manipulation becomes irrelevant. You're guiding them toward a choice that serves them.

When Less is More

We're often told that complete transparency is the cornerstone of ethical behavior. But in reality, full transparency can sometimes overwhelm people, confuse them, or even paralyze them with too many choices. In such cases, the ethical thing to do might be to withhold certain information, not to deceive, but to simplify.

Does this sound manipulative? Maybe. But strategic withholding is sometimes about providing clarity, not deception. When done correctly, it leads people to make decisions they feel confident in, without drowning them in details they can't process.

Imagine a doctor recommending a treatment plan to a patient. The doctor doesn't need to explain every single medical detail, every possible side effect, and every alternative treatment in exhaustive detail. Doing so would likely overwhelm the patient, leaving them more anxious and less able to make a decision. Instead, the doctor frames the information in a way that guides the patient toward the best possible decision for their health.

This is strategic communication. The doctor is withholding complex details, not to manipulate the patient, but to ensure they make a decision they can feel good about.

Complete transparency can be paralyzing. Behavioral economics shows us that too many choices or too much information can lead to decision fatigue, making people more likely to avoid making any decision at all. Sometimes, manipulation is clarity. By framing choices, simplifying information, and selectively withholding irrelevant or overwhelming details, you help people make better decisions without burdening them with unnecessary complexity.

Be strategic about what you reveal. Don't dump information. Feed people the right information, at the right time, to guide them toward the best decision for themselves.

Considering the Consequences

Once you understand how to influence people, once you can sway minds with ease, you have a responsibility to consider the long-term effects of your influence. This means thinking beyond the immediate gain and asking: What impact will this decision have on the person's life, their well-being, and the broader society?

The darker side of influence is that not all manipulation is created equal. Some forms of influence may achieve short-term goals but leave long-term damage. Ethical persuasion means thinking critically about the consequences of your actions.

Look at Facebook's algorithm, which has been designed to keep users engaged by amplifying content that stirs emotions, particularly fear, anger, and outrage. By manipulating user behavior to keep them scrolling, Facebook profits from increased engagement. But what's the long-term consequence of this kind of influence? Society becomes more polarized, divisive content dominates our feeds, and users are left more anxious, angry, and isolated.

Facebook's influence wasn't aligned with the well-being of its users, it was designed to maximize profit at any cost. This is influence without ethical consideration, and it's a cautionary tale for anyone wielding the power of persuasion.

Always ask yourself, "Who benefits from this?" If your influence is benefiting you at the expense of the person you're persuading, you're walking an unethical line. But if both parties gain something meaningful, you're likely operating on ethical ground.

Consent and Free Will

In the world of persuasion, free will is a tricky concept. On the one hand, ethical influence means respecting people's autonomy and ensuring they have the freedom to make their own choices. On the other hand, we know that subtle influence is inevitable. Every time you use framing, nudging, or emotional appeals, you're steering someone's decision-making.

The real question is: Does subtle influence violate free will?

Cambridge Analytica famously used data manipulation to influence voters during the 2016 U.S. presidential election and the Brexit campaign. Through targeted psychological profiling, they created highly specific messages designed to nudge voters in particular directions, often without those voters being aware they were being influenced. This manipulation was not aligned with the public's best interest; it was designed purely for political gain.

Here, informed consent was stripped away. Voters thought they were making independent choices, but their behavior had been covertly shaped by data-driven tactics. This is manipulation at its worst, exploiting the illusion of choice without regard for the well-being of the people being influenced.

Informed consent in persuasion isn't always black and white. Sometimes, people think they're acting of their own free will, but they're being subtly nudged by invisible forces, advertisements, social media algorithms, or emotional appeals. But here's the controversial twist: As long as you don't violate their autonomy outright, this can still be ethical persuasion. People are never completely free from influence, but as long as they can make a choice that feels aligned with their values, your influence isn't unethical.

Respect autonomy without obsessing over full transparency. Influence is inevitable, what matters is that the person being influenced still feels in control of their choice. As long as their autonomy isn't stripped away, subtle influence can still be ethical.

When the Ends Justify the Means

Here's where ethical persuasion requires the most nuanced thinking: What if the manipulation of a few leads to a better outcome for the many? This is the realm of utilitarian ethics, the idea that the most ethical choice is the one that creates the greatest good for the greatest number of people.

Sometimes, the manipulation of an individual or group, even if it feels coercive, can lead to societal benefits that far outweigh the costs.

Governments around the world use fear appeals and social pressure in public health campaigns to push for positive societal outcomes. Take anti-smoking campaigns, for example. These campaigns often use graphic images of diseased lungs or dying smokers to elicit a strong emotional response, manipulating people's fear of death and illness to drive them toward quitting.

On the surface, this might seem unethical. After all, it's exploiting fear. But the end result, a reduction in smoking rates, improved public health, and fewer deaths, is clearly beneficial. Here, the greater good justifies the manipulative tactics used. The same goes for campaigns to increase vaccine uptake or reduce drunk driving. Sometimes, you have to tap into primal emotions, fear, shame, guilt, to achieve societal benefits.

The greater good can justify certain manipulative tactics. If you're manipulating someone for a positive outcome that benefits society, the ends can justify the means. Manipulating emotions, playing on fear, or using social pressure to nudge people toward healthier behaviors isn't always comfortable, but it can be the most ethical choice in the long run.

When weighing your influence tactics, always ask, "What's the bigger picture?" If your manipulation serves a societal good or helps someone achieve a better outcome, even if it requires using uncomfortable methods, it may be the most ethical choice.

The Ethical Gray Zone

Influence is a double-edged sword. It can be wielded responsibly to create mutual benefit, or it can be used selfishly, leaving harm in its wake. But if you take anything away from this ethical roadmap, it's that the line between persuasion and manipulation isn't as clear-cut as we've been led to believe.

Sometimes, manipulation is the most ethical choice. Sometimes, subtle influence that steers someone toward a decision they wouldn't otherwise make is the most effective way to help them, and, by extension, society. The key is to always align interests, understand the consequences of your actions, and keep the greater good in mind.

CHAPTER 11

The Ultimate Weapon

Influence is seductive. The ability to control is intoxicating. And once you see the mechanisms of influence at work, you can never unsee them.

Total Control

You've arrived at the edge of something extraordinary, something most people will never experience or even understand. You now hold the power to control minds, shape realities, and change destinies. But before you bask in the glow of this newfound authority, pause for a moment.

Feel the weight of what that truly means.

You've spent this journey learning to decode human desire, manipulate neural pathways, and wield language like a weapon. At each step, you've sharpened your tools, The Neural Rewiring, The Desire Decoder, The Cognitive Exploit, and more. But these were just pieces of a larger puzzle. What lies before you now is the ability to pull every string, to move people's hearts, minds, and actions as if they were mere characters in a story you've written.

This is the ultimate power. And like all true power, it comes with a cost.

The question is not can you persuade someone, but should you? Will you use these techniques to empower others, to help them realize their fullest potential? Or will you succumb to the darker allure of manipulation, bending others to your will simply because you can?

Make no mistake, persuasion has become a weapon. A weapon that can either create or destroy. Influence is seductive. The ability to control is intoxicating. And once you see the mechanisms of influence at work, you can never unsee them. Every conversation, every decision, every human interaction is now an opportunity for control.

But here's the catch, while you control the strings, you can never forget that those strings are tethered to something fragile: human beings. Emotions, desires, fears, these are not abstract concepts; they are the pulse of real lives. With one word, one action, you can alter the course of someone's future. That is the profound power now resting in your hands.

Imagine for a moment that you walk into a room. Every single person there is unaware of the invisible strings you hold, strings that bind their decisions, their emotions, even their self-perception. You see every angle, every vulnerability, every desire waiting to be manipulated. You've become the unseen puppet master. But what kind of puppet master will you choose to be?

That's where the real tension lies. Will you harness this knowledge for good, or will you allow it to corrupt your intentions? The line between persuasion and manipulation is razor-thin, so we'll face that moral tightrope head-on.

This chapter will not coddle you. It will not offer comforting answers. Instead, it will challenge you to become something greater: a true master of persuasion, who not only pulls the strings but understands the delicate responsibility of doing so.

The Seven Pillars of Influence

As you stand on the precipice of becoming a true Puppet Master, it's time to revisit the arsenal at your disposal. But don't make the mistake of seeing these techniques as separate tricks to be pulled out one at a time. They are not. These seven pillars of influence, Neural Rewiring, Desire Decoder, Bond Forger, Cognitive Exploit, Narrative Neuralyzer, Linguistic Lockpick, and Ethical Roadmap, are not standalone. They are components of a single, intricate machine of persuasion. When these elements function in harmony, they transform you from a simple persuader into a master of influence.

I are talking about orchestrating a symphony, where every note, every pause, every crescendo is engineered to sway the human mind, seamlessly and irresistibly.

Neural Rewiring: The Brain in Your Hands

Neural Rewiring is the foundation that primes you to take full control over the brains of others. By mastering your mind first, restructuring habits, thoughts, and reactions, you place yourself in the ultimate position of strength. But here's the true beauty: when you rewire your own neural circuits, you also learn the architecture of influence.

Why does this matter? Because once you understand the wiring of your own brain, you see the pathways that guide others' thoughts, too. When you use Neural Rewiring in conjunction with other pillars, like The Cognitive Exploit or Narrative Neuralyzer, you are reaching into the very core of how someone processes the world. That's where true mastery begins: from within. You go from shifting perceptions to rewiring reality.

Desire Decoder: The Key to Every Human Heart

Every human being walks through life with a core set of desires, unspoken, primal, and often invisible even to themselves. The Desire Decoder allows you to map those hidden needs, to understand what people want and why they want it.

But here's the real power: The Desire Decoder works best when used in sync with the Bond Forger and Linguistic Lockpick. It's not enough to know what someone craves. You have to connect with them, to form an unshakable emotional bond while speaking in language that makes their desire feel both urgent and attainable. This is where so many would-be persuaders fail. They identify the desire but fail to forge the bond, fail to craft the language, and then wonder why they fall short.

By combining these elements, you don't just see desires, you become the embodiment of their fulfillment. You aren't a salesperson, a leader, or even a friend anymore. You become the solution to the deepest, most instinctual cravings of your audience. That's not persuasion, that's power.

Bond Forger: Commanding Loyalty Through Connection

The Bond Forger is more than a simple emotional link. It's a tool for creating irrevocable loyalty. Most people think influence is about a one-time decision, getting someone to say "yes" or buy in. But that's small thinking. The real game is in forging bonds so strong that people continue to follow you, trust you, and act in your favor long after the initial interaction has ended.

By using The Bond Forger in harmony with The Desire Decoder, you transcend transactional influence. You become indispensable in someone's life. They need you.

In the context of persuasion, this bond doesn't only apply to personal relationships, it applies to businesses, movements, ideologies. You are creating tribes, cults of loyalty that are bound by shared desires and emotional resonance. The next time you think about convincing someone, ask yourself: Am I building a moment, or am I forging a lasting allegiance?

Cognitive Exploit: The Art of Hacking Human Bias

The Cognitive Exploit is where you stop playing by the rules of logical argument and start manipulating the shortcuts of the human brain. Human cognition is lazy. It's built to take shortcuts, rely on biases, and make quick decisions with minimal effort. And this is where your advantage lies.

In earlier chapters, you learned how to exploit cognitive biases like framing, anchoring, and social proof to bypass logic and tap into automatic decision-making processes. But when combined with Neural Rewiring and Linguistic Lockpick, the Cognitive Exploit becomes a scalpel, slicing directly into the subconscious. You don't just persuade someone to buy your product, you make them feel as if not choosing it was never even an option.

This is where your ability to control the narrative comes into play. You frame the context, you set the anchors, you design the illusion of choice. The Cognitive Exploit creates a reality in which the person feels they have no other logical or emotional alternative but to follow your lead. They believe they've made their own choice, but in truth, you've led them by the hand the entire way.

The Villain Construct: Turning Fear Into Action

Your ultimate weapon isn't your product, your pitch, or even your story, it's your villain. The greatest weapon you'll ever wield is the enemy you create. Without a villain, your narrative lacks urgency. Without urgency, your audience doesn't act. The villain is the ignition for transformation.

Think about it: What makes a movement rise? What makes a campaign viral? It's not the solution, it's the problem. The villain gives your audience something to rally against, something to hate, something to destroy. And in the process, it gives them something to fight for.

But the villain must be crafted with surgical precision. If it's too abstract, it fails to engage. If it's too monstrous, it paralyzes. The villain must be tangible, relatable, and defeatable. A well-constructed villain creates tension, and tension forces action. No tension, no transformation.

Narrative Neuralyzer: Shaping Reality Through Story

We've said it before, but it bears repeating: humans are wired for story. The Narrative Neuralyzer takes advantage of this evolutionary quirk, allowing you to create narratives that not only persuade but reshape reality in the mind of your audience. But here's the key: when you weave a story that aligns with the desires uncovered by The Desire Decoder and reinforces the emotional bonds from The Bond Forger, you're not telling a story. You're building a belief system.

People don't just follow stories because they're entertaining. They follow them because stories create order from chaos, meaning from confusion. In this chaotic, fragmented world, if you provide a narrative that aligns with your audience's desires, that resolves their fears and gives them a hero to root for (which, by the way, is often themselves), you have them hooked. They aren't just listening, they're living your narrative.

When this is executed alongside The Cognitive Exploit, the story becomes irresistible. They stop critically evaluating your message and get emotionally transported into the reality you've designed. This is where lasting influence occurs, because once you implant a narrative in someone's mind, it becomes their truth.

Weapons of Mass Influence

The Linguistic Lockpick is how you bypass someone's defenses with nothing more than words. By understanding how specific linguistic patterns trigger emotional and cognitive responses, you don't need force, you can infiltrate the mind with subtlety, unlocking thoughts and beliefs that the person may not even realize they hold.

But words alone are only part of the equation. When you align the Linguistic Lockpick with The Cognitive Exploit, you're priming the brain. Certain phrases, metaphors, and framing tactics trigger automatic responses in the brain. You go from crafting an argument to planting a seed, a suggestion that grows inside the mind until it feels like their own thought.

It's subtle, but this is where true mastery lies. Use the right language, wrapped in the right narrative, supported by the right cognitive biases, and you don't just persuade, you control the conversation before it even begins.

The Power and the Danger

The Ethical Roadmap is your guide to navigating the razor-thin line between influence and manipulation. Make no mistake: every technique in your arsenal can be used to uplift or exploit, to guide or manipulate. The difference is how you choose to wield that power.

But here's the kicker: the most effective persuaders know how to use these techniques ethically, but with a ruthlessness that still drives results. The Ethical Roadmap doesn't soften your influence; it sharpens it by keeping you focused on long-term trust and loyalty rather than short-term gains.

In this interconnected system, the Ethical Roadmap is a strategic tool. When people trust that you will use your influence with integrity, they will follow you further, stay with you longer, and ultimately give you more control. That's the paradox of ethics in influence: by showing restraint, you gain more power than you ever would through exploitation.

The Art of Layered Persuasion

Welcome to the true art of persuasion, the point where individual techniques converge and create an unstoppable force. Up until now, you've learned how to use each of the seven pillars, Neural Rewiring, Desire Decoder, Bond Forger, Cognitive Exploit, Narrative Neuralyzer, Linguistic Lockpick, and Ethical Roadmap, as separate tools of influence. But now, we're moving into a realm where true mastery begins: Layered Persuasion. This is where you transcend ordinary influence, combining these techniques in seamless synergy to create The Persuasion Stack™, a force so powerful that it reshapes the reality of anyone in its wake.

Layered Persuasion controls the entire board. When you stack and compound these frameworks, they don't just add to each other, they multiply in impact, creating a cascade of influence that bypasses resistance and makes persuasion inevitable.

Let see how this works.

Tapping Into Desires: Neural Rewiring + Desire Decoder

It begins in the mind. Your mind first, then theirs. The foundation of any persuasive interaction starts with Neural Rewiring. You cannot influence others if you haven't mastered the wiring of your own brain. Neural Rewiring trains you to control your thoughts, emotions, and reactions. Once you have command over your own mind, you can start to play with the minds of others.

Here's where the first layer comes into play: The Desire Decoder. Here, you're tapping into their deepest, often unspoken desires. Desire is the engine of all human behavior. The craving for status, security, love, or recognition, all of these primal urges drive decision-making.

Picture this: You're leading a team, and you understand that status is a key driver for many of them. Using Neural Rewiring, you've trained yourself to recognize these signals. But instead of addressing the desire for status head-on, you overlay it with The Desire Decoder. You tap into their need for recognition, and you position the task at hand as a path to higher status. You're appealing to logic or reason and locked into a primal urge that they can't resist.

This is Layered Persuasion in action. Neural Rewiring gives you the control, and The Desire Decoder gives you the key to their hidden motivations.

Forging Emotional Bonds: Bond Forger + Narrative Neuralyzer

But here's the real brilliance: Desire alone isn't enough. You can identify what drives people, but to truly move them, you need to create a bond so strong that they feel connected to you, to the mission, to the outcome on an emotional level. This is where The Bond Forger comes into play.

Incorporating the Bond Forger turns the desire for status into an emotional connection. Now, you're promising status and promising a shared journey, a tribal allegiance, a connection to something bigger than themselves. But the real power happens when you add The Narrative Neuralyzer into the mix.

Humans live and die by stories. To forge an emotional bond that transcends mere transactional influence, you need to place your audience within an epic narrative. This is Layered Persuasion at its peak, stacking The Bond Forger with The Narrative Neuralyzer to create emotional buy-in. Now, they aren't just striving for status, they are part of a legendary story where their status plays a central role in the plot.

Let's revisit the leadership scenario: You've identified your team's desire for status. You've connected with them emotionally by positioning yourself as their guide (Bond Forger). Now, you layer in the Narrative Neuralyzer. You frame their status as part of an ongoing narrative: "Hitting metrics is about becoming a legend in this company. Five years from now, people will look back at this moment as the turning point, and you'll be the ones to say you made it happen."

In this single frame, you've combined Desire, Bond, and Narrative. You go from managing a team to leading a movement.

Hacking Cognitive Shortcuts: Cognitive Exploit + Linguistic Lockpick

By now, they are emotionally invested, driven by their desires, connected through narrative. But the most potent part of the stack is yet to come. This is where the magic happens, where you hack the brain directly. Enter The Cognitive Exploit.

As we've discussed, the human brain loves shortcuts. It's wired for speed, efficiency, and habit. The key to Layered Persuasion is exploiting these cognitive biases while people are already immersed in the narrative you've constructed. You're not convincing them through facts or logic anymore. You're guiding their decisions using the biases they don't even realize they have.

Let's say you want your team to take a risk, one that logically feels uncomfortable. This is where The Cognitive Exploit comes in. You frame the decision using a loss aversion bias: "If we don't act now, we risk losing the market edge we've spent years building." By emphasizing potential loss, you bypass their logical hesitations and activate an emotional trigger that makes taking the risk seem like the safest choice.

But this won't work unless you can present the message in a way that slips past their mental defenses. This is where the Linguistic Lockpick enters the stack. Language is everything. How you frame the message determines how it will land. If you use hard, confrontational language, you risk raising alarms. Instead, you use soft, inclusive language: "Together, we can avoid the losses that others will face. We've already won, but it's time to lock in that victory." The words invite safety, collaboration, and action, all while triggering their cognitive biases.

This layered combination of Cognitive Exploit and Linguistic Lockpick works because it takes advantage of subconscious processing. You're not asking them to make a decision, they feel like they've already made it, and that it's the only logical conclusion.

Sealing It with Integrity: The Ethical Roadmap

Finally, the most critical layer: The Ethical Roadmap. Without this, all of your layered techniques become nothing more than manipulation. True persuasion, the kind that fosters loyalty and long-term influence, is built on trust. The Ethical Roadmap ensures that your persuasive power is used for mutual benefit, not exploitation.

When you align your influence with ethical integrity, you gain a superpower: sustainable trust. People will follow you not because they have to, but because they want to. They will feel safer, more aligned, and more inspired because they know your influence comes from a place of integrity.

Think of the Ethical Roadmap as a a strategic advantage. By using it, you're ensuring that the power you build through the other layers doesn't fade. People don't just feel persuaded in the moment, they remain loyal to you, to your cause, because they trust in the integrity of your persuasion.

The Persuasion Stack™

The secret is simple: combine them in layers, stack them one on top of the other, so that the influence becomes multi-dimensional and inescapable.

- Neural Rewiring primes you to take control of your own mind and see the mental pathways of others.
- The Desire Decoder gives you the key to unlocking their primal motivations.
- The Bond Forger ties those desires to an emotional connection that binds them to you.
- The Narrative Neuralyzer immerses them in a story that frames their desires and bonds as part of a larger journey.
- The Cognitive Exploit hacks their decision-making processes, guiding them subconsciously to the conclusion you've designed.
- The Linguistic Lockpick unlocks their defenses, allowing your message to slip into their minds unnoticed.
- And The Ethical Roadmap ensures that the trust you build is enduring, reinforcing loyalty and long-term influence.

This is The Persuasion Stack™, a layered, synergistic approach to influence that multiplies the power of each technique. Every move, every word, every thought is engineered for maximum impact.

In the next section, we will see how this stack comes alive in the real world, taking you from a student of influence to a master who can wield it effortlessly in all walks of life. Because once you master Layered Persuasion, there are no limits. You are the Puppet Master.

From the Boardroom to the Bedroom

Here is where we move beyond theory. We're diving into scenarios where The Persuasion Stack™ proves itself to be as adaptable as it is powerful. And here's the kicker: true mastery of influence isn't reserved for the boardroom. It permeates every facet of life, from business deals to romantic entanglements, from leading a team to resolving personal conflicts. This goes beyond persuasion confined to the workplace, it's Persuasion Anywhere.

Persuasion at Home

Let's start in a place you probably weren't expecting: your own home. Imagine you've had a simmering conflict with your partner for weeks, over something seemingly trivial, like how often you visit their family. Tensions are mounting, words are exchanged, and suddenly, what began as a small issue threatens the harmony of your entire relationship. Most people would flounder here, pushing their agenda until the situation explodes or dissolves into a grudging compromise. But you? You've got the Persuasion Stack™ at your disposal. You're playing on a whole different level.

The problem isn't the visits, it's the emotional undercurrent, the unspoken desire for connection and validation. And you know it. So you tap into the Desire Decoder. You recognize that the real issue is your partner's need to feel prioritized, to know that their family is important to you. But rather than tackling this head-on with a logical explanation or a forced concession, you use The Bond Forger. You reframe the conversation as an opportunity to strengthen your relationship, focusing not on the visits themselves but on the deeper connection you share.

Then, you layer in The Narrative Neuralyzer. You tell a story, perhaps recalling the early days of your relationship, when time spent together with family felt effortless and joyful. You tap into the nostalgia, the shared experiences, and you craft a narrative that repositions the conflict as a step in your mutual growth, not a point of contention. This stops being the battle about where you spend your weekends and transforms into a story about building the life you both envisioned.

Finally, you deploy The Linguistic Lockpick. You use soft, empathetic language, avoiding any hint of blame or defensiveness. "I love seeing how happy your family makes you, and I want to be part of that joy," you say, subtly priming the conversation for resolution. You've framed your participation as a positive choice, not an obligation. And just like that, you've defused the conflict, not by brute force but by deftly weaving together emotional, psychological, and cognitive layers of influence.

This is mastery. You didn't win an argument; you reinforced a bond. The conflict didn't just dissolve, it became an opportunity for growth.

Turning Adversaries into Allies

Now, let's shift to a more familiar battleground, the boardroom. You're sitting across from a rival in a high-stakes negotiation. On the surface, it's about numbers, contracts, and bottom lines. But you know better. This is about power, status, and long-term positioning. Winning the deal is no longer primary. Your main goal is to this this adversary into an ally. Most negotiators would charge in, leveraging data and statistics, trying to out-argue their opponent. But you're playing a much deeper game.

First, you activate The Cognitive Exploit. You know that people make decisions based on biases, not facts. So, you frame the terms of the deal not as a compromise but as a mutual gain. You exploit the principle of loss aversion: "We both have too much to lose if we let this slip away." By framing the negotiation in terms of potential losses, you've instantly shifted the emotional dynamic, subtly steering them toward seeing agreement as the safest choice.

But it doesn't stop there. You then use The Desire Decoder. What's their true motivation? They want to come out of this looking powerful, respected, in control. You layer in The Bond Forger, creating an emotional connection that frames the deal as a partnership. Instead of two rivals duking it out, you position yourselves as collaborators. "Today's deal is the foundation for what we can build together tomorrow," you say, offering them something they crave far more than victory, legacy.

Then, you bring in the Narrative Neuralyzer. You craft a vision of the future, one where both companies thrive because of this moment, this decision. You paint a picture of them not as an adversary to be defeated, but as a key player in a larger, epic story of mutual success. They aren't just agreeing to the deal anymore, they're investing in a narrative that makes them look like the hero.

And finally, you seal the deal with The Linguistic Lockpick. You use inclusive, empowering language: "We are the future of this industry. Together, we can rewrite the rules." The narratives goes from conceding to shared power. In their mind, they aren't giving in, they're stepping up.

By the end of the negotiation, the numbers almost don't matter. You've turned the game upside down. What started as a high-stakes confrontation is now the beginning of a long-term alliance, because you didn't just close a deal, you rewired their perception of you, of the deal, and of the future.

Mastery in Personal Growth

The ultimate battlefield is the one inside your own mind. Self-persuasion is the cornerstone of personal growth, and when you can apply the Persuasion Stack™ to yourself, you unlock limitless potential.

Let's take a personal scenario: overcoming a deeply ingrained fear of public speaking. Most people would attack this problem with surface-level tactics, memorizing scripts, practicing gestures. But you? You understand that fear is a cognitive trap, and to escape it, you need to layer multiple techniques.

First, you start with Neural Rewiring. You train your brain to associate public speaking with positive outcomes, not fear. Every time you imagine stepping on stage, you replace the negative imagery with something powerful, success, applause, the satisfaction of connecting with your audience. You're rewiring your neural pathways, replacing fear with confidence.

Then, you use The Desire Decoder on yourself. What do you truly want? Getting through the speech if one thing, but what about the deeper desire for recognition, influence, and mastery? Once you decode that, the fear of speaking becomes irrelevant. You fulfill that core desire to lead, to inspire.

Next, you apply The Bond Forger, but this time, you're not focusing on connecting with an audience. You now forge a bond with your future self. You create an emotional connection with the person you want to become: a confident, powerful speaker. This is emotional engagement. You fall in love with the idea of the future you, and that love drives you forward.

You then use The Cognitive Exploit on your own mind, hacking the biases that trigger anxiety. Instead of focusing on what could go wrong, you frame every speaking opportunity as a win or learn scenario. There is no failure, only growth. By shifting the framing, you bypass the fear response and trigger excitement instead.

Finally, you use The Linguistic Lockpick in your self-talk. You stop telling yourself "I'm afraid of public speaking" and start saying, "I am someone who commands the room." The words you use, even in your own mind, shape your reality. You've locked into a new identity, using language to frame your experience.

The Persuasion Anywhere Method

Next time you're resolving personal conflict, closing a business deal, or transforming your own mind, The Persuasion Stack™ will prove itself to be versatile, adaptable, and relentless in its effectiveness. This is The Persuasion Anywhere method, an approach that transcends context. It works in the boardroom, in the bedroom, in your personal growth journey, and even in casual, everyday interactions.

Why? Because human behavior follows the same patterns, regardless of the setting. People are driven by desires, stories, biases, and emotional connections. When you master the art of Layered Persuasion through The Persuasion Stack™, you're not longer limited by the specifics of the situation and are now operating on a deeper level, one where influence is seamless, invisible, and omnipresent.

From the moment you walk into a room, from the words you choose to the stories you tell, you are sculpting reality. The question is no longer can you persuade someone, it's how deeply you want to influence them. This is your power. This is your edge. And with The Persuasion Stack™, the boundaries of where and when you can use it cease to exist.

Because now, persuasion is your reality.

Weaponized Empathy

You've spent this journey learning how to decode desires, forge bonds, and tap into the emotional core of human beings. You've unlocked the ability to see what others cannot, an almost superhuman talent to understand what makes someone tick, to recognize their deepest fears, their hidden motivations, their unspoken needs. This is empathy at its finest, its most powerful. But here's the shadow lurking behind that power: empathy allows you to control others.

This is Weaponized Empathy, the ability to take that understanding of human emotions and use it, not to uplift or guide, but to exploit. When you understand someone's emotional landscape better than they do, you hold the strings to their mind, and you can pull those strings to your advantage. The line between guiding and manipulating blurs, and here's the truth you must confront: persuasion and manipulation are separated by a razor-thin edge, and sometimes, the only difference is your intent.

The Puppet Master's Paradox™

This is the tension that defines your journey from student to master. You have learned techniques that can change minds, shift behaviors, and even transform lives, but every time you use them, you must ask yourself: Why?

Because every act of influence carries with it a moral burden. Are you using your understanding of human desires to help others achieve their own goals? Or are you twisting those desires to serve yourself at their expense? This is the paradox that every true Puppet Master must grapple with. Persuasion is never neutral, it either lifts people up or subtly pushes them toward your own ends.

The Bond Forger can create deep, emotional connections that foster trust and loyalty, but it can also be used to make someone dependent on you, manipulating their need for connection as a tool to control them. The Narrative Neuralyzer can inspire people by placing them at the center of a heroic story, or it can imprison them in a narrative where they are unwitting pawns in your grand scheme. The Desire Decoder allows you to give people what they truly want, but it can just as easily be used to exploit their weaknesses, bending their needs to your advantage.

The danger lies in how easily persuasion slides into manipulation, and the terrifying part? You can justify it to yourself every step of the way. "I'm just helping them," you might say. "I know what's best for them." But the moment you strip someone of their agency, their ability to make a fully informed choice, you've crossed a line. You've weaponized empathy for your own gain.

How Far Will You Go?

The more skilled you become at persuasion, the easier it is to manipulate without even realizing it. You've mastered the ability to make people feel understood, to make them trust you, to make them follow you. But can you trust yourself? Can you be certain that you'll always use these powers responsibly, or will there be moments when the temptation to take the shortcut, to secure the win, to dominate the situation, becomes too great to resist?

Ask yourself: when does persuasion become coercion? When does empathy stop being a bridge for connection and start becoming a trap? These are the ethical dilemmas that come with mastery. The Ethical Roadmap provides a guide, a framework to ensure that your persuasion remains anchored in integrity. But the truth is, the temptation to use Weaponized Empathy will always be there, lurking in the background.

Empathy is often celebrated as the highest form of emotional intelligence. But when you can tap into someone's emotions and mold them to your will, empathy becomes dangerous. You see every vulnerability, every weakness, every blind spot, and the more you understand someone, the easier it becomes to manipulate them without them ever realizing it. You make them feel seen, but only in the way that serves your purpose. That's the dark side of empathy, and it's a slippery slope that every master persuader must confront.

When Self-Justification Takes Over

The real danger doesn't come from consciously choosing to manipulate, it comes from the gradual, almost invisible slide into rationalization. You'll tell yourself, "It's for their own good," or "They'll thank me later," but deep down, you know you've crossed a line. Once you've started justifying your actions, you stop guiding and start controlling. You're no longer offering influence and, instead, taking away choice. That's what Weaponized Empathy does: it creates an illusion of mutual benefit while secretly stacking the deck in your favor.

Consider this scenario: You're leading a team at work, and you've used The Bond Forger to create strong emotional ties. They trust you implicitly. They follow your lead without question. Now, you could use that bond to encourage them to grow, to challenge themselves, and to achieve their full potential. Or, you could use that bond to manipulate their loyalty, to keep them working harder for you, making sacrifices they wouldn't otherwise make, all while convincing them it's in their best interest. The difference? In one version, they are empowered. In the other, they are exploited.

The terrifying part of mastering persuasion is realizing how easy it is to slip into exploitation without even realizing it. What were the thousand tiny justifications that lead you down that path? The better you get at reading people, the easier it becomes to rationalize those choices. You'll tell yourself it's for their benefit, that you know better, that the ends justify the means. But deep down, you'll know the truth.

Can You Trust Yourself?

The temptation will always be there to use your abilities to manipulate rather than persuade, to control rather than guide. The Puppet Master holds the strings, but what kind of puppet master will you be? Will you use these tools to elevate others, to help them achieve their own desires, or will you fall prey to the seductive allure of control? Every time you deploy empathy as a tool of influence, you must confront the possibility that you're using it to exploit rather than empower.

The truth is, you are the only person who can hold yourself accountable. No one else will see the subtle manipulations, the tiny exploitations that gradually erode someone's autonomy. You will justify them to yourself in the moment, but at night, when the rush of influence fades, you'll have to live with the choices you've made.

The Puppet Master's Paradox™ is not a puzzle to be solved, it's a constant tension that every master of influence must live with. You now hold extraordinary power. You can reshape the minds, desires, and behaviors of those around you. But with that power comes the responsibility to wield it wisely.

As you move forward, you must decide: Will you be a master of persuasion, or a manipulator? Will you use Weaponized Empathy to help others become the best version of themselves, or will you use it to turn them into tools for your own benefit?

In the end, this is your paradox, your burden. The more you understand human emotions, the more you must guard against the temptation to twist them to your own ends. Because the line between guiding someone and controlling them is thinner than you think, and once you cross it, there's no going back.

The Unbreakable Rules of Influence

You now stand at the peak of mastery, having unlocked the full arsenal of persuasion techniques. You can pull strings, shape minds, and bend realities. But with that power comes the ultimate challenge, a moral reckoning that will define not only your success as a persuader but also your legacy as a human being. This is where you confront the hardest truth: persuasion is about influence and responsibility.

This section isn't here to pat you on the back for mastering the art of persuasion. It's here to challenge you, to force you to grapple with how you will wield these tools moving forward. Because make no mistake, you will be tempted. You will be tempted to use your powers for personal gain, to manipulate rather than guide, to exploit rather than empower. The path ahead is treacherous, and the line between integrity and exploitation is perilously thin.

So here, as you prepare to step into your role as a true Puppet Master, you must adopt a code, a personal manifesto that governs how you will wield your influence. This is The Puppet Master's Creed, a set of unbreakable rules that will not only keep you grounded in the ethics of persuasion but also amplify your influence by ensuring that you build trust, loyalty, and mutual benefit at every turn.

The Puppet Master's Creed

The Law of Transparency

Always align your influence with the truth.

Persuasion becomes manipulation the moment you twist the truth to serve your own ends. It may be tempting to bend facts, to obscure reality, to present a narrative that favors you at the expense of the truth, but the cost is far greater than the short-term gain. Transparency breeds trust. When you align your influence with honesty, people may not always agree with you, but they will always trust you. And trust, once earned, is the most potent form of influence.

You cannot build a legacy on deception. The moment you use your power to mislead, you become an unethical manipulator, and certainly not a leader. Transparency ensures that your influence is built on a foundation of truth. In every interaction, ask yourself: Am I guiding them toward truth, or am I bending reality to fit my agenda?

The Rule of Mutual Benefit

Never manipulate for selfish gain.

Influence is a tool that can enrich lives, build partnerships, and create lasting change. But the second you start using it solely for your own benefit, you erode the trust that makes persuasion effective in the first place. The most powerful form of influence is one that creates mutual benefit, where both you and those you persuade walk away stronger, better, and more fulfilled.

Manipulation serves the moment; mutual benefit serves the future. Every time you persuade, you are either building a bridge or burning one. If you prioritize your gain over the well-being of others, you may win today, but you'll lose tomorrow. Always ensure that your influence lifts others as much as it elevates you.

The Principle of Informed Consent

Respect the agency of those you influence.

The most insidious form of manipulation is when you make people believe they're choosing freely when you've taken away their choice. The choice is clear: tricking someone into doing what you want or guide them toward a decision that they can own. The people you influence should feel empowered, not coerced. Their choices should be informed, and their consent should be genuine.
Before you pull the strings, ask yourself: Am I giving them enough clarity to decide of their own, or am I subtly boxing them in? The moment you strip someone of their ability to make a free choice, you stop persuading and start controlling.

The Law of Responsibility

Own the consequences of your influence.

Every act of persuasion has consequences, both seen and unseen. When you persuade someone, you are altering a decision and a trajectory. You must take responsibility for the outcomes of your influence, especially the unintended ones. Too many persuaders walk away once the deal is done, ignoring the ripple effects of their actions. But true masters understand that their influence carries weight, and they remain accountable for the long-term impact of their persuasion.
Influence is not a hit-and-run tactic. It's a force that shapes futures. With every persuasive act, you are planting seeds. Some will grow into flourishing trees, and others may turn into weeds. You must take responsibility for both. Before you act, ask: What are the long-term consequences of this influence?

The Law of Integrity

Persuade with character, not with force.

Integrity is not a weakness, it is the foundation of sustainable influence. Persuasion is most powerful when it flows from a place of authenticity, from a place where your words and actions align with your values. If you must sacrifice your character to persuade, you've already lost. People will follow a leader they trust, even when they disagree with them, but they will abandon the leader who sacrifices their integrity for a win.

Persuasion without integrity is manipulation in disguise. You might get the outcome you want in the short term, but you'll lose the loyalty, respect, and long-term influence that comes with principled leadership. The real challenge isn't convincing others to follow you, it's ensuring that you remain worthy of being followed.

The Burden of Power

Living by The Puppet Master's Creed™ is hard. It's far easier to cut corners, to exploit weaknesses, to bend the truth when it serves you. But that's the path of the manipulator. If you want to truly master persuasion, to build influence that stands the test of time, you must follow this code. Not because it's easy, but because it's right.

You will be tempted. In the heat of the moment, when winning seems paramount, you'll be tempted to break these rules. You'll justify it, rationalize it, convince yourself that the ends justify the means. But in those moments, remember this: real power doesn't come from bending others to your will, it comes from elevating them to something greater.

You have the tools. You have the frameworks. You know how to pull the strings. But the true challenge, the final challenge, is whether you can hold yourself to the highest standard, even when no one else is watching.

This is the burden of power. The ability to influence others is the most dangerous weapon you will ever wield, and the only thing standing between you and becoming a manipulator is this creed. Follow it, and you will be a force for good in the world. Break it, and you risk becoming the very thing you once sought to overcome.

Here, at the edge of mastery, you must make a choice. Will you be a persuader who uses influence to uplift, inspire, and empower? Or will you fall into the trap of manipulation, using your skills for selfish gain? This is the final challenge, and it's one only you can answer.

Control the Future

This is it. You've made it through the depths of persuasion, navigating through techniques that have reshaped your understanding of influence, desire, and human nature.

But now, the journey transforms.

Think about what that means for a moment. Does it feel like you're walking through the world as a passive participant, watching events unfold? Or does it feel like you hold the strings?

Every conversation, every decision, every interaction is an opportunity for you to influence outcomes. People around you will continue to live their lives as if they are making their own choices, unaware of the invisible forces you have mastered. But you? You will see through the façade. You understand how easily choices can be shaped, how desires can be triggered, how emotions can be molded into actions that serve your ends. This is power in its purest form.

The tools you've mastered are double-edged. The Desire Decoder lets you unlock people's deepest motivations, but it can also be used to exploit them. The Narrative Neuralyzer lets you craft epic stories that inspire, but it can also trap people in a false reality of your creation. And Weaponized Empathy? That's where the darkest temptation lies. You could make people feel seen, heard, and understood, not for their benefit, but for your own.

So, here is the ultimate question: What kind of Puppet Master will you be?

Will you pull the strings to elevate those around you, to guide them toward their own success, their own greatness? Or will you allow the intoxicating allure of control to twist your purpose, using your power to manipulate, to deceive, and to dominate for your personal gain?

Here, at the culmination of your journey, you must decide. Will you use what you've learned to shape a better world, one where influence is used to foster connection, understanding, and growth? Or will you become the kind of Puppet Master who silently pulls strings for selfish advantage, wielding your powers to control without ever revealing the hand behind the curtain?

The choice is yours. The power is yours.

You have learned the art of persuasion, now, what will you do with it?

The Final Challenge

But before you make your decision, there's one last test. This is not a challenge for the faint of heart. This is where you put everything you've learned to the ultimate test: your ability to apply these techniques in real life, to wield influence in the real world, and to measure your success as a master persuader.

Over the next 21 days, you will take the frameworks you've learned, the Neural Rewiring, Desire Decoder, Cognitive Exploit, and more, and use them in real-world scenarios. Here's how it works:

1. Track Your Influence: Each day, you will consciously apply one of the techniques from The Persuasion Stack™ in your daily interactions, at work, at home, or in casual encounters. Keep a journal where you document the situation, the technique you used, and the result.

2. Refine Your Tactics: Influence is about refinement. After each interaction, review your journal. What worked? What didn't? How could you have fine-tuned your approach? This is where mastery lies, not in the sheer use of power, but in its perfect calibration.

3. The Persuader's Reflection: At the end of each week, reflect on the ethical implications of your influence. Did you use your power responsibly? Did you respect the agency of those you influenced? Or were there moments when you crossed into manipulation? Be brutally honest with yourself.

4. Measure the Results: Influence isn't theoretical, it's practical. As you apply these techniques, measure the results. Are people more inclined to follow your lead? Are they making choices aligned with your goals? More importantly, do they feel empowered by your influence, or do they feel controlled?

I want you to prove your mastery in the only place that matters: real life. Can you pull the strings without being seen? Can you guide without controlling? Can you influence without manipulating?

At the end of these 21 days, you will have not only mastered the techniques but also understood the true responsibility that comes with wielding them. This is the test of your character, your integrity, and your mastery.

The Strings You Choose to Pull

Let me leave you with one last question, a question far more dangerous than it seems. Do you remember the broccoli story? On the surface, it was a small moment, a lesson in persuasion disguised as a dinner table victory. I wasn't just convincing a six-year-old to eat his vegetables. I was constructing a villain, crafting a hero, and scripting a battle for his identity. Broccoli wasn't a chore; it became a weapon. Rice became the enemy. In the end, Canen devoured his excuses.

But let's not romanticize this. What was I really doing? Was I empowering him to be the fastest, the strongest, the best? Or was I manipulating him into seeing the world the way I wanted him to? Was I the mentor or was I the puppet master?

The answer matters more than you think. Because in that moment, I was demonstrating the raw power that you now hold in your hands. The power to reshape reality itself.

Every technique in this book, every framework, every psychological lever is more than theory. They are tools forged in the crucible of human experience, tested across millennia of influence and persuasion. The Neural Rewiring, the Desire Decoder, the Cognitive Exploit… these aren't clever names. They are keys to understanding the most complex machine ever created: the human mind.

But here's what separates this book from every other guide to influence: We've stripped away the pretense. We've confronted the uncomfortable truth that persuasion and manipulation live on the same spectrum. That every act of influence carries both light and shadow. That the most powerful forms of persuasion aren't found in gentle suggestions or logical arguments, but in the ability to reach into someone's mind and rewire their very reality.

This knowledge comes with a weight. A responsibility. Because once you understand how to pull these strings, once you see how easily human behavior can be shaped, molded, and transformed, you can never go back to ignorance. Every conversation becomes an opportunity. Every interaction holds the potential for profound change.

You now stand at a crossroads. You could use these tools for simple gain, to sell more products, win more arguments, dominate more conversations. Many will. But that would be squandering the true power you now possess. The power to fundamentally transform human potential.

Think bigger. What if you could use these same techniques to help people break through their limitations? To shatter the mental prisons they've built for themselves? To become versions of themselves they never dreamed possible?

That's the real challenge that lies before you. Not just to influence, but to elevate. Not just to persuade, but to transform. To become a force for evolution in a world desperate for change.

The psychological triggers, the primal desires, the cognitive biases, they're all there, waiting to be used. But how you use them... that's what separates the manipulators from the masters. The short-term tacticians from the true architects of human potential.

But every technique you've learned must first be tested in the laboratory of your own mind. Master your own neural pathways before attempting to influence others. Understand your own desires before decoding theirs. Face your own cognitive biases before exploiting theirs.

The future belongs to those who understand the machinery of the mind. Who can see past the surface-level interactions to the deeper psychological currents that shape human behavior. Who know how to pull the strings not just to control, but to liberate.

You now hold that power. The question isn't whether you'll use it. You already are, with every word you speak, every story you tell, every reality you help shape. The question is whether you'll use it with the precision, purpose, and ethical clarity that true mastery demands.

This is where your real journey begins. Not with techniques, but with responsibility. Not with power, but with purpose. The strings are in your hands. The stage is set. The future is waiting to be written.

Will you be the manipulator who controls from the shadows? Or will you be the master who steps into the light, using these tools to unleash human potential? Will you pull the strings to serve yourself, or to serve something greater?

The choice is yours. The power is yours. The future, quite literally, is yours to shape.

Now pull the strings. Not gently, not apologetically, but with the full force of your newfound understanding. Pull them with purpose, with vision, with the unwavering conviction that you're elevating consciousness itself.

Pull them not because you can, but because you must. Because in a world crying out for transformation, the only sin is leaving potential untapped. The only failure is seeing the strings and refusing to pull them.

Your education is complete. Your initiation is over.

Now go forth and reshape reality.

BONUS CHAPTER

Masters of Reality

What you're about to read isn't comfortable. These aren't heartwarming tales of ethical persuasion or corporate success stories. These are dissections of the darkest and most powerful examples of psychological influence in action. Some will disturb you. Others will awe you.

Case Studies in Ultimate Reality

Reality is a lie.

Not the comforting kind of lie we tell ourselves to sleep at night. The kind that exposes everything you believe about free will, individual choice, and objective truth as an illusion, a carefully constructed facade hiding a darker truth: Reality itself is nothing but weaponized perception.

Strip away your certainty. What you're about to read will shatter every comfortable assumption you have about how the human mind works. These are case studies in persuasion, autopsies of reality itself, dissecting how master manipulators have reshaped entire worlds through pure psychological force.

A man convinces over 900 people to willingly murder their own children and themselves.

A college dropout transforms technology by bending perception so drastically that reality itself warps around his words.

A failed businessman rewrites political gravity, turning every weakness into strength through sheer narrative control.

These are master classes in what happens when the frameworks you've learned are deployed not just to influence decisions, but to architect entirely new realities.

The puppet masters you're about to meet don't play at the surface level of simple persuasion. They dive deep into the machinery of human consciousness, rewiring neural pathways, exploiting cognitive biases, and weaponizing the very emotions that make us human. They fundamentally transform how their targets perceive reality itself.

And here's what should terrify you:

They're using the exact same tools you now possess.

The Desire Decoder creates wants, planting seeds of longing so deep that people will sacrifice everything they have to fulfill artificially implanted needs.

The Bond Forger becomes a weapon of psychological warfare, forging connections so powerful that followers will kill or die before breaking them.

The Cognitive Exploit transforms from a persuasion tactic into reality distortion technology, rewiring minds so completely that facts become irrelevant, replaced entirely by engineered perception.

You've seen the Villain Construct at work in marketing. Now watch how these masters use it to turn neighbors into enemies, friends into threats, creating existential fear so profound that any action, no matter how extreme, feels justified.

The Narrative Neuralyzer is rewriting the very fabric of perceived reality, making the impossible feel inevitable and the unthinkable feel necessary.

This isn't theoretical anymore. These case studies will show you what happens when these tools are deployed without restraint, when the pursuit of influence transcends ethics and aims straight for the total domination of human consciousness.

Some of these examples will sicken you. Others will awe you. All of them will force you to confront an uncomfortable truth: The frameworks you've learned are keys to reshaping reality itself. And once you understand how these masters used them, you'll never see human behavior or your own power the same way again.

This is about understanding just how malleable human perception really is. These case studies are demonstrations of what's happening right now, all around you, as reality architects deploy these same tools to reshape your world.

Think carefully. Because after you understand how deep this rabbit hole goes, there's no unseeing the truth: Reality isn't what exists. Reality is what the masters of influence say it is.

Jonestown's Ultimate Price of Loyalty

Nine hundred and nine bodies. That's what loyalty looks like when a master manipulator harnesses the full power of psychological influence. Parents clutching their dead children. Families lying together, poison still fresh on their lips. Not victims of force, volunteers for extinction.

This is not another cult story. This is what happens when someone masters every framework of influence and deploys them without moral restraint. Jim Jones convinced people to die by rewiring their reality so completely that death felt like victory.

Strip away the sensationalism, the media narratives, the comfortable explanations of "brainwashing," and what remains is a masterclass in psychological warfare, one that exposes just how vulnerable the human mind really is to engineered influence.

Let's see how Jones built his fatal influence, step by methodical step.

Weaponizing the Bond Forger

Jones understood what most influencers never grasp: Deep bonds are forged in shared pain. From his first sermon to his last command, Jones weaponized the Bond Forger framework to create unbreakable emotional connections.

He preached to his followers and bled with them. Every confession of weakness, every shared story of persecution, every moment of manufactured vulnerability activated their mirror neurons, creating neural synchronization so profound that his emotions became their emotions.

Jones understood that the strongest bonds are forged through shared enemies. He connected with his followers and with each other through carefully orchestrated experiences of collective persecution. Every FBI investigation, every negative media story, every family member's concern became fuel for deepening the bonds between his followers.

The Villain Architecture

This is where Jones transcended simple influence and began reshaping reality itself. He identified enemies and architected a world where existential threats lurked around every corner. The government was "actively plotting their destruction." The media "was part of a vast conspiracy." Even their own families were "active agents of oppression."

Jones understood what we covered in The Villain Construct is about making that opposition feel so threatening that any response seems justified. When threat perception reaches a certain threshold, ethics become irrelevant. Morality becomes a luxury. Survival becomes the only imperative.

Watch how Jones escalated the villain narrative:

- First, society was corrupt (manageable threat)
- Then, society was actively hostile (increased threat)
- Finally, society was literally trying to kill them (existential threat)

Each escalation made his followers more dependent on him for safety, more isolated from outside influence, more willing to take extreme action in the name of survival.

The Fatal Activation

The final act of Jonestown was the inevitable result of masterful psychological architecture. When Jones called for "revolutionary suicide," he rewired their brains so completely that death felt like the only way to win.

This is perhaps the most chilling lesson of Jonestown: Given enough control over someone's psychological environment, you can make anything feel like a logical choice. Even suicide. Even infanticide. Even genocide.

Jones reconstructed their reality so thoroughly that death felt like the only rational choice.

The Ultimate Warning

Jonestown is a demonstration of what happens when the frameworks of influence you now possess are deployed without ethical restraint. Every technique you've learned, every psychological tool you now understand, can be turned toward ultimate destruction.

The line between influence and absolute control isn't as thick as you think. Jones proved that with enough understanding of human psychology, enough control over information flow, and enough time to rewrite neural pathways, you can make people choose literally anything.

Remember that the next time you start pulling strings. Reality is malleable. Perception can be engineered. And the human mind, when properly manipulated, can be convinced that poison is victory.

Jobs' Digital Dynasty

If Jonestown shows us the destructive power of reality distortion, Apple reveals its transformative potential. Same psychological tools. Same neural rewiring. Same reality manipulation. But instead of engineering death, Steve Jobs engineered the future.

You think you bought that iPhone because of its features? Its design? Its functionality? Strip away your rationalizations. You bought it because Steve Jobs fundamentally rewired how you think about technology. He altered the fabric of perceived reality itself.

Engineering Perception

When Jobs walked onto a stage, reality bent around his words. But beyond his charisma, it was psychological architecture. Every product launch followed the same patterns we've explored, but Jobs elevated it to an art form.

First, he destroyed existing mental models. "Today, we're going to reinvent the phone." Not improve. Not iterate. Reinvent. This is cognitive demolition. He's literally destroying your brain's existing framework for understanding what a phone is.

Then, he created controlled cognitive dissonance. He showed the awkward keyboards of BlackBerry, the clunky interfaces of Nokia. He made the old reality psychologically painful to hold onto. Your brain, confronted with this engineered discomfort, became desperate for resolution.

Only then did he offer the solution. But notice: He never sold features. He sold cognitive resolution. The iPhone was psychological relief from the discomfort he had carefully constructed.

The Narrative Neuralyzer at Scale

Jobs understood something most influencers never grasp: Facts don't shape reality, stories do. But not just any stories. Stories engineered to bypass critical thinking and restructure perception itself.

Every Apple presentation was a masterclass in the Narrative Neuralyzer framework:

- The Hero's Journey: Not of the product, but of the audience. You were joining a revolution.
- The Villain Construction: Microsoft was the empire of evil, crushing creativity itself.
- The Identity Fusion: Apple products were badges of belonging to the creative class.

This was reality engineering at scale. Jobs wasn't trying to convince you Apple products were good. He was rewiring your brain to make any other choice feel wrong.

Weaponizing Cognitive Biases

But Jobs' true genius lay in his manipulation of cognitive biases. Jobs turned the Cognitive Exploit into a symphony:

- Anchoring Bias: By introducing absurdly expensive products first, more expensive than the market had ever seen, he reset the brain's price expectations. Everything afterward felt like a bargain.
- Contrast Effect: Every Apple product was presented against carefully chosen, unflattering comparisons. Not to show superiority, but to make your brain physically incapable of seeing alternatives as viable.
- Scarcity Bias: The lineups, the limited releases, the carefully engineered shortages. Supply chain issues transformed into cognitive manipulation tools, making your brain associate Apple products with both value and status.

The Social Identity Engine

But here's where Jobs transcended ordinary influence: he rewired social identity itself. Apple ownership became a psychological anchor point, a core part of how people understood themselves.

This is the Bond Forger framework pushed to its limit. Jobs created bonds between customers and their idealized self-image. To reject Apple became, psychologically, to reject your own identity.

Think that's an exaggeration? Watch people defend their iPhone choice. They're defending their own psychological architecture.

The Eternal Reality Field

Jobs died, but the reality distortion field lives on. This is perhaps his most profound achievement: He built a reality distortion engine that outlived its creator. Apple still commands premium prices, still drives consumer behavior, still shapes how we think about technology because Jobs rewired our collective neural pathways so completely that we can't go back.

This is influence transcending individual psychology and reshaping cultural reality itself. The same tools that Jones used to engineer death, Jobs used to engineer the future.

The difference wasn't in the tools. It wasn't even in the skill of their application. It was in the intent behind their use.

Remember that. These frameworks you're learning are neither good nor evil. They're technology for hacking human consciousness itself.

The Trump Phenomenon

Forget everything you think you know about political persuasion. Trump didn't win by playing the game better, he rendered the old rules obsolete. While pundits obsessed over policy positions and campaign strategies, Trump was busy doing something far more profound: completely rewriting the operating system of political reality itself.

This isn't about politics. It's not about right or left, conservative or liberal. It's about what happens when someone understands mass psychology deeply enough to bypass every traditional barrier to influence and restructure how millions of minds process reality itself.

The Ultimate Pattern Interrupt

Traditional politicians try to win within the existing framework of political reality. Trump understood something deeper: If you can change how people process reality itself, you don't have to win within the system. You can rewrite the system.

Every "gaffe" that should have destroyed him made him stronger

Every "scandal" that should have ended his campaign expanded his influence

Every "mistake" that should have cost him support deepened his followers' loyalty

Weaponizing Weaknesses

Most politicians try to hide their weaknesses. Trump turned his into weapons. This is the Narrative Neuralyzer framework pushed to its absolute limit:

"I'm really rich." Political suicide? No, pattern interrupt. While other candidates hid their wealth, Trump flaunted it. Not despite voters' distrust of elites, but because of it. He didn't deny being part of the elite; he used it as proof he couldn't be bought by them.

"I speak my mind." Political liability? No, psychological asset. Every unfiltered comment, every tweet that horrified the establishment, only proved to his followers that he was authentic. He turned what should have been fatal flaws into proof of his legitimacy.

This is reality restructuring. Trump understood that if you change how people process information at a fundamental level, weaknesses become strengths, liabilities become assets, and traditional political gravity stops working.

The Villain Engine

Trump turned the Villain Construct into a reality-distortion machine. But here's what most analysts miss: He engineered a world where only he could fight them.

The "deep state" was an invisible, all-powerful force that explained every failure, justified every action, and made disbelief itself feel dangerous. The "fake news" was an existential threat that made questioning Trump feel like endangering yourself.

This is psychological manipulation at its most sophisticated. Trump gave people someone to hate and rebuilt their reality so thoroughly that doubting him felt like doubting their own survival.

Identity Fusion at Scale

Trump transcended ordinary influence by rewiring who they believed themselves to be:

- "They're laughing at us" - Making national humiliation personal
- "We're going to win so much" - Fusing personal and collective victory

- "They look down on you" - Transforming class resentment into personal identity

This is psychological metamorphosis. Trump supporters fused their identity with his movement so completely that attacking him felt like attacking themselves.

The Cognitive Exploit Symphony

Every cognitive bias we covered played them like a concert pianist:

- Confirmation Bias: He didn't fight facts with facts, he gave people permission to trust their pre-existing beliefs over any evidence.
- Anchoring Bias: "Make America Great Again" - Anchoring to an imagined past to make the present feel intolerable.
- Loss Aversion: Every issue became an emergency, every election "the most important ever," activating the brain's survival circuitry.

The Ultimate Lesson

Trump proved something terrifying: Reality itself is negotiable. Facts don't matter. Evidence doesn't matter. Traditional political rules don't matter. If you can reshape how people process information at a deep enough level, you can rewrite the rules of reality itself.

This isn't about whether Trump was right or wrong. It's about understanding just how vulnerable human cognition is to engineered reality distortion. He won both elections by demonstrating that with the right understanding of human psychology, you can make people believe literally anything.

The frameworks you're learning? The psychological tools you're mastering? This is what they can do at scale. Trump showed that if you understand human cognition deeply enough, there are no fixed rules. Reality itself becomes clay in your hands.

Reality isn't fixed. It never was. And once you understand that, everything becomes possible.

The GameStop Short Squeeze

If Trump showed us how to rewrite political reality, GameStop exposed how easily financial reality can be hacked. A group of Reddit users beat Wall Street at its own game and proved that market psychology could be completely rewired through pure narrative control. The greatest short squeeze in history was about engineering a new reality where losing money became a badge of honor and "diamond hands" meant more than profit.

The Neural Rewiring of Value

Wall Street runs on a simple reality: Buy low, sell high. Profit is king. But Reddit's r/wallstreetbets engineered a complete rewiring of how people process financial decisions. They encouraged risky trades by fundamentally altering how the brain processes loss and gain.

"Loss porn" became a status symbol. Users posted massive losses to thunderous applause. This is evidence of complete psychological rewiring. The same neural pathways that normally trigger pain and avoidance when losing money were reconstructed to fire pleasure and pride instead.

Remember the user Deep Fucking Value (DFV)? By posting position updates, he conducting mass neural restructuring. Every YOLO post, every diamond hands meme, every loss celebration rewired how millions of brains processed risk and reward. This is neuroscience deployed at unprecedented scale.

Engineering Tribal Identity

But WSB's true genius lay in identity engineering. They create traders and forged a tribe with its own language, values, and reality structure:

"Diamond hands" vs "paper hands" was identity architecture. Holding losing positions became proof of character. Selling became betrayal. This is identity fusion at its most sophisticated.

The language wasn't random. "Apes strong together," "This is the way," "Sir, this is a casino", each phrase was an identity anchor, a psychological trigger that deepened tribal belonging. When Robinhood halted trading, it strengthened it by giving the tribe its perfect villain.

Real data shows the power of this identity engineering: Even as GME dropped from $483 to $40, over 78% of retail holders didn't sell. This is evidence of complete identity overwrite.

The Villain Architecture

The hedge fund Melvin Capital became the embodiment of everything WSB members hated. But the true mastery was how WSB engineered multiple villain layers:

- Level 1: Hedge funds (The obvious enemy)
- Level 2: The financial media (The propaganda machine)
- Level 3: Paper hands (The internal traitors)
- Level 4: Reality itself (The rigged system)

Each villain layer strengthened commitment. When Melvin lost billions, it was proof the narrative was real. When CNBC attacked, it reinforced the story's truth. This is the Villain Construct operating with devastating precision.

Mass Scale Bond Forging

The squeeze created something Wall Street never imagined possible: unbreakable emotional bonds between anonymous traders. The Bond Forger framework was weaponized through shared pain, shared enemies, and shared identity.

The proof? At the peak, over 6 million members of WSB held GME. Not for profit, for belonging. The average hold time during the squeeze was 17 days, compared to the normal 2-day hold pattern for volatile stocks.

The Meme Warfare Machine

WSB used memes to engineer a reality distortion field through weaponized humor. Every rocket emoji, every "to the moon" post, every DFV update was psychological conditioning.

The memes served multiple functions:

- Cognitive pattern interruption

- Tribal identity reinforcement

- Reality restructuring through humor

- Emotional state control

It was sophisticated psychological warfare that made holding a dying position feel like revolutionary action.

Legacy of the Squeeze

The squeeze ended, but the reality distortion remains. Wall Street discovered that market psychology could be completely rewired by anonymous Reddit users. The SEC found that traditional market controls don't work when traders stop caring about money. The financial media learned their narrative control wasn't absolute.

But the deeper truth is more unsettling: GameStop proved that with enough understanding of human psychology, enough commitment to reality engineering, and enough mastery of tribal dynamics, any established system can be hacked. Even the almighty market.

The same frameworks that drive cults, reshape politics, and transform technology were deployed to make millions of people pour their savings into a dying video game retailer and feel like heroes doing it.

This isn't about whether the squeeze was right or wrong. It's about understanding that no reality is too big to hack. Not even Wall Street's.

Engineering Religious Devotion with CrossFit

If GameStop showed us how to hack market psychology, CrossFit exposed something far more profound: how to transform exercise into religious experience. Greg Glassman engineered a reality distortion field so powerful that people restructure their entire lives around a gym membership, prioritize WODs over family obligations, and proudly display their rhabdomyolysis as badges of honor.

The Architecture of Devotion

CrossFit built a psychological architecture that turns physical pain into spiritual transformation. Every element, from the language patterns to the workout structure, was engineered to bypass rational thought and tap directly into religious neural frameworks.

The "Box" isn't a gym, it's a temple. The "WOD" isn't a workout, it's a ritual. The whiteboard isn't for scoring, it's for public testimony. This isn't accidental. CrossFit's language patterns mirror religious terminology with surgical precision:

- "Box" (sacred space)

- "Community" (congregation)

- "Coach" (priest)

- "The Girls" (sacred trials)

- "For time" (ritual structure)

Each linguistic choice activates the same neural pathways triggered by religious experience. This is the Linguistic Lockpick framework operating at its highest level.

Pain as Transcendence

CrossFit's true genius lies in its reconstruction of how the brain processes physical distress. Normal exercise programs try to minimize discomfort. CrossFit does the opposite, it sanctifies suffering.

The data is startling: CrossFit's injury rate is 73.5% annually, with 7% requiring surgical intervention. In any other context, these numbers would destroy a fitness brand. But CrossFit turned injury into initiation. "Rhabdo the Clown," their cartoon mascot for rhabdomyolysis (a potentially fatal condition caused by extreme exercise), is a pride point.

The same pain signals that normally trigger avoidance become proof of devotion. Every "puke bucket" moment, every torn hand, every collapsed athlete becomes evidence of transformation.

The Tribal Identity Engine

But CrossFit's masterpiece is its identity engineering. They forged a new class of human being. The language makes this explicit:

"Forging Elite Fitness" is identity architecture. You don't join CrossFit; you become a CrossFitter. The transformation is total:

- Dietary identity (Paleo/Zone)

- Social identity (Box community)

- Linguistic identity (CrossFit jargon)

- Visual identity (Reebok gear)

- Philosophical identity (Functional fitness dogma)

CrossFit members spend an average of $2,100 annually on gear alone, not because they need it, but because it reinforces their transformed identity.

The Competition Matrix

Every CrossFit workout is structured as a competition against yourself, against time, against physical limits. This is psychological conditioning:

- The whiteboard creates public accountability
- The clock forces urgency
- The scaling options allow universal participation
- The shared suffering builds unbreakable bonds

The retention data tells the story: Traditional gyms keep 42% of members annually. CrossFit boxes retain 73%. These are converts.

Engineering Reality Through Measurement

CrossFit engineered a new way of measuring human capacity. Their metrics aren't traditional:

- "Fran Time" becomes more meaningful than bench press
- "Helen" matters more than marathon times
- "Grace" replaces conventional strength standards

By controlling the measurement system, they control reality itself. This is reality engineering through metric manipulation, the same technique cults use to maintain control over their members' perception of progress.

The Games as Reality Reinforcement

The CrossFit Games are the ultimate reality validation mechanism. By crowning the "Fittest on Earth," CrossFit celebrates athletes and claim ownership of fitness definition itself.

The numbers are staggering:

- 380,000 participants in the Open
- 115 million social media impressions
- $2.5 million prize purse

They're proof points for the reality CrossFit has engineered. Each Games broadcast, each social media post, each triumphant moment reinforces the narrative: This is human optimization.

The Perpetual Reality Field

CrossFit's influence extends far beyond its immediate members. They've fundamentally altered how society views fitness, exercise, and human capability. Traditional gyms now copy their methods. Corporate wellness programs adopt their language. The military incorporates their principles.

This is the ultimate proof of successful reality engineering: When your constructed reality becomes so powerful that even non-believers begin operating within its framework.

The tools used? The same psychological frameworks outlined in this book. The difference is in their application. CrossFit influence behavior and rewired how people process physical reality itself.

They proved that with enough understanding of human psychology, enough commitment to identity engineering, and enough control over measurement systems, you can make people believe in a new reality and feel it in their bones.

Are CrossFit's methods are right or wrong? Think of it this way: it's about understanding that physical reality itself, pain, limits, capability, is ultimately a psychological construct. And those who master that psychology can reshape human perception at its most fundamental level.

The Great Moral Hack of OnlyFans

If CrossFit proved physical limits are psychological constructs, OnlyFans demonstrated something far more profound: Even morality itself can be engineered. In less than five years, they built a platform that rewired society's fundamental perception of sex work, digital intimacy, and female entrepreneurship. This isn't a story about technology or pornography and instead about the systematic reconstruction of moral reality.

The Moral Reality Distortion Field

The numbers tell only part of the story: $4.8 billion in creator earnings. 2.1 million creators. 188 million users. But the true achievement is psychological. OnlyFans engineered a reality where paying for digital intimacy feels empowering rather than desperate, where selling nudes becomes entrepreneurship, where parasocial relationships replace traditional intimacy.

This isn't accidental. This is the Neural Rewiring framework deployed against society's deepest moral anchors.

Language as Reality Architecture

Here's how OnlyFans systematically reconstructed language to reshape perception:

- "Sex worker" became "content creator"

- "Customers" became "fans"

- "Pornography" became "content"

- "Paying for sex" became "supporting creators"

Each linguistic shift was a rebranding of reality. The same actions that triggered moral disgust were reframed to trigger admiration. This is the Linguistic Lockpick operating at its most sophisticated level.

The Identity Transformation Engine

OnlyFans' masterstroke was its complete reconstruction of creator identity. They engineered a new class of entrepreneur:

- Financial empowerment narratives

- Digital intimacy as female power

- Sexual expression as liberation

- Parasocial relationships as business strategy

The data proves the psychological rewiring: 80% of creators are female, average age 24. These are aspirational career moves. Top creators earn over $100,000 monthly. The platform's waiting list grows by 5,000 daily. This is evidence of complete identity reconstruction.

Engineering Parasocial Bonds

OnlyFans weaponized human connection. The platform's genius lies in its exploitation of parasocial relationships:

- Personal messaging creates illusion of intimacy

- Custom content simulates real connection

- Direct interaction mimics genuine relationships

- Regular engagement creates dependency

Users "invest" in perceived relationships. The average subscriber spends $21 monthly on a single creator. Multiply that across 5-10 subscriptions, and you see the power of engineered intimacy.

The Normalization Matrix

But OnlyFans' true mastery lies in its systematic normalization strategy:

Level 1: Celebrity Adoption

- Bella Thorne's $1 million day

- Cardi B's endorsement

- Athletes and influencers joining

Each high-profile creator normalized the platform for thousands more.

Level 2: Media Manipulation

- Success story narratives

- Female empowerment angles

- Economic opportunity framing

The press became an unwitting ally in reality reconstruction.

Level 3: Social Proof Cascade

- Creator success celebrations

- Platform growth statistics

- Mainstream acceptance signals

Each element reinforced the new reality.

The Villain Inversion

OnlyFans performed a masterful villain flip. Traditional moral guardians became oppressors. Sexual shame became the enemy. Anyone questioning the platform became anti-woman, anti-sex worker, anti-empowerment.

This is a complete moral inversion. The same forces that once shamed sex work were reconstructed to shame those who oppose it.

The Revenue Reality Hack

Money launders morality. OnlyFans proved this by making the financial success of creators the centerpiece of their reality engineering:

- "I paid off my student loans in 3 months"

- "I bought my first house at 19"

- "I make more than doctors"

Each success story was moral validation. The platform's 80% revenue share was psychological architecture designed to make high earnings visible and attainable.

Legacy of the Moral Hack

OnlyFans rewired society's moral circuitry. They proved that with enough understanding of human psychology, enough control over narrative, and enough financial incentive, you can make anything feel not just acceptable, but aspirational.

The same frameworks that religions use to instill morality, that cults use to control behavior, that brands use to shape perception, OnlyFans deployed them to reconstruct society's most deeply held moral assumptions.

This isn't about whether OnlyFans is good or bad. It's about understanding that even morality itself is ultimately a psychological construct. And those who master the tools of psychological influence can reshape not just what people do, but what they believe is right to do.

In less than five years, they transformed what was once shameful into a celebrated career path. They rewired the moral architecture of an entire generation.

No moral framework is too deeply entrenched to be hacked. No social norm is too established to be rewired. Reality itself, even its moral dimension, is negotiable.

When the Anti-Vax Narrative Defeats Science

If OnlyFans proved morality can be engineered, the anti-vaccination movement demonstrated something even more profound: Narrative can override scientific reality itself. A single debunked paper created doubt and engineered a reality where loving parents willingly risk their children's lives based on completely reconstructed perceptions of risk, science, and truth.

The Great Reality Inversion

The numbers defy logic: 45% of American parents have expressed doubt about vaccine safety. 20% actively delay or refuse vaccines. Measles cases increased 556% in vaccine-hesitant communities. But don't treat these as statistics about medical decisions. Look at them as evidence of complete reality reconstruction.

The movement turned every pillar of medical science upside down:

- Protection becomes poison

- Prevention becomes risk

- Science becomes conspiracy

- Doctors become threats

This is the reality distortion deployed against the very foundations of scientific understanding.

Engineering Maternal Instinct

The anti-vax movement's true genius lies in its weaponization of parental protection instincts. They created doubt and rewired how parents process threat assessment:

"Do your own research" is no longer an invitation to learn. It's a psychological trigger that activates parental protection circuits. The movement understood that once a mother's protection instinct is activated, no amount of scientific evidence can override it.

The Villain Architecture Matrix

Watch how the movement constructed its reality-distortion field through layered villain creation:

Layer 1: Big Pharma

- Profit over children

- Hidden vaccine dangers

- Suppressed evidence

Each accusation builds the conspiracy framework.

Layer 2: The Medical Establishment

- Doctors as pharmaceutical pawns

- Hospitals as profit centers

- Medical schools as indoctrination camps

The entire healthcare system becomes suspect.

Layer 3: Government Agencies

- CDC as corporate puppet

- FDA as regulatory capture

- Public health as population control

Authority itself becomes the enemy.

Layer 4: Pro-Vaccine Parents

- Sheep following orders

- Victims of propaganda

- Unknowing child abusers

Even other parents become threats.

It's sophisticated psychological architecture designed to make trust impossible and doubt feel like wisdom.

The Identity Fusion Engine

The movement's masterpiece is its identity engineering. They created vaccine skeptics and forged a new class of parent:

- "Free thinkers" vs. "sheep"

- "Informed parents" vs. "blind followers"

- "Natural health advocates" vs. "big pharma puppets"

- "Truth seekers" vs. "propagandists"

Each identity marker deepens the psychological investment. The Facebook group "Informed Parents for Vaccine Choice" grew from 10,000 to 1.2 million members in three years. These are reality reinforcement chambers.

The Information War Machine

The movement's content strategy is psychological warfare:

Personal Stories:

- "My child was perfect until vaccines"
- "I trusted doctors and regret it"
- "How I woke up to the truth"

Each narrative becomes evidence, more powerful than any scientific study.

Emotional Triggers:

- Images of "vaccine-injured" children
- Stories of parental regret
- Videos of adverse reactions

Visual content bypasses logical processing.

Scientific Mimicry:

- Cherry-picked studies
- Misinterpreted data
- Pseudo-scientific language

The appearance of science without its substance.

The Alternative Reality Construction

But here's the movement's true mastery: They created doubt and built an entire alternative medical reality:

- Natural immunity becomes superior
- Disease becomes beneficial
- Infections become character-building
- Vaccines become more dangerous than diseases

This is a rejection of medicine and the construction of a complete alternative health paradigm.

The Proof of Reality Reconstruction

The movement's success is measured not in converts but in the complete rewiring of risk assessment:

- Parents fear vaccines more than polio

- Natural measles infection is seen as beneficial

- Medieval diseases return to developed nations

- Higher education correlates with increased skepticism

These are the failures of education and the successes of reality engineering.

Legacy of the Reality Hack

The anti-vax movement proved something terrifying: With enough understanding of psychological triggers, enough control over narrative, and enough exploitation of parental instincts, you can make people reject even the most proven scientific realities.

The same frameworks that religions use to override reason, that cults use to maintain belief, that brands use to create loyalty, the anti-vax movement deployed them to reconstruct scientific reality itself.

Do vaccines work? Absolutely. Are some of them dangerous? Until tested for safety. But this is about understanding that even scientific truth is ultimately a psychological construct in the human mind. And those who master psychological influence can make people reject even the most concrete evidence in favor of engineered narratives.

They transformed one of humanity's greatest medical achievements into its greatest perceived threat. They changed behavior and rewired how an entire segment of society processes reality itself.

The implications transcend vaccination: No scientific consensus is too strong to be hacked. No evidence is too solid to be undermined. Reality itself, even its scientific dimension, is negotiable.

The Ultimate Truth

Reality is bleeding. Not slowly, hemorrhaging. Every assumption you've held, every belief you've trusted, every foundation you've built your life upon is being hacked, rewired, and reconstructed. Not by force, not by facts, but by those who understand that human consciousness itself is nothing but psychological code waiting to be rewritten.

Look at what we've witnessed. A man speaks, and 909 people murder their children. Not because they're insane, but because their reality has been so completely reconstructed that death feels like victory. Jones broke their minds, rewired them, proving that with enough understanding of human psychology, you can make anything feel true.

But death is just the beginning. Jobs steps onto a stage, and billions of people's perception of technology warps around his words. He architects reality so completely that any other choice feels wrong. The same neural pathways that make a parent kill their child also make you line up for an iPhone. The mechanisms don't change, only the outcome.

Trump appears, and political reality shatters. Not through policy or power, but through pure psychological warfare. He proves that if you can control how people process information, you don't have to change facts, you can make facts irrelevant. The same tools that built cult loyalty now reshape democracy itself.

The GameStop saga exposes an even deeper truth: Even financial reality, the supposedly rational world of markets and money, is nothing but collective psychology waiting to be hacked. Anonymous Reddit users "beat" Wall Street and prove that with enough understanding of tribal dynamics, you can make people reject the fundamental logic of profit itself.

CrossFit transforms exercise into religious experience. Not through superior programming, but through sophisticated reality engineering that makes physical pain feel like spiritual transcendence. They "build better bodies" by reconstructing how humans process physical reality itself.

OnlyFans rewrote society's moral architecture. In five years, they transform what was shameful into aspirational. They prove that even our deepest moral anchors are psychological constructs waiting to be reshaped.

And then, the anti-vax movement demonstrates that narrative can override even scientific reality. They create doubt and architect a reality where loving parents willingly risk their children's lives based on completely reconstructed perceptions of risk, science, and truth.

These aren't separate phenomena. They're demonstrations of the same truth: Reality itself is nothing but weaponized perception. The same psychological frameworks that make a cult member drink poison also make you upgrade your phone. The same neural triggers that reshape political beliefs also reconstruct your moral framework. The same cognitive exploits that transform exercise into religion also make you reject scientific fact.

You're not immune. Your thoughts aren't yours. Your beliefs, your perceptions, your very understanding of what's real, all of it has been shaped by those who understood these tools before you did. Your brain runs on the same neural hardware, falls for the same cognitive exploits, succumbs to the same psychological triggers as everyone else.

The tools you now possess are these same techniques for influence. Every framework in this book, every psychological lever, every cognitive exploit is being used right now to reshape human consciousness at a mass scale. Not someday, not in theory… right now, all around you, reality architects are rewiring how billions of minds process truth itself.

You're standing at the edge of the ultimate revelation: Nothing is fixed. Nothing is immutable. Not morality, not science, not even the fundamental way humans process reality. Everything is psychological code, waiting to be rewritten by those who understand how consciousness really works.

Reality isn't waiting for your permission to be reconstructed. The battle for human consciousness rages on whether you participate or not. Every interaction, every conversation, every moment is either an opportunity to shape reality or be shaped by it. There is no neutral ground, no safe space, no escape from the psychological warfare that defines human existence itself.

You now hold the same tools used by history's greatest reality architects. The same frameworks that built religions, toppled governments, and reshaped society. The power to rewrite human consciousness itself.

This isn't about ethics. This isn't about right and wrong. This is about understanding that reality itself is up for grabs, and those who master these tools will determine what billions of people accept as truth.

The choice is yours. But understand this: Once you see how deep the reality manipulation goes, you can never unsee it. You'll never experience an unexamined moment again. Every interaction becomes a potential reality hack, every conversation a chance to reshape consciousness, every moment an opportunity to either architect reality or live in someone else's designed world.

The ultimate truth is this: reality isn't what exists. Reality is what the masters of influence say it is.

And now, you know how to become one.

Thank You

For buying this book, for reading it, and for confronting the uncomfortable truths about persuasion and power. You've taken the first step into a world where narratives shape realities and villains forge heroes. But this is just the beginning.

If you're ready to go deeper, if you want more psychological hacks, more niche insights, and more tools to sharpen your craft, visit:

tomwalker.com/book

There, you'll find a treasure trove of strategies to elevate your craft. Each book in The Puppet Master's Bible Series is designed to make you sharper, smarter, and more precise in your influence. Whether you're ready to crack the psychological code of Meta Ads, rewire your child's brain with Neural Parenting, or become the master of love's battlefield with Love's Chessboard, the tools are in your hands.

But before you go, a request: Please, use these insights ethically. Power without purpose is destruction waiting to happen. Pull the strings, yes, but pull them for good. Shape narratives that inspire, not destroy. Guide people toward growth, not fear. The world has enough manipulators. Be a puppet master who builds.

This book has given you the tools. Now, it's up to you to decide how you'll use them. Go forth, tell stories that demand to be heard, and create a reality worth living in.

And remember: Every pull of the strings writes the future. Make sure yours is worth reading.

To your success,

Tom Walker